THE SINS OF SCRIPTURE

OTHER BOOKS BY JOHN SHELBY SPONG

Honest Prayer

Dialogue in Search of Jewish-Christian Understanding
(with Rabbi Jack Daniel Spiro)

Christpower (compiled and edited by Lucy Newton Boswell)

Life Approaches Death—A Dialogue in Medical Ethics
(with Dr. Daniel Gregory)

The Living Commandments

The Easter Moment

Into the Whirlwind: The Future of the Church

Beyond Moralism (with the Venerable Denise Haines)

*Survival and Consciousness: An Interdisciplinary Inquiry into the
Possibility of Life Beyond Biological Death* (Editor)

Living in Sin?: A Bishop Rethinks Human Sexuality

*Rescuing the Bible from Fundamentalism: A Bishop Rethinks the
Meaning of Scripture*

*Born of a Woman: A Bishop Rethinks the Virgin Birth and the
Role of Women in a Male Dominated Church*

This Hebrew Lord: A Bishop's Search for the Authentic Jesus

*Resurrection: Myth or Reality? A Bishop Rethinks the Meaning
of Easter*

Liberating the Gospels: Reading the Bible with Jewish Eyes

*Why Christianity Must Change or Die: A Bishop Speaks to
Believers in Exile*

The Bishop's Voice: Selected Essays (1979–1999)
(compiled and edited by Christine M. Spong) (Crossroad)

*Here I Stand: My Struggle for a Christianity of Integrity, Love,
and Equality*

*A New Christianity for a New World: Why Traditional Faith Is
Dying and How a New Faith Is Being Born*

THE SINS OF SCRIPTURE

Exposing the Bible's Texts of Hate
to Reveal the God of Love

JOHN SHELBY SPONG

HarperSanFrancisco
A Division of HarperCollins*Publishers*

All Bible quotes are from the Revised Standard Version unless otherwise noted.

Readers may write the author by email at CMSCTM@aol.com.

Readers may direct questions and comments to the author and join in chat-rooms on issues he raises by becoming subscribers to his weekly newsletter at www.johnshelbyspong.com.

FIRST EDITION

Library of Congress Cataloging-in-Publication Data
    Spong, John Shelby.
        The sins of Scripture : exposing the Bible's texts of hate to reveal the love of God / John Shelby Spong. — 1st ed.
            p. cm.
    Includes bibliographical references (p.) and index.
    ISBN 0–06–076205–5 (cloth)
        1. Bible — Criticism, interpretation, etc. 2. Liberalism (Religion) — Episcopal Church. I. Title.
    BS511.3.S69   2005
    220.6—dc22   2—4060665

05 06 07 08 09 RRD(H) 10 9 8 7 6 5 4

For

CHRISTINE MARY SPONG

My Partner

in Every Sense

of the Word

CONTENTS

Preface   ix

SECTION 1. THE WORD OF GOD

Chapter 1. Why This Book, This Theme, This Author   3

Chapter 2. A Claim That Cannot Endure   15

SECTION 2. THE BIBLE AND THE ENVIRONMENT

Chapter 3. The Ethics of Overbreeding   29

Chapter 4. The Virtue of Birth Control   41

Chapter 5. The Earth Fights Back   49

Chapter 6. Bad Theology Creates Bad Ecology   59

SECTION 3. THE BIBLE AND WOMEN

Chapter 7. Creation:

The Woman Is Not Made in the Image of God   71

Chapter 8. Sexism in Christian History   79

Chapter 9. The Woman as the Source of Evil   87

Chapter 10. Menstruation and the Male Fear of Blood   95

Chapter 11. Recasting the Negativity   101

SECTION 4. THE BIBLE AND HOMOSEXUALITY

Chapter 12. The Ecclesiastical Battle over Homosexuality: 113

Intense, Irrational, Threatening and Hysterical

Chapter 13. The Holiness Code from the Book of Leviticus   121

Chapter 14. The Story of Sodom   127

Chapter 15. The Homophobia of Paul   135

SECTION 5. THE BIBLE AND CHILDREN

Chapter 16. The Appeal in the Text "Spare the Rod"   145

Chapter 17. Violence Is Always Violent, Whether the   151
Victim Be a Child or an Adult
Chapter 18. God as Judge:
Searching for the Source of the Human Need to Suffer   161
Chapter 19. God as Divine Child Abuser: 169
The Sadomasochism in the Heart of Christianity
Chapter 20. Moving Beyond the Demeaning God   175
into the God of Life

SECTION 6. THE BIBLE AND ANTI-SEMITISM

Chapter 21. Searching for the Origins of Christian Anti-Semitism   183
Chapter 22. Anti-Semitism in the Gospels   193
Chapter 23. The Role of Judas Iscariot in the Rise of Anti-Semitism   199
Chapter 24. The Circumstances That Brought Judas   205
into the Jesus Story

SECTION 7. THE BIBLE AND CERTAINTY

Chapter 25. The Symptoms: 213
Conversion, Missionary Expansion and Religious Bigotry
Chapter 26. Creedal Development in the Christian Church   219
Chapter 27. Since I Have the Truth, "No One Comes   231
to the Father, but by Me"
Chapter 28. My Vision of an Interfaith Future   239

SECTION 8. READING SCRIPTURE AS EPIC HISTORY

Chapter 29. The Hebrew Scriptures Come into Being   247
Chapter 30. Escaping the Limits of the Epic: 267
The Prophets, the Writings, the Dream
Chapter 31. Jesus and the Jewish Epic   277
Chapter 32. Jesus Beyond Religion: 285
The Sign of the Kingdom of God—the Epic Universalized
and Humanized

Notes   299
Bibliography   305
Scripture Index   311

PREFACE

Several years ago we were enjoying an evening with friends, watching the sunset from the deck of their summer home on Fire Island off the southern shore of New York State. I was due to retire in six months and our conversation turned not unnaturally to that issue and what retirement now means, when many people are living healthy, productive lives for twenty or thirty years after the end of their "working" careers. Retirement is no longer appropriately viewed as one or two years sitting in a rocking chair looking back on life. It was then that our hosts, Phoebe and Jack Ballard, introduced my wife and me to the concept of the "third half of life." I was intrigued with this phrase, which the Ballards had used while leading retirement conferences. Their thesis was that if this part of life was to be as long, rewarding and satisfying as the first two halves of our lives had been, it needed to be given similar thoughtful and intentional planning. It was a new and exciting idea.

My father died at age fifty-four; his father at a similar age. Consequently I was not programmed to think in terms of longevity. Yet when I retired as the bishop of Newark I was sixty-eight years old. I had served for twenty-four wonderful and exciting years in that dynamic, mind-stretching and life-giving community of faith. I assumed that it was time to end my professional career and to step out of public life. I had no intention of behaving like many retired bishops who are not able to give up their former symbols of power and influence and thus succeed only in making the lives of their successors miserable. The new bishop of Newark, a good friend and a very able priest, would not have to put up with that. So I severed all connections other than Sunday worship that I had with the Episcopal Church I had served in my forty-five-year career and that I still love very deeply. I was sure I would miss being the bishop, but I intuitively knew that it would be the people with whom I had worked so closely that I would miss rather than the power or position of that office. What I did not know, however, was where I would direct my energies in the future. I had to feel my way into that.

Today, from a vantage point five years removed from my life as the bishop of Newark, I am happy to say that this first part of the "third half of life" has been the most exciting, the most enjoyable and perhaps even the most creative of all the years that I have known. If this is what the rest of life looks and feels like, then it is the greatest and most incredible part of life's various adventures.

I originally intended for my last published book to be my autobiography: *Here I Stand: My Struggle for a Christianity of Integrity, Love, and Equality*. Surely, I thought and stated, "one does not write another book after an autobiography has been published." Autobiographies come at the end of life. The first chapters describe one's origins and the last chapter should be the summation of one's life from a vantage point near its end. Perhaps someone might even add to certain autobiographies a postscript to take note of the author's death. My autobiography was set and programmed to come out as I retired, and it was to announce my intended destiny to walk quietly into the sunset! That, however, has not been my experience. Perhaps Ed Stannard, writing about my retirement in the national Episcopal newspaper called *Episcopal Life* (February 2000), had it right when he concluded his article with these words: "His life will be different but don't expect him to keep quiet."

The first sign that I might be in for a surprise came when a letter arrived prior to my retirement inviting me to become the William Belden Noble Lecturer at Harvard University during the first semester of the year 2000. Indeed, that semester began on February 1, the very next day after my official date of retirement. The invitation stated that a requirement of this lectureship was that the lectures "had to be publishable." It was that requirement which forced me to think well beyond my work in *Why Christianity Must Change or Die* and to begin to dream of what the Christianity of the future might look like. The Harvard lectures were destined to form the core of the book *A New Christianity for a New World*, which was published a year later. That book was not only my "second last book," but it was also, along with my other work at Harvard, destined to form the first great opportunity in my "third half of life."

The Harvard lectureship was later augmented by an invitation to teach two classes at the Harvard Divinity School and thus it served to focus anew my lifelong commitment to the vocation of teaching as the primary component of my ministry. Prior to my election as bishop, for many years in my parish ministry I had taught an adult class each Sunday morning before the worship service. That class had become the center around which my ministry was organized. While I was bishop, I followed a pattern of delivering twelve to fifteen public lectures a year within the diocese. I also accepted lecture invitations from outside my diocese in which I sought to relate biblical scholarship to scientific, economic and political concerns. I insisted on filtering the biblical stories through the crucible of contemporary knowledge, so making them pertinent to our day.

I also instituted in our diocese a sabbatical program consisting of a three-month study leave for every five years of service for our clergy. I used that time myself not only to set the example for our clergy about the importance of regular, disciplined study time, but also to immerse myself in contemporary biblical scholarship at such places as Union Theological Seminary in New York City, Yale Divinity School, Harvard Divinity School and the storied universities in Edinburgh, Oxford and Cambridge. With that study background and the publication of my books, the orbit of my influence began to extend beyond my diocese and my denomination. When I retired as bishop, to my great surprise the number of invitations I received to lecture literally exploded. Now that I finally had the time to be a full-time teacher I discovered that I would also have the opportunities. In the last five years I have delivered more than two hundred public lectures each year, the venues for which have moved, just as my books have moved, from the United States first to other English-speaking nations of the world and then ultimately to the nations of Europe, Asia and the South Pacific.

Lecturing and traveling are inevitably stretching experiences. Both stimulated my mind and that proved to be the catalyst for driving me back into a writing career that I assumed had been completed. It began in a very different and unexpected place when I was invited to become a columnist with an Internet start-up company called Beliefnet.com. In that capacity I not only filed columns on a regular basis, usually twice a month, but I was also given special assignments. For example, I covered and filed a daily report from the Democratic National Convention of 2000 that nominated the ticket of Al Gore and Joseph Lieberman. It was a great treat to end each day's story with the sign-off words: "This is John Shelby Spong reporting to you live from the floor of the Democratic National Convention in Los Angeles!" I would have covered the Republican National Convention also, but a long-standing lecture commitment made that impossible. Gary Bauer was my substitute!

I was now beginning to experience life as a journalist. This was a world that I had barely known before and it forced me to realize that I had lived in a fairly narrow orbit inside the church. When Beliefnet.com went into bankruptcy, I trust not because I was writing for them, a new company called Agoramedia.com that grew out of Beliefnet was launched, and the people heading that new Internet venture invited me to become one of their weekly columnists. They began to market the column to subscribers late in 2002. I was now writing a column on religion, politics, social affairs, ethics and even economics each week. It was a struggle at first, both to get the column established in the public arena and to master the discipline of preparing a five-page essay every Friday, plus a question-and-answer feature to allow dialogue with my readers, for release the following Wednesday. These hurdles were, however, overcome and the column appears to be a growing success. Agoramedia changed its name to WaterfrontMedia.com and my column now has a core of regular readers that grows by several hundred subscriptions a month. WaterfrontMedia traced one column I wrote as an open letter to political columnist George Will after he had attacked my church in general and me in particular over our stand in favor of the full inclusion of gay and lesbian people. That exercise discovered that this column had been opened over one hundred thousand times, which confirmed its growing influence.

Journalistic writing is not like authoring a book. It is hot, reactive, contemporary and quickly dated. Books probe deeper and tend to last longer. Because both my career and my audience seemed to be expanding in retirement rather than contracting, the people at HarperCollins suggested that I consider resuming my book-writing career. It was Mark Tauber, now my HarperSanFrancisco publisher, who first suggested that I might create a book examining the hurtful texts of the Bible; that is, those texts that have been used through history to justify the denigration or persecution of others, all the while carrying with them the implied and imposed authority of the claim that they were the "Word of God." Mark especially urged me to examine and challenge the texts that Christians of a conservative bent were regularly using to keep their homophobia intact, since that was the major debate going on in Christian churches all over the world.

I was not enthusiastic about this task at first. I had moved beyond that debate and considered it to be essentially over. I do not mean that all prejudice against homosexual persons is over, but the back of this prejudice has been broken in both church and society and no one doubts the final outcome. To me such a book was fighting yesterday's war. But then the project expanded and my eagerness to engage the task grew. There was also the history of the church's anti-Semitism to explore. It is still alive and well in the Middle East and around the world today and the Bible is regularly used to undergird it. The comment attributed to Pope John Paul II, "It is as it was!" upon viewing Mel Gibson's anti-Semitic motion picture *The Passion of the Christ* only reveals how deep and systemic that prejudice really is.

In addition to homosexuality and anti-Semitism, there was the way women have been treated in Christian history. The two largest Christian churches in the world, the Roman Catholics and the Orthodox tradition, still refuse to ordain women and the conservative Protestant churches continue to argue about something they call "headship," which means that no woman should be allowed authority over a man. After this, other themes began to occure to me with some regularity. There was the issue of child abuse in the Western world that has operated under the rubric of "proper discipline," which constituted another offense historically rooted in biblical quotations. There was that enormous religious negativity that attacks family planning and the subsequent environmental impact of overpopulation, all the while rooting itself in biblical authority in order to give its negativity credibility. Christian voices in our world continue to employ words that reveal nothing less than arrogance toward other religions, whose adherents they regard as fit subjects not for dialogue but for conversion. This attitude is regularly enforced with biblical claims that a particular religious tradition possesses the certainty of the ultimate truth of God that is seen first as religious bigotry and later as religious persecution. So the idea of doing a book to expose and challenge what I began to call first the "terrible texts of the Bible" and later "the sins of scripture" grew in its appeal. My purpose was to lay bare the evil done by these texts in the name of God.

Even that, however, was not enough to convince me to undertake the discipline required to write another book. As a committed Christian who has spent a lifetime studying the Bible and whose life has been deeply shaped by that study, I was not interested in writing what was beginning to sound like a negative, Bible-bashing book. I have passed the point in life when I find fulfillment in doing deconstruction. There had to be more to it than that. Exposing the misuse of scripture can, I believe, be done only in the context of introducing people to a proper way to engage this holy book of the Judeo-Christian tradition. So I began to research the "terrible texts of the Bible," not just to lay bare the negativity, but with the hope of recovering that ultimate depth of the texts which I believe enables me to acknowledge the divine image in the face of every person, to see the love of Christ for every person and to assist in the call into life by the Spirit for every person. Only when the way to connect these positive ideas to an analysis of the "terrible texts of the Bible" became clear did this book finally take shape. It would be another, and I hope timely, attempt to rescue the Bible from those who first literalize it and then so badly misuse it.

As my lecturing career grew, it was inevitable that my study of these biblical ideas would begin to be incorporated into my lectures. That, of course, meant that audiences interacted with, questioned and challenged my thinking. This in turn brought refinement and more study. There were several venues that were particularly significant in developing the material for this book which I would like both to acknowledge and to thank. These include St. Deiniol's Library in Hawarden, Wales, where the warden, Peter Francis, and his wife Helen run an incredibly open, groundbreaking conference center; the Lutheran Church in Finland, especially Lutheran pastors Hannu Saloranta and Jarmo Tarkki, as well as Bishop Wille Riekkinen and Heli Vaaranen, who served as my guides and translators while I was in that incredibly beautiful country; the Anglican Church in Montreal, Canada, especially the Reverend Canon Tim Smart, who invited me, and Archbishop Andrew Hutchinson and his wife Lois, who extended to Christine and me the gracious hospitality of their home and the more special gift of their friendship. I rejoice that the Canadian Anglican Church has since then made Archbishop Hutchinson their primate. Others include the Wilmot United Church of Canada in downtown Fredericton, New Brunswick, and the interim minister, Chris Levan, who invited me, and Peter Short, their permanent pastor, who was on leave from that church to serve as the moderator of the United Church of Canada; the First Methodist Church of Omaha, Nebraska, and its pastor Chad Anglemyer and lay leader Joan Byerhof, who organized my lectures there; the Asbury United Methodist Church of Phoenix, Arizona, and its pastor Jeff Proctor-Murphy, and the Via de Cristo Methodist Church in

Scottdsale, Arizona, and its pastor David Felten, who are two of the most gifted young clergy I have ever met; SPAFER (Southern Points Associations for Exploring Religion) in Birmingham, Alabama, and its founder Ken Forbes, who stirs the water in a constant battle against confining and prejudiced southern Christian fundamentalism; the people who call themselves the Gathering of Friends at Capital Manor Retirement Home in Salem, Oregon, and their leaders, Chuck Woodstock and Jack Powers, along with the Reverend Gail McDougle at the First Congregational Church in Salem and the Reverend Charles Wallace, the chaplain at Willamette University, who organized the series of lectures that I gave in Salem. This was the most energetic retirement community I have ever known. At Payap University in Chiang Mai, Thailand, I addressed a worldwide interfaith conference and had the privilege of being in dialogue with Muslims, Buddhists, Hindus and Jews, and at the Satya Wacana Christian University in Salatiga, Indonesia, President John Titaley invited me to address the students over two days on the subject of the Bible. Finally, when the book was finished but not yet published, I lectured on its specific content in Bay View, Michigan, where the Bay View Association led by R. Robert Kimes invited me to be their Chautauqua lecturer in the summer of 2004, and I also spoke on the book's content in Houston, as the fall lecturer for the Foundation for Contemporary Theology, an opportunity that came in an invitation from Ruth Seliger. There were others, but these are the primary places in which the ideas of this book first began to see the light of day.

I want to thank my publishers at WaterfrontMedia.com, Mike Keriakos and Ben Wolin, as well as my editors Mark Roberts and Tony Brancato for their encouragement in the use of my weekly columns to hammer out these ideas in that forum, and my subscribers who through their letters have engaged, challenged and deepened my thinking. Others at HarperCollins for whom my gratitude is great are Stephen Hanselman, John Loudon, Kris Ashley, Michael Maudlin, Lisa Zuniga, Cindy DiTiberio, Margery Buchanan, Claudia Boutote and Julie Rae Mitchell. These people have undoubtedly made me a better writer than I ever could have been apart from them, and their friendship has been sustaining. I look forward to other proposed projects with them in the future.

Finally, there are a number of individuals who assisted in the production of this book in ways the reader would never know unless I gave them the credit they are due. The Reverend Dr. Larry Meredith, the former head of the Department of Religion at the University of the Pacific in Stockton, California, who served as my expert on motion pictures, novels and Broadway plays, especially as they reveal biblical phrases and themes; Steven Blackburn, the librarian at the Hartford Theological Seminary in Hartford, Connecticut, who has been enormously helpful in locating not just the quotations that open each chapter but in finding their sources for proper footnotes; Mabel and Gus Allen, who came up with the subtitle; Marilyn (Lyn) Conrad, who was my executive secretary when I was the bishop, and who put retirement aside and undertook the task of translating my legal-pad notes into Microsoft Word. It was a joy to work with Lyn once more on what will be the sixth book of mine to bear her imprint; and Rosemary Halstead, secretary at St. Paul's Church in Morris Plains, New Jersey, who has worked for me part-time in my retirement and who makes my weekly column possible. I am most grateful to each of these people.

Finally, I pay tribute to my wife Christine, to whom this book is dedicated. If this book's title page were accurate it would say "written with the cooperation, editorial skills and brilliance of Christine Mary Spong." Not only is this lady my beloved and treasured wife; she is also my editor, my source of encouragement, the refiner of my ideas, the organizer of my professional life, an extra pair of eyes and ears wherever I speak and the person without whom I could not possibly live the life I lead. Not every author is in love with his editor, but I am, and I am unbelievably fortunate that she is also my wife.

Christine and our primary family members Ellen Spong and her husband Gus Epps, Katharine Spong and her husband Jack Catlett, Jaquelin Spong, Brian Barney and his wife Julieann, and Rachel Barney make up the first generation of that family. Shelby, Jay, John, Lydia, Katherine and Colin are the grandchildren who extend that family to the next generation. We love them all and of each of them I am forever proud.

—*John Shelby Spong*
Morris Plains, New Jersey, 2005

THE WORD OF GOD

WHY THIS BOOK, THIS THEME, THIS AUTHOR

The Bible is a subject of interpretation: there is no doctrine, no prophet, no priest, no power, which has not claimed biblical sanctions for itself.

Paul Tillich[1]

I t is a mysterious book, this Bible. It possesses a strange kind of power. It has been the best-selling book in the world every year since printing began. It comes as no surprise to recall that when the Gutenberg press was invented, it was the Bible that first bore the imprint of its metal letters. There is hardly a language or a dialect in the world today into which the words of the Bible have not been translated. Its stories, its words and its phrases have permeated our culture, infiltrating even our subconscious minds. One thinks of motion picture titles that are direct quotations from scripture: *Lilies of the Field* (Matt. 6:28), a 1968 film that earned Sidney Poitier an Oscar for best actor; *Inherit the Wind* (Prov. 11:29), the classic film about the Scopes trial set in the Tennessee of 1925 with Spencer Tracy starring as Clarence Darrow and Fredric March as William Jennings Bryan; and *Through a Glass Darkly* (1 Cor. 13:12), an Ingmar Bergman masterpiece. Beyond these titles there have also been motion pictures dramatizing biblical epics, frequently in overblown Hollywood style: *The Ten Commandments,*

Samson and Delilah, David and Bathsheba, Barabbas and in more recent days *The Passion of the Christ.*

Beyond overt references, biblical allusions are constantly used in literature. Without some knowledge of the sacred text, many expressions in our language would be meaningless. John Steinbeck's novel *East of Eden* comes to mind, along with *Exodus* by Leon Uris, *The Green Pastures* by Marc Connelly and *The Four Horsemen of the Apocalypse* by Vicente Blasco Ibanez, which became a motion picture directed by Vincent Minnelli.

The words of the Bible enrich our everyday speech whether we are aware of it or not: "for crying out loud," which refers to Jesus on the cross; "land of Goshen," a reference to that section of Egypt which housed the Jewish slaves; "sour grapes," a phrase which derives from Jeremiah 31:39 that is widely used to explain behavior; and "the olive branch" as a sign of peace, which comes from the story of Noah. Far more than anyone realizes, all of Western life has been deeply shaped by the fact that the content of this Bible has washed over our civilization for more than two thousand years. Biblical concepts are so deeply written into our individual and corporate psyches that even nonbelievers accept them as both inevitable and simply a part of the way life is.

In the history of the Western world, however, this Bible has also left a trail of pain, horror, blood and death that is undeniable. Yet this fact is not often allowed to rise to consciousness. Biblical words have been used not only to kill, but even to justify that killing. This book has been relentlessly employed by those who say they believe it to be God's Word, to oppress others who have been, according to these believers, defined in the "hallowed" pages of this text as somehow subhuman. Quotations from the Bible have been cited to bless the bloodiest of wars. People committed to the Bible have not refrained from using the cruelest forms of torture on those whom they believe to have been revealed as the enemies of God in these "sacred" scriptures. A museum display that premiered in Florence in 1983, and later traveled to the San Diego Museum of Man in 2003, featured the instruments used on heretics by Christians during the Inquisition. They included stretching machines designed literally to pull a person apart, iron collars with spikes to penetrate the throat, and instruments that were used to impale the victims. The Bible has been quoted throughout Western history to justify the violence done to racial minorities, women, Jews and homosexuals. It might be difficult for some

Christians to understand, but it is not difficult to document the terror enacted by believers in the name of the Bible.

How is it possible, we must ultimately wonder, that this book, which is almost universally revered in Western religious circles, could also be the source of so much evil? Can that use of the Bible be turned around and brought to an end? Can the Bible once again be viewed as a source—even an ultimate source—of life? Or is it too late and the Bible too stained? Those are the themes I will seek to address in this volume.

My qualifications for telling this story are twofold: first, I have had a lifetime love affair with this Bible; and second, I am a church insider, who yearns to see the church become what it was meant to be. I will not give up on the Bible or the church easily, but I will insist that the Bible be looked at honestly in the light of the best scholarship available and that the church consciously own its historical destructiveness.

I do not know exactly when my love affair with the Bible began. Perhaps its first seeds were planted when I was a child and began to notice that the family Bible was displayed prominently on the coffee table in our modest living room. I do not recall my parents ever reading it, but there was no question that it was revered. I did see it used to record the family's history in a special section that bore titles like "Births," "Deaths" and "Marriages." Nothing was ever to be placed on top of that holy volume—not another book, not a glass or a bottle, not even a piece of mail. This sanctified book could brook no cover, nor could it be seen as secondary in any way to any other entity. This attitude was certainly encouraged and my passion for this book was enhanced by the schools, both weekday and Sunday, that I attended eagerly as a young pupil.

Yes, as hard as it is for citizens of the twenty-first century to imagine this scenario, stories from the Bible were read or told to the children of my generation in both church school and public school with regularity. I suspect that if one had to compare the two places, it would be the public schools in my region that were even more fervent about revering the Bible than were my church's Sunday school sessions. There is a sense in which the public schools in the southern part of the United States where I grew up were, in an earlier day, little more than Protestant parochial schools. Every public school day in my childhood began with both a Bible story and a prayer, most often the Lord's Prayer, led by a teacher. I suppose that a sense of awe was communicated to me during this daily opening exercise, for inattentiveness was said to be "rude to God." Following these opening religious rituals we recited the pledge of allegiance to the flag. Devotion to both God and my nation were regularly placed side by side with God always coming first. Indeed, my nation was said to be the instrument through which God worked in this world. These sentiments were not far from a concept of America being a new divinely chosen people.

The intensity of these public school religious exercises depended to some degree on the piety of the particular teacher. To this day I can bring to mind indelible memories of the public school teacher I had when I was ten years old. Her name was Mrs. Owens—Claire Yates Owens, to be specific. She started our class each day by reading a chapter from a children's Bible storybook. These tales were not unlike radio soap operas in that they left the listener hanging in anticipation of what the next episode would reveal. Most of us could not wait to see what was going to happen to Moses in the midst of the Red Sea or to Joshua in the battle of Jericho. We hung on Paul's every adventure and reveled in his most recent shipwreck or snakebite. The stories from this book were so natural to our lives and so deeply a part of our culture that none of us could imagine a time when the Supreme Court of our land would declare this activity to be unconstitutional. Mrs. Owens even required us to memorize the Ten Commandments in the long form directly from the book of Exodus. None of those *Reader's Digest* shortened versions would do for her! That meant we had to repeat all of those intimate details found in the second commandment about how the "sins of the fathers would be visited upon the children to the third and fourth generation." We all hoped our great-grandparents had been virtuous people lest we be forced to pay the price of their evildoing. There was also that long list of both people and creatures that the fourth commandment ordered to refrain from labor on the Sabbath. Memorizing these convoluted and intricate passages was worth the reward of special public commendation that Mrs. Owens both promised and delivered. If one wanted extra credit in this class, or at least the satisfaction of impressing our demanding teacher and being recognized as extraordinary by our peers, we were encouraged, although not required, to memorize in order all of the sixty-six books in our King James Protestant version of the scriptures. I passed that test then and can still recite them to this day.

Yet from even that early date as I perused the sacred text I would come across a narrative from time to time that was brutal or insensitive. Still, no matter what I discovered on those hallowed pages, the fact that it was in the Bible surrounded each passage with an aura that was designed to reaffirm my trust in the ultimate goodness of all its words. I recall even in this early part of my life asking questions about the Bible. Those questions, however, were still relatively safe. "Why," I wondered, "was the language of the Bible different from all of the other books we read?" By "language" I really meant "English," since that was the only language I knew. "Why was this book filled with words like 'thee' and 'thou' or verbs like 'shalt' and 'beseecheth'?" "Why was it that in the Bible when Jesus wanted to make an important pronouncement, he would introduce it by saying: 'Verily, verily, I say unto you. . . '?" I could not imagine anyone else saying such stilted, silly-sounding words in any other setting. These unusual words and phrases communicated to me that this book was somehow profoundly different from all others. I had not yet confronted the Elizabethan English of William Shakespeare and knew nothing about how my native tongue had developed. I suppose my classmates and I made lots of unconscious assumptions. I know I identified this holy-sounding language of the Bible with the language of God. Perhaps, I reasoned, God was so old that the divine language was the classical English of long ago. The idea that God or Jesus had spoken anything other than English had not yet dawned on me. I was told this book revealed God's language and that assumption was reinforced in my mind every time someone referred to this book as the "Word of God."

There were other issues about this book that were different, but I did not yet even wonder, much less ask, about them. For instance, why was this book typically printed with two columns of type on each page? Sometimes these columns were separated by a simple line, but on other occasions by a narrow center section that ran down the entire page and was filled with small, italicized type and other strange hieroglyphics. No other books that I knew of except dictionaries and encyclopedias were printed this way. This was a particularly interesting insight when it finally dawned on me that no one was ever supposed to sit down and *read* a dictionary or an encyclopedia. These were, rather, resource books to which one turned to get specific answers to particular queries. Was the Bible printed this way to encourage me to think of it as a kind of holy dictionary or sacred encyclopedia that possessed all the answers to all the questions that I might ever ask? Even now when I raise these possibilities they sound a bit sinister, so you may be sure they were not allowed to enter my mind as a child. But I still wonder if this was a conscious or an unconscious decision. Did that layout reflect the position of the hierarchy in the Western Catholic tradition? Was that part of the church leaders' campaign to keep the Bible from being read, at least not by the uneducated masses? Does that printed style itself reflect their need to guard the Bible's secrets in order to protect their authority? I suspect it does and that even then I was being trained, quite unconsciously, to view the Bible as a resource book to which I would turn only to get the final answers to my questions, and thus to accustom myself to think of the Bible as an ultimate, undebatable authority from which there was no further appeal in the quest for truth. That is certainly consistent with the way the Bible has been used in Western history. Whatever the motives were which produced these realities, conscious or unconscious, they surely worked on me. The Bible was different from every other book in its ultimate power.

I approached this book and its holiness rather tangentially as a child. Children's Bible storybooks were my absolute favorites. The more graphic the pictures, the better I liked them. I am sure that both this affinity and my affection for Bible stories were noticed and encouraged by my mother, for on the Christmas following my twelfth birthday—perhaps not coincidentally it was also the Christmas following the death of my father—I received as my primary present, my "Santa gift" as our family called it, my very own personal copy of the Holy Bible.

I was thrilled with this gift. Nothing could have pleased me more. This particular Bible was large in size with gilt-edged, tissue-thin pages and a cross on its leather cover. That cover was both thin and pliable, so that my Bible could be held in one hand with its cover and pages flopping down on each side of the hand of the holder just as they did when preachers held the Bible while expounding on its various texts at revivals and from church pulpits. This Bible also had a concordance in the back that would guide me to places where particular words or characters might be located. It possessed all kinds of introductory material and page after page of notes. Included in its appendix were colored maps of the Holy Land. On one of those maps I could see visually the boundaries of each of the twelve tribes of Israel and could even locate the little-known lands of Naphtali, Dan and Benjamin. On another map I could follow in minute detail both the journey of Jesus from Galilee to Jerusalem and the travels of Paul, first into the desert of Arabia and later across the lands contiguous to the Mediterranean Sea. Most special of all to me was the fact that this Bible was a "red letter edition," in which all the words believed to have been spoken by Jesus were printed in red, so that these words literally leaped off the pages in importance. I am sure that part of my excitement over this Christmas gift was contained in the realization that it was in some sense an acknowledgment on my mother's part that I was growing up and that the time had come for me to give up childish things like children's Bible storybooks and to start feeding my soul on the "red meat" of the Bible's own words. Whatever motives were operating in my psyche or even my mother's psyche, I took to this book like a duck to water and immediately began to immerse myself in its content. I cannot imagine my grandchildren today responding in a similar fashion.

When the excitement of Christmas Day was over that year, I placed my treasured new gift on the table beside my bed and began that night a regular practice of reading it, day after day, week after week, month after month and year after year. That was more than sixty years ago. There have been few days in my life since that Christmas that I have not intentionally and intensely read and studied these words. I suppose I have worked through this sacred text from cover to cover some twenty to twenty-five times. Some individual books, like the four gospels, the Acts of the Apostles and Genesis, I have read many more times than that. Because I loved this book so much and because I read it so carefully, I could not fail to notice its gory passages that did not jibe with what I had been told about either God or religion. I met in its pages things that were disturbing, malevolent and evil. That was how the dark side of the Bible first began to dawn on my consciousness.

Looking back, I believe now that these insights would have come to me even sooner had I not been what the Bible seems to regard as a privileged person. I do not refer to my social or economic status, which was modest to say the least, but to the fact that I was white, male, heterosexual and Christian. The Bible affirmed, or so I was taught, the value in each of these privileged designations. It was clearly preferable to be white than to be a person of color; male, in whom the image of God was clear, rather than female; heterosexual and therefore "normal" rather than homosexual and therefore "abnormal"; and Christian, which was, of course, the only true religion. I grew up secure in each of these definitions.

I hope these brief autobiographical comments will make it clear that I do not come to this biblical interpretive task as an enemy of Christianity. I am a Christian, a deeply committed, believing Christian. I am not even a disillusioned former Christian, as some of my biblical scholar friends now identify themselves. I recognize that the Christian faith has traditionally claimed that its beliefs and practices are based on and supported by the Bible. I understand the centrality of this book. I write as one whose entire professional life has been lived in the service of that Christian church with which I am still joyfully identified. I was ordained a priest in the Episcopal Church at age twenty-four and elected one of its bishops at age forty-four. I am a person who organized my priestly vocation after the analogy of a seminary professor, by interpreting my ordained role to be that of a teacher and the church primarily as a teaching center. The textbook that I taught my congregations Sunday after Sunday and year after year was the Bible. At diocesan centers, first across the South and later across the nation, I led conferences on the Bible. In parishes where I was the rector I initiated adult Bible classes for an hour prior to the Sunday worship service each week. The content I presented each Sunday using a lecture format would not have been dissimilar from that found in any seminary or theological college. I believed that my parishioners could learn everything that I had been taught. I regarded those classes as my highest priority and prepared for them more rigorously than I prepared for anything else I did. If the people in my congregation did not want to drink from the fountain that I was offering, there were plenty of other churches available from which they could choose. I never believed in tailoring the class to the security level of its members by hedging the truth. My aim was to challenge people with the insights of the scholars and to make contemporary biblical thinking available to them.

I would normally spend an entire year on a single book of the Bible, choosing a commentary to guide my thinking from among the world's great biblical scholars. I would work on that book of the Bible and that commentary week after week until both became part of what I know and who I am.[2] It was my ambition to work through the entire Bible with my congregations in the course of my ministry. I did not plan to skip even Obadiah or Nahum and figured I could complete this study in the years of my priestly career.

My election as a bishop tempered that ambition but did not diminish my zest for teaching. Like my great mentor John A. T. Robinson in England, I interpreted the office of bishop as a teaching and writing office. The result of this commitment was that I both know and love the Bible deeply. I also recognize where its warts are.

I know what parts of it have been used to undergird prejudices and to mask violence. I have discovered that there is a strange ability among believers not to see the negative side of their religious symbols. It did not take a genius to realize that human conflicts the world over always seemed to have a religious component. Slowly I was also forced to acknowledge that every great battle that I had joined both as a priest and as a bishop, to call the church into being what I believed the church had to be, was ultimately a battle against the way the Bible had been used throughout history. It was out of the Bible that pious and devout people drew the definitions they sought to impose on powerless people and to justify the oppression that those powerful religious voices seemed eager to impose. It was strange and uncomfortable to come to the awareness that the people who quoted this book most often were opposed to the justice issues that I found so compelling. At first I convinced myself that the problem was not in the Bible itself, but in the way the Bible was used. That, however, was a defensive and ultimately dishonest response. I had to come to the place where I recognized that the Bible itself was often the enemy. Time after time, the Bible, I discovered, condemned itself with its own words.

This was certainly true in the battle to overcome the racism and segregation that so deeply affected my childhood church in North Carolina. Quotations from the Bible were frequently employed in the racist battle to maintain segregation in which I, as a white person, was judged to be of greater worth than a black person. Quotations from the Bible were also the chief source of that very patriarchal prejudice by which I, as a male, profited and through which women were diminished.

The Bible was clearly the enemy when I began to address the way that Christians had treated the Jews throughout Christian history. My church had filled me with a deep-seated but Bible-based religious bigotry. I breathed it inside my congregation's life. Whenever the gospels said "the Jews," there was no escaping the fact that something evil was meant. This evil was acted out in the Western world again and again, culminating in the Holocaust, but not ending with it. I have dealt with the defacement of synagogues even in the twenty-first century. Religious bigotry is certainly still present in the rhetoric of certain preachers, such as the former president of the Southern Baptist Convention who said on national television not only in my presence but in the presence of his Jewish interviewer, Larry King: "God almighty does not hear the prayers of a Jew."[3]

Later other forms of this same religious bigotry filled the pronouncements of popular American televangelists when they talked about both Jews and Muslims and certainly when they talked about their other favorite victims, the homosexuals of the world. Much as I wanted to think otherwise, I had to conclude that the Bible is not always good. Sometimes the Bible is quite overtly evil. Sometimes its texts are terrible. It was not a comfortable insight, but it grew into being a crusade to lift the Bible above its own destructiveness and to force the Christian church to face its own terrifying history that so often has been justified by quotations from "the scriptures."

As the twenty-first century dawned, the citizens of the United States had to face for the first time the reality of international terror which came at us in killing fury from a religious tradition different from our own. The only positive thing about the evil of terrorism was that it forced Christians to face the same kind of religious bigotry and hostility that we had long acted out with clear consciences toward others. That was a new learning for citizens in the dominant nations of the Christian West. So terrorism created for me a new imperative, indeed a compelling vocation. I had to deal with the destructive and terrifying side of my own religion. I had to face openly and admit honestly those things about which most Christians are neither knowledgeable nor aware. I had to document the evil that Christians have so frequently rendered to others in the name of our religion, including the way we have justified violence with biblical quotations. No, we Christians are not the only violators. But Christians have been major players in the realm of violence, and that must not be denied. There is plenty of guilt to go around. It appears to be in the nature of religion itself to be prejudiced against those who are different in looks, language, habit and religion. Violence is almost always the result of such prejudice.

Is it not a fact that Osama bin Laden invoked God when he directed his hijacked suicide airliners into the World Trade Center and the Pentagon in 2001?

But is it also not a fact that President George W. Bush invoked God when he unleashed his missiles and bombers on the people of Iraq?

Palestinians have likewise invoked God when they have strapped dynamite to their waists and boarded a crowded bus or entered a public restaurant in Israel to destroy themselves and anyone else who happened to be near.

The Jews in Israel have invoked God as they sent their tanks into the West Bank and the Gaza Strip to knock down houses that were thought to provide shelter to their enemies, believing this to be the appropriate and righteous response to the terror that victimized them.

Catholics and Protestants have both invoked God as they killed each other in Ireland, the last gasp of a dying fury that spawned a thirty-year religious war and in 1588 propelled the Spanish Armada to a watery grave as it sought to win back Protestant England for the Vatican.

Religious evil gets even more complicated and even more uncompromisingly destructive as we press our gaze into very sensitive areas. Priests in our day still invoke God when they violate and abuse the little children who have been entrusted to their care. The church taught its people that these priests were to be respected as their spiritual fathers, so abuse was not only morally wrong, it was a violation of trust. It gets worse still. The superiors of these priests—the bishops, the archbishops and the cardinals—also invoked God when they acted to cover up these violent crimes and protect the victimizers and ultimately themselves and the church rather than the victims.

Other worldwide religious leaders, including both the pope and the archbishop of Canterbury, invoked God when each allowed the homophobic prejudices of some parts of the Christian world to be honored while homosexual people were violated again and again for the "sin" of being who they are. Both placed the unity of the church above truth. It has not been a pretty picture.

The source for the invoking of God in each of these instances was the sacred scriptures of the person speaking. For Christian victimizers it has regularly been the Bible. That is why it is the Bible that I seek now to explore. I believe the Bible must be preserved, but not the Bible that people have used to enhance the pain and evil present in human history.

Exploring these areas has not always been a comfortable journey for me and I am well aware that many of my conclusions will not be comfortable for those who think of themselves as "simple believers." Many of them will become quite threatened, even angry. That is why it is essential for my readers to be aware that I am doing this as a Christian, as a believer. That will surely be apparent before my readers complete these pages. My pledge is only that I will seek the truth openly. Duplicity has lived for far too long inside the leadership of the Christian church for me to be content to allow it to continue unchallenged.

2

A CLAIM THAT
CANNOT ENDURE

Idolators and doubters, oppressors and oppressed—
The Bible gives a record of searching and unrest;
Today we see how power can harden and corrupt,
How greed can cause dissension and conflict to erupt.

The truth is always larger than one event in time,
God's truth is not restricted to place or paradigm,
Each Bible story echoes our present faith and fears,
The ancient and the modern unite across the years.

Jean Holloway [4]

Perhaps the strangest claim ever made for any written document in history is that its words are or somehow contain the "Word of God." Such an assertion assumes that God is a very humanlike being who has the ability to speak to a particular people in a language that they understand and that God is intimately invested in the minutiae of human life. Yet without any apparent embarrassment such claims have been made throughout Western history for what we call the holy scriptures of the Christian church. Similar claims have also been made for the sacred writings of other religious traditions, but Christians have never taken these "pagan" claims seriously. Somehow the claims coming from non-Christian sources are just too obviously absurd. One does not have to travel far, however, to hear the Christian version of this claim stated with liturgical precision.

"This is the Word of the Lord." That is the phrase that mainline Christian churches most frequently use following a reading from the Bible in the Sunday liturgy. The congregation responds dutifully with the words "Thanks be to God." In the more unstructured or evangelical Christian churches, the phrase might be a little more flowery, but its claim is no less clear. Many times I have heard some variation on these words after the Bible has been read in these places of worship: "May God add his blessing to this reading from his Word." The use of these masculine pronouns for God has never been a large concern in evangelical circles.

"I do believe the holy scriptures of the Old and New Testaments to be the Word of God and to contain all things necessary to salvation." That is the vow, called the Oath of Conformity, that is required of every candidate for ordination in my Episcopal/Anglican Church. I have recited that vow three times: once when I was ordained a deacon, then when I was ordained a priest and finally when I was ordained a bishop. Having graduated from one of my own church's accredited theological seminaries, where I was well trained in a critical approach to the Bible, it did not occur to me to see any conflict between that oath and my education. To call the Bible the "Word of God" is so commonplace in the tradition that it rolls off our tongues by rote with little thought as to what it means. However, when a debate begins in the church over some major social issue, the ultimate authority quoted most regularly is a biblical text. The assumption of these Bible quoters is that the Bible is in fact invested with the authority of God.

I suspect that we still call the Bible the "Word of God" because everyone reserves to himself or herself the right to interpret what that claim means. When some Christians say of the Bible, "This is the Word of God," they mean quite literally that they believe this book was written or dictated by God and is therefore inerrant. That is the popular point of view asserted by America's well-known television evangelists. One wonders, however, upon hearing that claim whether these people have ever read the entire biblical text! Others, attempting to find a more moderate position which will allow a bit more interpretive space, suggest that to call the Bible the "Word of God" simply means that God inspired the Bible's human authors. It is still God's word, but some room is created to allow for human error in the sacred text. At least people holding this position give evidence of the fact that they know enough about the biblical text not to want to ascribe it all to God!

Others, who are still bound, albeit even more loosely, to the traditional claim that the scriptures contain or reveal the "Word of God" suggest that what this phrase really means is that people in every generation continue to hear the "Word of God" through the reading of these ancient and time-bound texts. This position is frequently adopted by those who are moving toward the edges of institutional Christian life. It is as if they sense that without an authoritative Bible undergirding their faith, there is little or nothing holding it up. The struggle to secure the authority of the Bible is therefore an enormously important issue.

The content of this debate turns on exactly what is meant by the verb "to be," with its various forms of "is" and "are." The verb "to be" is the basic building block in every human language. "I do believe the holy scriptures of the Old and New Testament *to be* the Word of God." "This *is* the word of the Lord." Are not those fairly specific claims? We might argue that the verb "to be" is more complex than we imagined. One remembers with some amusement from the vantage point of history a former president of the United States, under political pressure for his indiscreet private behavior, defending himself by suggesting that there are various meanings to the word "is."[5] Is the word "is" or the verb "to be" that imprecise? Literalists do not think so.

Historically the evidence is clear that the verb "to be" has been employed in church circles for centuries to give authority to the Bible. Nor is there any doubt that these claims for the Bible have also shaped traditional Christianity for its entire history. I now, however, want to open this debate to new possibilities by asking a few simple but very direct questions: Was this claim for the Bible to be the "Word of God," no matter how it is interpreted, ever appropriate for this volume which contains sixty-six books (or even more if you count the Apocrypha) that were written over a period of perhaps twelve hundred years? Can such a claim stand even the barest scrutiny? Is Christianity so shaped by this strange claim as to be unable to extricate itself from its biblical moorings and still be recognizable? Is this claim not the primary source from which evil has flowed so freely from the Christian church throughout Christian history? Has not this definition been the very thing that has produced the religious mentality that has perfumed prejudice, violated people literally by the millions and created an idol out of the scriptures that even in our somewhat enlightened generation is still allowed in some circles to masquerade as if it were the final inerrant authority? It is quite clear to me that it is the assumption that the Bible is in any sense the "Word of God" that has given rise to what I have called in the title of this book "the sins of scripture." By "the sins of scripture" I mean those terrible texts that have been quoted throughout Christian history to justify behavior that is today universally recognized as evil.

To face this reality is essential for my integrity as a Christian, but it is not easy. My religious critics say to me that there can be no Christianity apart from the authority of the scriptures. They hear my attack on this way of viewing the Bible as an attack on Christianity itself. I want to say in response that the claim that the scriptures are either divinely inspired or are the "Word of God" in any literal sense has been so destructive that I no longer want to be part of that kind of Christianity! I do not understand how anyone can saddle God with the assumptions that are made by the biblical authors, warped as they are both by their lack of knowledge and by the tribal and sexist prejudices of that ancient time. Do we honor God when we assume that the primitive consciousness found on the pages of scripture, even when it is attributed to God, is somehow righteous? Do we really want to worship a God who plays favorites, who chooses one people to be God's people to the neglect of all the others? When we portray the God of the Bible as hating everyone that the chosen people hate, is God well served? Will our modern consciousness allow us to view with favor a God who could manipulate the weather in order to send the great flood that drowned all human lives save for Noah's family because human life had become so evil God needed to destroy it? Can we imagine human parents relating to their wayward offspring in this manner? Can we really worship the God found in the Bible who sent the angel of death across the land of Egypt to murder the firstborn males in every Egyptian household in order to facilitate the release of the chosen people? Can the Bible still be of God when it portrays Joshua as stopping the sun in the sky for the sole purpose of allowing him the time to slaughter more of his enemies, the Amorites (Josh. 10:12–15)? Can the Bible be the "Word of God" when it has Samuel order King Saul in the name of God to "Go and smite Amalek, and utterly destroy all that they have; do not spare them, but kill both man and woman, infant and suckling, ox and sheep, camel and ass" (1 Sam. 15:3)? Is it the "Word of God" when the Psalmist writes about the Babylonians who have conquered Judah: "Happy shall he be who requites you with what you have done to us! Happy shall he be who takes your little ones and dashes them against the rocks" (Ps. 137:8–9)? These are but a few of the questions I want the Bible quoters to answer. Is Christianity somehow irrevocably linked to this mentality because of our continuing claims for the Bible?

One can easily descend from these serious questions to those that are a bit more frothy, frivolous and fun. Many of these biblical assertions have floated across the Internet in a variety of versions, making good reading for a biblically illiterate nation. According to the Bible, one of these Internet offerings noted, it is permissible to sell one's daughter into slavery (Exod. 21:7). It is of interest that sons as candidates for slavery are never mentioned. One may possess slaves, says the Bible, but only if they come from neighboring countries (Lev. 25:44). One wonders, as an American, if that makes both Canadians and Mexicans eligible!

The execution squads would have to work overtime to keep up with the number of texts from the Bible that call for the death penalty. Violating the Sabbath (Exod. 35:2), cursing (Lev. 24:13–14) and blaspheming (Lev. 24:16) are among them. Such judgments would fall most heavily on athletic locker rooms used in preparation for Saturday or Sunday football games! But of course no one should be playing football anyway, for Leviticus also prohibits touching anything made of pigskin (Lev. 11:7–8)! Perhaps this great American fall sport should be played with rubber gloves! Even stubborn and rebellious children are at risk of capital punishment, according to the Bible. If children do not obey their parents, if they overeat or drink too much, they are to be stoned at the gates of the city (Deut. 21:18–21). That is a bit stricter than even right-wing biblical moralists and ideologues care to go. Yet if one wishes to search the scriptures sufficiently, this rather bizarre list of texts can be expanded almost endlessly.

The case against the Bible, however, does not stop at the end of clever lists. It is quite easy to demonstrate that the Bible is simply wrong in some of its assumptions. It is hard to maintain the claim of inerrancy in the face of biblical statements that are obviously incorrect. The "Word of God" is not infrequently simply wrong.

Moses did not write the Torah: Genesis, Exodus, Leviticus, Numbers and Deuteronomy. Moses had been dead for three hundred years before the first verse of the Torah achieved written form. Those books reflect multiple strands of material that were put together over a period of at least five hundred years. One of those Torah books, Deuteronomy, even provides us with the account of Moses' death and burial (chapter 34). Is it not a rather remarkable author who can record in his writing that particular moment in his own life? Yet Jesus himself makes the traditional claim for Mosaic authorship of the Torah in multiple places in the gospel record (see Mark 1:44; Matt. 8:4, 19:7, 8, 22:24; Luke 5:14, 20:28, 24:27). It is also a working hypothesis in parts of the Old Testament.

David did not write the Psalms. Scholars locate the writings of most of the Psalms during the period of Jewish history called the Babylonian Exile, which started with the fall of Jerusalem in 596 BCE and lasted in some of its forms until the mid-400s. That would be between four and six hundred years after the death of King David. Yet, once again in the gospels, the Davidic authorship of the Psalms is asserted by Jesus (see Mark 12:36–37; Matt. 22:43–45 and Luke 20:42–44). Such a claim made today on a final exam, even at the seminary where I was trained, would result in a failing grade. Jesus, or those who thought they were quoting Jesus, was simply wrong about that.

The case for the Bible possessing the authority of being the "Word of God," or at the very least having been divinely inspired, gets even murkier when the biblical claim is made that epilepsy and mental illness are both caused by demon possession, or that profound deafness, what we once referred to pejoratively as being "deaf and dumb," is caused by the devil tying the tongue of the victim. Can the "Word of God" be bound to levels of knowledge that were transcended centuries ago? Yet once again in a variety of biblical passages Jesus is portrayed as making these specific claims (see Mark 1:23–26, 9:14–18; Matt. 9:13 and Luke 9:38–42).

The fact that we know today that the earth is not the center of the universe, with heaven above the sky, renders the worldview of the biblical writers seriously inaccurate. Was God ill-informed or did God choose not to reveal such truth to the authors of the biblical books? Yet an earth-centered, three-tiered universe underlies such biblical stories as the Tower of Babel (Gen. 11), manna falling from heaven (Exod. 16:4ff.), the wise men following the star of Bethlehem (Matt. 2) and even the cosmic ascension of Jesus (Luke 24; Acts 1).

The Bible tells us that the Israelites wandered nomadically in the wilderness between Egypt and the Promised Land for forty years, guided by the magic signs of a pillar of cloud by day and a pillar of fire by night, which connected them with the God who lived just above the sky (Exod. 13, 16:35).

The Bible makes assumptions that most of us who live in a post-Newtonian world of "natural law" could never make. Special people in the Bible were said to have had their lives marked by signs of divine favor. Elijah and Elisha, for example, both had miracle stories connected to their lives in the developing traditions. These miracles included the ability to expand the food supply (1 Kings 12:8–16, 17:8–16); the ability to enable an iron axe-head to float on the river (2 Kings 6:5) and even the experience of raising the dead (1 Kings 17:17–24 and 2 Kings 4:8–37).

When we come to the Jesus story, a literal reading will reveal either unbelievable miracles or a land of make-believe. Like all great mythical heroes, Jesus was said to have had a supernatural birth. He was conceived without benefit of a male agent (Matt. 1:18–25 and Luke 1:26–38). It was a bit more spectacular than the birth of John the Baptist, who was simply conceived when his father was elderly and his mother was postmenopausal (Luke 1:5–25). Before these two boys were born, we are told, their relative importance was announced when the fetus of John the Baptist, while still in the womb, leaped to salute the fetus of Jesus (Luke 1:41–44). Surely no one would seriously argue that this story was literal history! The birth of Jesus gets more spectacular yet. It is announced to the world by a star that illumined the heavens. The star was said to have had the power to wander through the sky so slowly that it could guide wise men from the East first to the palace of Herod and second to a house in Bethlehem where Jesus could be found (Matt. 2:1–12). Next Luke tells us that on the night of his birth angels split the night sky, behind which they were presumed to live, in order to sing to hillside shepherds. The angels must have sung in Aramaic, for that was the only language the shepherds understood (Luke 2:8–14)!

In a narrative about the child Jesus at age twelve, we are told that he was capable of confounding the greatest teachers of the land (Luke 2:41–52). Stories showing the hero possessing godlike wisdom as a child constitute a familiar theme in the mythology of many great leaders.

We cannot read the rest of the gospel narratives without confronting the image of Jesus as a worker of miracles, from walking on water to stilling the storm. If we believe these stories in any literal way, we have to presume that God suspended the laws of the universe in the first century to allow Jesus to demonstrate his divine origins. The only alternative is to be forced to face the fact that we have in the gospels only mythical accounts of Jesus' life. In either of these rather sterile choices it becomes very difficult to assert that these narratives are the "Word of God."

When we turn to the writings of Paul, the claim that the words of this rather passionate, intensely human and clearly conflicted man were in any sense the "Word of God" borders on the absurd. Since no one would ever confuse Paul with God, there appears little rationality in the attempt to confuse the words of Paul with the "Word of God." Paul was many things, but divine was not one of them.

When Paul says in his letter to the Galatians, "I wish those who unsettle you would mutilate themselves" (5:12), is there something godlike in his words that I am missing? How about his advice to women to keep their heads covered in worship or his assumption that the ancient Hebrew myth of Adam and Eve proved that women were inferior to men (1 Cor. 11:2–16)? When Paul or one of his disciples instructs women to subject themselves to their husbands (Eph. 5:22), slaves to obey their masters (Col. 3:22 and Eph. 6:5) and children to obey their parents (Col. 3:20 and Eph. 6:1–3), surely that is not the eternal "Word of God" speaking. These are the reflections of a rather discredited cultural sexism, an immoral oppression of human life and an obsolete guide to good parenting being revealed here. When the holy God is identified with such bankrupt ideas, surely God is not well served.

In contemporary studies of the way the gospels came into being, scholars are all but unanimous today in asserting that Mark was written first and that both Matthew and Luke incorporated Mark into their narratives. The problem for the excessive claim of a divine origin for the scriptures then comes when we discover that both Matthew and Luke changed Mark, expanded Mark and even omitted portions of Mark. That is not exactly the way one treats something identified as the "Word of God," or even something thought to be inspired by God. The problems grow when these same studies reveal that Matthew and Luke periodically disagreed with Mark and thus contradicted him. Luke went so far as to edit Mark's poor grammar, treating his Marcan source very much as an English professor might treat a freshman's term paper.[6] Mark ended his gospel with the dangling phrase "for they were afraid" (16:8), which Luke simply omitted (24:1–12). Clearly the gospel writers themselves had no concept that either they or their sources were writing the "Word of God." Luke indeed insists that he is writing only after consulting other, presumably conflicting accounts, to compose an "orderly one" (Luke 1:1–4).

The gospel writers are also not averse to ripping biblical stories out of their Hebrew context and using them to buttress their arguments for Jesus as the fulfillment of the prophets. A defensive writer who twists or tweaks his sources so that they will serve his purpose hardly gives evidence of the fact that he is writing something that might be referred to either as the revealed "will of God" or the inspired "Word of God." Matthew is, in my opinion, the writer most guilty of this abuse. He bases his virgin birth story, for example, on Isaiah 7:14. Yet he translates that text to read that a virgin shall conceive (see Matt. 1:23) when the text in Isaiah not only does not use the word "virgin" but says that a young woman *is* with child. In the world I inhabit, if a young woman is with child, she is hardly a virgin! He also twists either a passage that refers to a holy man as a nazirite (Judg. 13:5), or a passage that uses the word *nasir*, which is translated "branch" (Isa. 11:1), to suggest that the Hebrew scriptures had centuries earlier referred to Jesus growing up in the village of Nazareth (see Matt. 2:23). That is a rather huge stretch even for a gospel writer!

Later, the church fathers would build the superstructure of the Christian creeds, doctrines and dogmas on the same shaky foundation of assuming that the Bible contained the irrefutable words or "Word of God." So the virgin birth was placed into creeds along with the cosmic ascension, though I know of no reputable biblical scholar in the world today who thinks that either ever happened in any literal way. Nor do scholars today believe that the prophets predicted things that Jesus actually did. That is a gross distortion of scripture. Yet much of the Christology debate in early church history depended on that assumption. Not only was the Jesus story in the gospels written some forty to seventy years after the earthly life of Jesus had come to an end, but it was written quite deliberately with the Hebrew scriptures open so that the story of Jesus could be conformed to those expectations. Various doctrines of the Christian church quake in instability with this undoubted recognition.

The idea that God would plant holy hints of Jesus' life into the writings of Jewish prophets some six to eight hundred years before the birth of Jesus is fanciful enough, but when you then suggest that as these books were being copied anew in each generation—for that is the only way an ancient text could be preserved—God watched over the copiers to make sure that they did it correctly, and that in times of war and natural disaster God guarded these sacred texts from destruction so that when Jesus came people would recognize him as Messiah because he fulfilled these expectations, rationality rebels and proclaims, "There is something wrong in this equation." It violates everything we know about how the universe operates. It defines God as a super manipulator.

When all these things are put together, it becomes clear that the traditional claim that the Bible is in any literal way the "Word of God" is problematic at best and absurd at worst. To the degree that the historical liturgies of the church are themselves dependent on these same biblical claims, it becomes obvious that they too will collapse as soon as these things become consciously evident. The future of the Christian enterprise, therefore, does not look secure, at least to the extent that it is based on the premise of the authority and literal historicity of scripture. The hysterical denial of these obvious biblical truths that mark the life and rhetoric of right-wing churches, both evangelical Protestant and conservative Catholic, is not a sign of hope. It matters not that these churches attract thousands of worshipers who come craving both authority and certainty. This is rather just one more sign of an internal sickness that has not yet been adequately faced by Christian leaders. The constant attack of these right-wing voices on Christian scholarship is a clear tip-off that they cannot face reality. When people cannot deal with the message, the ancient and still regularly practiced tactic is to shoot the messenger.

The greatest tragedy that has arisen because of the way these claims have been made for the Bible, however, is not just the impending collapse of organized religion, as frightening as that now is to many; it is rather in the moral dilemma that comes when religious people face the evil and pain done to so many people over the centuries in the service of these biblical claims. It is high time to call the church and this use of the Bible itself to accountability.

Text by text I will seek to disarm those parts of the biblical story that have been used throughout history to hurt, denigrate, oppress and even kill. I will set about to deconstruct the Bible's horror stories. But destruction is neither my aim nor my goal. I want above all else to offer believers a new doorway into the biblical story, a new way to read and to listen to this ancient narrative. I want to lead people beyond the sins of scripture embedded in its "terrible texts" in order to make a case for the Bible as that ultimate shaper of the essence of our humanity and as a book that calls us to be something we have not yet become. I want to present a different portrait of Jesus, not as a mythical hero, not even as a divine invader of humanity, but as a God presence, a new dimension, even a new vision, of what human life was meant to be.

There is a story told about Elijah in the book of 1 Kings (19:4–18) that guides my efforts. Elijah had been defeated and hounded by his enemies, who thought him responsible for the fact that the popular religion of the people was collapsing. He prayed in his despair for God to take away his life, since in his mind the original covenant had been forsaken, the altars thrown down and the prophets slain. God, instead, invited Elijah to stand upon a mountain and to watch a great and mighty wind rend that mountain into pieces. Then came an earthquake that broke open the great rocks and finally there came a fire of consuming power. God was not in any of these. Yet each of these incredible and fearful acts of destruction had to be endured before Elijah was able to hear "the still small voice." God was in that small voice, and the divine message urged him to return to the work to which he had been called.[7]

I am now convinced that institutional Christianity has become so consumed by its quest for power and authority, most of which is rooted in the excessive claims for the Bible, that the authentic voice of God can no longer be heard within it.

So I want to invite people to a mountaintop where together we can watch the mighty wind, the earthquake and the fire destroy those idols of creed, scripture and church, all of which have been used to hide us from the reality of God.

When that destruction is complete, my hope is that we too will then be ready to hear that still, small voice of calm that bids us to return to that vocation which is, I believe, the essence of what it means to be a disciple of Jesus. We are to build a world in which every person can live more fully, love more wastefully and be all that God intends for each person to be. In that vocation we will oppose everything that diminishes the life of a single human being, whether it is race, ethnicity, tribe, gender, sexual orientation or religion itself. That is what I see Jesus as having done, and because he did exactly that, people were able to see, to meet and to experience God in him in a radically new way.

That is the Jesus I hope to sketch out when the deconstruction is complete, so that my readers will close this book not with the shreds of a destroyed Bible in their hands, but with the vision of a new humanity before them. An ambitious task? Perhaps! But that is the primary task of reformation.

THE BIBLE AND THE ENVIRONMENT

THE TERRIBLE TEXTS

Be fruitful and multiply, and fill the earth and subdue it.

Genesis 1:28

Let us make man in our image after our likeness and let them have dominion over the fish of the sea and over the birds of the air, and over the cattle, and over all the earth, and over every creeping thing that creeps upon the earth.

Genesis 1:26

3

THE ETHICS OF OVERBREEDING

She runs at him and he melts before this whirling dervish with
a damaged child in her arms and a healthy one stirring
inside. . . .

A year later another child is born. . . .

The McNamara sisters said Angela was nothing but a
rabbit. . . .

No one was paying any attention to him because we have two
new babies who were brought by an angel in the middle of the
night. . . .

There is a new baby soon, a little girl and they call her
Margaret. . . .

Frank McCourt[1]

These lines occur in the first chapter of Frank McCourt's award-winning memoir entitled *Angela's Ashes*. It is the moving story of growing up poor in Ireland, being subservient to and shaped by a radical nationalism that was deeply infused by tribal religion. Indeed, this book comes out of a world where to be Irish is to be Roman Catholic. It reveals with dramatic power the impact on this struggling family as birth after birth after birth is endured as their way of being loyal to their religious heritage. After all, the Bible urged reproduction on the people, and those injunctions have been interpreted by the Roman Catholic Church to be a divine command against birth control. Those who find their identification in this religious system must be loyal to its teachings and therefore they must walk in lockstep with its pro-hibitions against anything that contravenes God's order to reproduce. *Angela's Ashes* chronicles the human cost of poverty, as well as the loss of life to death and the diminishment of life to disease that poverty constantly exacerbates. It portrays a father so overburdened with the anxieties of his life and by the ab-sence of any hope for a way out in the future that he drowns his pain in alco-hol. It also portrays a mother, old and haggard before her time, beaten down by the combination of inadequate diet and constant pregnancies and endur-ing the traumas that a woman in those circumstances has to confront. The most trying trauma was quite obviously the history of both the births and the deaths of her own children. She was able neither to care adequately for these children nor to keep them from being born. She could neither protect them once they were born nor change her circumstances.

Two things sustained this family emotionally, and both were radically in-terconnected. One was the delusional hope that Ireland would someday be not only free and independent, but mighty and admired among the nations of this world. The other was their devotion to the "true faith" of the Catholic Church, which, they believed, would secure for them a better life in the world to come. The corollary of this heavenly dream was, of course, their fear that if they were not faithful and obedient to Mother Church, they would have to absorb the wrath of Father God. They would then face the eternal punishment of the literal hell that was said to await not only all Protestants, but also those Catholics who compromised one of their church's principles or deviated in any detail from their church's "true faith."

If the Catholic Church said that birth control was sinful, then sinful it was. There was no further debate. The Church of Rome told its people that all of its teachings were based on the clear dictates of the "Word of God" found in the Bible, where God's first commandment to the original man and woman was "Be fruitful and multiply." It did not seem to register or even to matter in any ultimate sense that many of the McCourt family babies died prematurely. Indeed, it happened so often that McCourt reports in this memoir that he and his siblings actually looked forward to such deaths be-cause they got a day off from school to attend the funeral, an occasion that was accompanied with much sympathy and even increased amounts of food to eat. It did not seem to matter that the lives of both parents were being destroyed in this process, since through it all the teachings of the church were affirmed and the fires of hell were averted. McCourt's parents were taught constantly by the one they called "Father" that the sex act was sinful unless it was used for reproduction. The choice between sexlessness and hell had no great appeal. So they opted for the practice of sex that was indivisible from reproduction, no matter how desperate life was, no matter what each new pregnancy did to the entire fabric of this family, whose dietary, emotional and financial resources were never sufficient to absorb one more baby. Mother Church had spoken and this loyal Irish Catholic family would not think of refusing to obey the pope. One wonders where morality lies in this sad story. Were responsible choices available? Is the absence of family planning holy or is it evil? Is the text "Be fruitful and multiply," as it has been traditionally interpreted, the "Word of God"? Or is it a "terrible text" that reveals one of the sins of scripture, since it has been used inappropriately throughout history to maximize the authority of the leaders of the church?

Agatha Yarnell is not a Roman Catholic. She is rather an evangelically oriented, Protestant fundamentalist Christian. As a psychologically damaged woman, she had sought medical help and counseling after a prolonged post-partum depression following her third pregnancy. Her doctor urged her and her "born-again" husband not to have any more children, warning them both that the emotional resources of this family were simply not adequate to encompass another pregnancy. But in the "Word of God," Agatha and her husband read that God had enjoined the people of the world to "be fruitful and multiply." We must obey the Bible, this couple concluded, rather than the words of some doctor, who may not even be a "true believer." He could be an agent of Satan tempting us to deviate from the revealed divine truth. So another baby was conceived, and then another, until Agatha was the mother of five.

Then came that all but inevitable break. It was so sudden, so severe and so final. Agatha Yarnell systematically took her five children, beginning with the youngest, and drowned them one by one in the bathtub. She had to chase the oldest one in order to catch him after he saw that his four brothers and sisters, lined up side by side on the mattress, were lifeless. But he was caught and soon took his place beside his siblings on that same bed.

Agatha next placed a call to the police and announced, "I have just drowned my five children." Today she is in a jail in the southwestern part of the United States under a life sentence with the conviction of murder written indelibly across the record of her life.[2] The court judged the obvious fact. This woman was guilty of this heinous crime. It did not occur to the members of the jury, charged with rendering a verdict, that it was their responsibility either to judge the motive or to explore any extenuating circumstances. All that mattered to them was that this was a criminal act and Agatha Yarnell had clearly done it.

Yes, she is guilty. Is she, however, the sole guilty party? Were there any accomplices? Of course there were. No human being is an island. We now know that each of us is created by millions of interactions and actions that have taken place in our lives. Her husband, for example, was hardly without some fault, some responsibility, even if it was nothing more than the sin of bad judgment. He heard and he ignored the medical opinion. Yet he was judged by the law to have been innocent, since he took no overt action to destroy his children's lives. He walks the streets today as a free man.

Was her church guiltless? Are institutions responsible for expressing what they believe are divine laws, even if those laws turn out to cause enormous destruction? Ignorance has certainly never been declared a crime. But this question does raise the issue of the responsibility of an institution that becomes obsessed with its ability to tell the gullible and easily manipulated what God thinks. Can anyone say that this particular church, which placed its rules ahead of a woman's health and her children's safety, acted in Agatha's best interest or that of her children? Or is this not one more place where what some call the "Word of God" turned out to be nothing more than a "terrible text" that has yet one more time brought destruction on the lives of innocent people? Is it not time that we raise to consciousness the destructiveness of the sins of the Bible and the terrifying price they exact? How can words like "Be fruitful and multiply," which brought such pain to Frank McCourt's mother and siblings and to Agatha Yarnell, her husband and their five children, be called the "Word of God"?

My journey into these destructive aspects of the Bible begins with an examination of the biblical setting of this particular text. It occurs at the end of the first story of creation in the book of Genesis.[3] In this narrative God's wondrous work of creation is almost complete. The sun has been fashioned to give light by day and the moon to give light by night. The firmament that separated the waters above from the waters below has been established. Fish swim in the sea. Plants have taken root in the soil of the earth and birds have been made to populate the sky. Then the climactic sixth day arrives. We are told that on that day, by the hand of God, the earth brings forth "living creatures," which are identified as "cattle and creeping things and wild animals of the earth" (Gen. 1:24, NRSV). God then pronounces the world, as it exists thus far, to be good (Gen. 1:25). The crown jewel of this divine creative act, however, is still to come. So God is quoted as saying, on that same sixth day, "Let us make man in our image, after our likeness; and let them have dominion over the fish of the sea, and over the birds of the air, and over the cattle, and over all the earth, and over every creeping thing that creeps upon the earth" (Gen. 1:26). The text goes on to be specific: "God created man in his own image, in the image of God he created him; male and female he created them" (Gen. 1:27).[4]

It was at this moment on the final day, before God was to begin the holy rest from all the divine labors that would establish the Sabbath, that God is said to have spoken these words: "Be fruitful and multiply." The first rule, the first divine command that God issued, was given to the only creatures who bore the divine image, and these words clearly stated that these human creatures were intended to be dominant over all the other creatures on this planet earth. "Be fruitful and multiply," that is your divine duty. Doubt it not, for this is the "Word of the Lord."

Since the idea of God speaking to give commands to the created ones seems somewhat inappropriate in our age, the question we need to ask is, What did these words mean to those ancient people who framed them? How were they first understood? What was the human experience that caused our ancestors to "hear" God say these words? Why did this message gain such power that people began to say that God commanded us to "be fruitful and multiply"?

Understanding the context in which anything is written is essential to grasping the import of the message. The context of the words "be fruitful and multiply" is both specific and universal.

On the level of specificity it must be noted that these words are generally attributed to one of the priestly writers who penned them during the period of Jewish history known as the Exile. The Jews were captives, deported to the foreign land of their Babylonian conquerors. They had dreams about someday returning to the sacred soil of Judah, but they had no very realistic hopes. They had few rights in captivity. To reproduce and to grow their tribal numbers so that some of them might someday return home was keenly important.

The universal context out of which these words must be heard drives us deeply into our understanding of the nature of our humanity. Part of what it means to be human is to accept the fact that we carry within ourselves long-standing and chronic anxieties. From the moment in which human beings achieved the dramatic step into self-consciousness, the evolutionary struggle to survive became primary, carrying with it enormous emotional consequences. Self-conscious human beings knew the dangers of existence in a way no other creatures did. It was as if human life was hardwired to endure the traumas of an existence in which danger was always anticipated and unrelieved fear was a part of what it meant to be human. Human beings now lived in the stream of time with a remembered past and an anticipated future, so that they were forced to contemplate daily what might actually happen at any moment. To be human was always to be on guard against external enemies, both human and subhuman. The desire to survive compelled our ancestors to the task of subduing whatever might threaten them. It created for them an atmosphere of vigilance and life-and-death competition. Success in both tribal warfare and the hunt was the key to survival and many of our forebears died in both enterprises.

In this struggle a driving motivation developed that would help these self-conscious creatures to achieve success in battle against their enemies and to establish viable defenses behind which they could live in safety. Both offensive and defensive tactics took many forms. On the offensive side more and more lethal weapons were devised to enable both warfare and the hunt to be successfully engaged at greater and greater distances of safety. Rocks and sticks gave way to spears and then to bows and arrows. The animal world was mastered. When the species we call Homo sapiens could not defeat human enemies, they learned to build defensive walls to protect themselves. Death began a slow but steady retreat.

On a different front, this one in their battle against the enemy of hunger, our ancestors learned to cultivate the land, to grow crops and to build food surpluses so that the anxiety of the daily quest for food that made our ancestors pray "Give us this day our daily bread" was diminished. Better diet combined with access to clean water contributed to a growing longevity. Once again death was postponed and the population expanded. Our survival anxieties began to be banked.

An enormous boost was given to that longevity process in recent centuries when increased knowledge and developing skills in the healing arts began to defeat the causes of sickness. Once germs and viruses were identified as causative factors in illness, counterattacks were launched against these enemies with penicillin and other antibiotics. Surgical procedures, selective radiation and chemotherapy were developed to fight tumors and cancers. Cardiovascular accidents, now called heart attacks and strokes, were subjected to angioplasty procedures, valve replacements and drugs that opened clogged arteries. Preventive measures such as lowering cholesterol levels were introduced to combat coronary disease. The fact that we talk routinely today of double, triple or quadruple bypass heart procedures only emphasizes the depth of the revolution through which we human beings have moved in the treatment of heart disease. With the introduction of prenatal care for expectant mothers, there has been a sharp decline in the number of women who die in childbirth and a huge increase in the number of healthy babies. All of these forces have combined to change our lives dramatically and to enhance our rate of survival. The result has been a geometric rise in the human population.

So the need to "be fruitful and multiply" has over the centuries slowly but surely lost its urgency. But if you have been programmed since the dawn of conscious time by a survival mentality and are convinced that this injunction was somehow the command of God, then the power of the injunction lives on when the need to obey it is no longer relevant. That is where we are today. The command originally given to enhance life has now become a command that threatens to destroy life. At first the human ability to prolong life so dramatically was a source of great joy and a reason for much celebration. We seemed, as our medical technologies advanced, to be constantly successful in our quest to survive. No downside was visible.

There were also some setbacks along the way, however, that tempered our optimism and restored momentarily the sense of an eternal and divine command found in the words "Be fruitful and multiply." The Black Death—or the bubonic plague, as it was sometimes called—occurring in the fourteenth century, was the most recent illustration of such a setback in the historic memory of the Western world. Somewhere between 20 and 35 percent of the citizens of Europe, depending on which statistics you accept, died as the result of that infection. It is hard to imagine the psychological impact of that much death on human life in that region of the world. The population of

Europe actually declined and it took generations before human beings felt that their extinction was not once more right around the corner. That disaster served to enhance the power of the ancient command to continue our reproduction rate.

Other plagues or disasters, some natural and others human-made, that occurred throughout the world were much more localized, if no less devastating to those involved. Massive deaths administered by human hands were sometimes directed against a specific segment of the world's population. We now call that ethnic cleansing. Sometimes these murderous outbreaks were conducted in full view on the stage of human history. Sometimes they occurred in parts of the world where human prejudice or limited communications muted their full horror. One thinks first of the Holocaust in Nazi Germany in the 1930s and 1940s, in which perhaps 50 percent of the Jews of the world, plus great numbers of the mentally sick, the physically impaired, the known homosexual population and others Hitler thought unfit to continue living and therefore breeding, were destroyed. Then there was the enormous slaughter carried out in the civil war in the late twentieth century in Rwanda and Burundi, where millions from among the two competing tribes—the Tutsis and the Hutus—were annihilated. More widespread still was nature's slaughter in the AIDS epidemic in Africa in the late twentieth and early twenty-first centuries, in which whole villages were decimated all over the continent and the population growth of that vast land was dramatically affected. Each of these horrors raised anew the possibility of extinction and revivified among those affected the sense that the first divine command to the human creature, who in the biblical story was appointed by God to be the master of all that God had made, was to multiply. In time, however, these horrors faded and the relentless march toward overpopulation began anew.

The reality for human beings has been that slowly but surely the enemies of human survival have been defeated, one after another. The proof of this is recognized when one looks at the statistics of human population. Human life emerged on this planet, according to the best estimates of anthropologists, between one and two million years ago. Yet it took from that point of origin until 1750 CE for the number of human beings to top one billion. It then took only about one hundred and eighty years for the human population to reach the two billion number plateau, which demographers believe was achieved around the year 1930 CE. It then took only forty years until 1970 to add the third billion. Since then, in the thirty-plus years between 1970 and the present, the world's human population has doubled to approximately six billion people. Even now, when the rate of growth has finally begun to slow, the actual expansion of human beings has not.

Current estimates are that before the twenty-first century fades into history, the human population will reach a figure of somewhere between nine and ten billion people. There are still some who do not see this as an impending disaster. We hear them saying, "There is no need to curb our breeding habits." We can do it all, they seem to say. We can "be fruitful and multiply," because we can conquer anything.

Human accomplishments have indeed been spectacular, as a quick look at our history will reveal. We have demonstrated that as our numbers expanded we could respond by forcing the land to produce more and more food per acre until the land itself was all but exhausted. We then learned how to revive the land with a variety of chemical fertilizers. We developed electric milking machines designed to extract from the cow every ounce of its milk for human use. To expand our livable space we built air conditioners to push back the heat and heating systems to push back the cold. We created combustion engines and installed them in cars, planes, trucks and tanks, as well as in tractors, lawn mowers, leaf-blowers, snowmobiles and golf carts. We electrified life so that we could cook with convenience, have our dishes and clothes washed and dried for us and our garbage disposed of easily. We built irrigation systems to push back the desert and used our water supplies as if they were unlimited. We were not concerned about the waste products that we pumped into our atmosphere because space seemed limitless.

We developed genetically modified foods and scientific methods for increasing the supply of livestock, poultry and fish to satisfy the needs of our ever-expanding human population. In the process we performed that biblical calling to have dominion over all the earth. We also assumed that human life was the only kind of life that ultimately mattered, so whatever it took to support human life was deemed to be both necessary and good.

We began to lower our sense of what it meant to guarantee some reverence for all living things. We castrated cows, sheep and hogs to make their meat more tender. We created stockyards and slaughterhouses, where brutality is practiced daily so that meat markets may be filled with steaks and chops. We created, thereby, what animal rights activists call a holocaust for subhuman creatures. We now grow poultry to the desired weight with scientifically de-vised feeding programs that number the days from hatching to dispatching on huge chicken farms where these creatures never escape the confines of their cages. We pour chemicals into what the chickens are fed to fatten them for human tastes and human profits. We freeze fish at sea, making it possible to extract even bigger catches until some species have begun to be extinct. We have developed the "farming" of fish such as salmon and talapia, again feed-ing them chemically to increase their size quickly for the market. We took a large wild bird called a turkey and domesticated it, turning it into a mis-shapen, big-breasted creature so top-heavy it can barely stand up, its bulk pro-ducing abundant quantities of that white meat that consumers seem to prefer. I think it is fair to say that we have obeyed what we took to be the divine com-mand. We have reproduced ourselves in abundance and now we clearly have dominion over all the earth.

That was an enormous achievement not to be denigrated. But instead of seeing our accomplishment as building that mythical kingdom of God on earth, we looked again at our world and discovered that human life now seems to be quite vulnerable all over again. The conquered earth over which we today exercise dominion still has trump cards to play and in that fact lies a new challenge to our survival.

We discovered that the chemicals we used to expand the capacity of the land to produce great quantities of grain and other foods are now showing up in the breast milk of young mothers and poisoning our infants. The salmon we farmed on our quick-growth plans is not now regarded as safe for a preg-nant woman to eat, because it contaminates the unborn. There is a price to pay when profits are given a higher value than health. The antibiotics that we have used on cattle, sheep, hogs and chickens are now discovered to be low-ering human immunity to the next generation of germs and viruses. The water that once seemed abundant is now both polluted and in short supply. Bottled water is today sold in supermarkets at a cost beyond what we pay for soft drinks or beer. The air we breathe is now making us sick in such numbers that health alerts about air quality are issued daily along with the weather re-ports. The fossil fuels we burn are giving us global warming and their increas-ing shortages are tilting inflation ever upward. No end is visible in these spiraling realities. Indeed, increasing demand for fossil fuels, clean air and pure water are undeniable.

The developed nations of the Western world, by which I mean that belt that stretches across the northern hemisphere from Japan through Russia to Europe and on to North America, once had a monopoly on the resources we need to create the life of ease for our citizens. But today the world's fastest-growing economies are in China and India, two nations that claim between them about 30 percent of the world's population. One can only imagine the environmental disaster that will occur when the Chinese and Indians want to have the same percentage of automobiles, air conditioners, gas-fired appliances, telephones and computer terminals that are available in the United States today. Our excessive lifestyle in the developed nations has destroyed any moral ground we might have had to seek to hold developing nations to the standards our common environment might be able to absorb. Since we have no credibility and thus no ability to temper the coming disaster to the environment, our world will almost inevitably and relatively soon be pushed over the brink of destruction.

Can this pending tragedy be averted? I see no way to achieve that hope without a limitation on human expansion. Once the supposedly divine command to "be fruitful and multiply" was seen as necessary to enable the human race to survive. Now it must be seen as nothing less than a prescription for human genocide. Once it was accepted as the "Word of God." Now it must be viewed as a terrible and life-threatening text. Once we were able to see and embrace this terror primarily on the level of individual family tragedies. Our hearts ached at the pain endured by the McCourts in Ireland and the Yarnells in the southwestern United States. But now these family tragedies threaten to become global disasters. A text attributed to God and created to enable life to survive has become one of the sins of scripture that, if followed literally as the "Word of God," all but guarantees our annihilation. A new way to read the scriptures becomes a crying, even a frantic need.

The Word of the Lord to us can no longer be "Be fruitful and multiply." We wonder if we can hear a new "Word of the Lord" that will save us from this pending disaster.

THE VIRTUE OF BIRTH CONTROL

Effective family planning has become a new moral imperative.

James A. Pike[5]

The most apparent fact about the public face of Christianity in recent history is that it is continually in conflict over issues of human sexuality. The battles being fought represent a major war within the Christian community. In order to place the crisis of our burgeoning human population into a context where it can be discussed meaningfully, we need to look at this contemporary conflict in the light of the history of our cultural understanding of both religion and sexuality. Religious people think that it is a moral battle. Nonreligious people think of it in survival terms. Light needs to be thrown on this debate that today produces mostly heat.

Historically, the leadership of the Christian church has always attacked vigorously any procedure that might separate sexuality from procreation. That leadership has consistently stated that if this separation were ever allowed to occur, the door to moral anarchy would be opened so wide that it could never again be shut. The only constraining power, they have argued, capable of keeping sex in line and therefore moral is the fear of pregnancy. Out of this belief has arisen the prohibition against anything that might come between sexual activity and conception. As the issues facing the world have changed, however, the human birthrate has begun to threaten the survival of the whole ecosystem. As reproducing life has faded in importance across our society it has been replaced by the concern that appears to dictate a compelling need to slow down the human birthrate. Survival replaced morality as the driving emotion in this conflict, and in response the major religious institutions of the West began to experience a dramatic identity crisis. The Christian church, which historically had claimed for itself the right to define and to defend public morality, suddenly discovered itself still supporting the expansion of the human population as the highest good. Christians justified this behavior with the claim that they were preventing the gift of sexuality from becoming "irresponsible" or from being practiced without the "punishing" consequences necessary to secure control over all sexual activity. Today those same Christians fail to understand that this is no longer the substance of the conflict.

Throughout human history an ancient dance has been conducted between religion and sex. They have been bound together like the yin and the yang. It will be helpful, therefore, to see the present phase of this dance as only one more part in an ancient and long-term relationship.

Sex and religion have never been separated in human history. It is almost amusing to listen to church leaders, caught up as they are in the debates of this present generation, discussing questions about the acceptability of various changing patterns in sexual behavior. How many times have I heard some form of this pious yearning, "I wish we could quit talking about sex and get back to concentrating on the church's mission." They do not seem to recognize that sex is and has always been at the heart of the mission of every religious system. Sex and religion have moved in tandem since the dawn of human self-consciousness. Sex is such a powerful force that religion has always felt it must master and control it in order for religion to have credibility. Organized religion has also related to sexual activity as something to be feared, which in turn has led to enormous efforts throughout history to tame it, incorporate it, deny it or in some manner make it the servant of religion.

On one side these efforts were seen in those ancient religious systems, shaped by the agricultural cycle, which believed that God was worshiped by co-opting sex to serve the fertility needs of that culture. That was when temple prostitutes, both male and female, became part of religious liturgies. On the other side of this debate has been the Western Catholic tradition which, reacting to loose sexual practices in the Mediterranean world, made the suppression of sex the first prerequisite for the holy life of both the ordained and what they called "the religious"; that is, monks, nuns, sisters and brothers who lived under vows in various orders. In this view holiness and sexual practice were defined as mutually antithetical.

To undergird this conviction, church leaders in this period of Christian history began to teach people that bodies were unclean, even loathsome, and physical desire was nothing other than the mark of the evil one, manifesting itself in our "fallen natures." This attitude reflected, far more than the church has ever recognized, not a biblical perspective so much as a Neoplatonic Greek worldview that separated bodies from souls, flesh from spirit and material things from spiritual things. In this Western tradition marriage itself came to be regarded as a compromise with sin, while virginity was installed as the highest virtue. It was St. Paul who proclaimed that he was "captive to the law of sin which dwells in my members" (Rom. 7:23). He spoke of a war that went on inside him, enabling his mind, which was spiritual, to follow one law, while his body, which was carnal, followed another. "Wretched man that I am! Who will deliver me from this body of death?" (Rom. 7:24), he asked. His words would later be used to equate celibacy with holiness. The only virtue found in sex was ongoing procreation and the preservation of the human species. Outside of that purpose, it was believed, sex had no redeeming features.

The church had by this time clearly lost that part of its own biblical creation story in which God was portrayed as creating ex nihilo—out of nothing—and calling good all that God had made, including the physical earth and presumably the physical bodies of human beings together with their sexual desires (Gen. 1:25). The battle in religious circles over birth control was, therefore, a battle that pitted a religion of control and repression against a religion that celebrated the goodness of creation. It is certainly not accurate to portray it as a battle between morality and the breakdown of morality, as so many religious spokespersons, even today, like to assert.

Primitive attempts at birth control have been around since human beings became aware of the relationship between sex and procreation and were motivated primarily by the inconvenience of an unwanted pregnancy. There is even a biblical story about a man named Onan who did not want to produce an heir by his deceased brother's widow, so he practiced what came to be called "coitus interruptus" and, as the Bible said, "spilled his seed on the ground" (Gen. 38:9, KJV). This "seed" was thought of as the "source of life," and its "holiness" was not to be wasted. Religious negativity toward masturbation finds some of its roots here.

Before DNA evidence could trace parenthood so precisely, the only way a man could guarantee the legitimacy of his own offspring was to keep his wife confined in a place where no opportunity for sexual indiscretion existed. As one person observed, the primary difference between knowledge and faith was that the woman knew she was the mother of the baby while the man had "faith." A desire to make the man's faith as certain as his wife's knowledge led to social prohibitions on women's mobility. That too was a form of birth control, but it was thought of as godly, not sinful. There were also techniques developed to produce a "spontaneous abortion," but none of them was particularly satisfactory or safe. The only sure method of birth control in those days was abstinence and the primary force undergirding abstinence was public opinion, enforced by the moral pronouncements of ecclesiastical leaders. Hence in the Western world, the Christian church staked its claim to being the guardian of this powerful sexual force, which they believed had to be controlled or public morality would be doomed. Birth control became, therefore, the implacable enemy of the church and thus was by definition evil.

In earlier parts of history, the number of women appears to have been greater than the number of men. This was because of the predominantly male casualties suffered in both warfare and the hunt. The extra women in the tribe could be cared for only with a system of multiple wives, so polygamy was not only encouraged, it was said to have been blessed by God. Religious systems have always accommodated reality in ways such as this. The Hebrew Bible is filled with stories that illustrate this principle. The patriarchs of Israel's history—Abraham, Isaac, Jacob and Joseph—all had numerous wives.

Since women were considered to be the property of men, wives were a sign of wealth and power. Alliances were frequently sealed when one king gave his daughter to the harem of another king. The Bible tells us of Solomon's one thousand wives and concubines. The day had not yet dawned when this male-imposed stereotype of the female and her purpose was thought of as immoral. Women's feelings were given no consideration, since controlling the woman's body for the sexual benefit of the male was the only priority and men claimed that right exclusively for themselves.

When monogamy, reflecting an increasing appreciation of women, became the norm, the sense of a woman's worth was a potent force that contributed to the importance of family planning. Some natural processes of birth control then came to be called moral by the church. These included postponing the weaning process in the belief that pregnancies were less probable while the mother was nursing, thereby resulting in better spacing for the children. Then religious institutions began to encourage couples to practice periodic withdrawal from sexual activity for pious reasons. A couple might give themselves to prayer and abstinence for the forty days of Lent, for example, which would, not coincidentally, take the woman out of production temporarily. The modern attempt to predict the moment of ovulation by the woman so that sexual intercourse might be withheld at the time of fertility is still regarded by the Roman Catholic Church as a natural (and acceptable) form of family planning. Critics refer to it by the less generous term "Vatican roulette." These crude forms of birth control received ecclesiastical blessing because none of them committed what the church regarded as the cardinal sin of separating sexuality from procreation.

There was also in Christian history a widespread use of mistresses—especially postmenopausal mistresses, who posed no threat of pregnancy and whose presence meant that wives could be spared the regular risk of childbirth. This was a reflection of that well-entrenched double standard of morality. It was quite public, and yet no word of disapproval from the church was forthcoming. The church condoned the morality of sexual activity outside of marriage by men much more quickly than it allowed any restriction on conception inside a faithful marriage. Many parts of the Christian church are still locked in this antiquated position.

In the twentieth century, however, many new things coalesced to produce a dramatic sexual revolution. First, there was the development of the sanitary napkin, which did more to free women from the old stereotypes than has yet been fully understood. The inhibiting "bustle," designed to keep the bulky clothing worn during menstruation from being obvious, was doomed once the sanitary napkin gained ascendancy. Such cover-up styles were quickly replaced by the form-fitting dresses worn by the "flappers" of the 1920s when they celebrated this new freedom by doing the Charleston. Next there was the rise of other powerful emancipating forces. The suffragette movement established women's right to vote and thus their right to full citizenship. The opening of the doors of higher education to women followed quickly. Teachers' colleges were set up primarily for women to alleviate the teaching shortage, a crisis created when the profession paid so poorly that men stopped seeking this role. The same source of cheap labor would also open nursing and secretarial positions to women.

Progress was slow, however, until World War II created the need for women to enter the workforce in massive numbers. It even sent women into heavy industry. "Rosie the Riveter" entered our consciousness and has never departed. Following World War II there was a rush into coeducational university life in all of the most prestigious centers of higher learning. This, in turn, opened the doors for women to enter the workforce in the professions and at executive levels in business from which they had previously been prohibited. These new freedoms meant that women had an ever-rising need to balance career with family. Birth control became increasingly necessary. A safe, relatively efficient condom was developed. This was by every measure the most successful method of birth control yet devised, and it is not surprising that condoms are still today readily available through dispensers in almost every public restroom in America. Finally, "the pill" was created through medical and scientific research and birth control had at long last become convenient, safe and fully effective. It was also increasingly socially acceptable.

These were the forces that created the era of sexual freedom that appeared to justify the worst fears of the most righteous moralists, including strident voices from both the Protestant and Catholic sides of the Christian church. The 1960s were a decade of rampant sexual experimentation. The pill separated women once and for all from living under the burden of a male-imposed biological definition. The pill also began finally to affect population growth. Every nation in the developed Western world today has slowed its birthrate substantially, with some nations, like Italy—incidentally, a predominantly Roman Catholic country—no longer even reproducing their present population.

The people of the Western world have now simply risen up and discarded the family-planning repression of Western religion. The Protestant churches, by and large, adapted to these new realities and ceased condemning birth control. The Roman Catholic Church held firm to its condemnation of all "unnatural" means of birth control only to see its constituency abandon their church's teaching on this subject almost totally. Polls indicate that Roman Catholic women in the developed nations of the world practice birth control in exactly the same percentages (90-plus percent) as do Protestant women, Jewish women and nonreligious women. Papal teaching on this subject is simply ignored. The only place where the traditional sexual teaching of the church fuels emotion today is on the issue of abortion, which I regard as nothing more than the last gasp of the birth control battle. Abortion would be minimal today if sex education and birth control were available to all of our citizens. But, of course, conservative Catholic and Protestant churches would never allow that. It is, however, a battle they are destined to lose. The increasing popularity of the so-called morning-after drugs, such as Plan B and Preven, now legally available in the United States without a prescription, will quickly diminish the need for abortion. The great moral battle of the previous century is destined to die without a whimper.

The population of the world continues to explode today only in the third world, where poverty, ignorance and traditional religious teachings combine to produce a senselessly high number of births, a burgeoning that results in starvation and shocking rates of infant mortality. Relief efforts to feed these children, without a corresponding program of education and birth control, will only guarantee a population explosion in the next generation that will make infant mortality even worse. Unfortunately, that effort is periodically impeded by American politicians who seek the conservative religious vote by prohibiting funding that goes to any family-planning clinic where abortion or abortion counseling might be available, which of course includes almost every family-planning center in the third world.

"New occasions teach new duties. Time makes ancient good uncouth."[6] These words from James Russell Lowell, written in 1845, articulate a daring truth. The time has come for the Christian church in all its forms to recognize that its traditional negativity toward birth control has itself become immoral and that limiting births has become a new virtue. Religious teaching must turn from its fear-driven moralism and concentrate on deepening relationships, articulating a new, responsible human maturity and recovering the essential goodness of life. The day has arrived when people no longer believe that God commands them to "be fruitful and multiply." This "terrible text," this sin of scripture, has become a dated expression of an ancient survival fear and the literal understanding of the Bible that gave this verse its power must now be jettisoned.

Human survival means that human beings must cease our outrageous over-breeding and learn to live in harmony with this world, not as the dominators of its life, but as an essential part of a common and fragile ecosystem. Perhaps our hope now resides in our increasing fear. There are plenty of reasons to assert that this fear is rising. The question is, Will that fear be of sufficient magnitude to change the human habits of the ancient past? Time will tell, but to those fears we now turn.

5

THE EARTH FIGHTS BACK

Unbridled striving for power was to make human beings like
their God—so these human beings invoked God's almighty
power in order to furnish a religious justification for their own.
The Christian belief in creation, as it has been maintained in the
European and American Christianity of the Western Churches, is
therefore not guiltless in the crises in the world today.

Jürgen Moltmann[7]

The purpose of being fruitful and multiplying, according to Genesis
1:28, was to subdue the earth and to have dominion over all living
things. This text set the stage for seeing the earth as the enemy of human beings. Increasingly we exercised that dominion, but today the earth is fighting
back.

Traveling through Australia and New Zealand several years ago, my wife
and I came upon a scene that was both ordinary and yet quite bizarre. In both
countries we saw schoolchildren six, seven and eight years of age or so who
were playing on the school grounds at recess. They were running, laughing
and engaging in games of competitive skill. That was certainly ordinary;
nothing unusual there. In both countries, however, we noticed that each
child was wearing a wide-brimmed Australian-style hat. There is nothing
quite so weird to the American eye as the scene of children running on a
playground wearing not baseball caps or football helmets, but wide-
brimmed, sun-shading Aussie hats. Upon inquiry about this strange scene,

we were informed that these hats were now required by law. In both Australia and New Zealand children in the state-supported public schools must wear uniforms. The government had recently added to the mandated standard dress code these hats designed to screen the children from the harmful rays of the sun. Both nations are situated deep in the southern hemisphere. The ultraviolet radiation from the "hole" that has recently developed in the ozone layer over Antarctica is now believed to present a serious health danger to the people who live in the southern hemisphere. The farther south the nation extends, the greater the danger. Hats are therefore encouraged for adults in Australia and New Zealand, but they are required by law for the children. Welcome to the twenty-first century!

On the other side of the southern hemisphere, in the town of Punta Arenas, Chile, part of the regular curriculum for schoolchildren is instruction on how to survive in the sun. I cannot recall that being part of my curriculum as a child. Children in this town, however, live under the same thinning in the ozone layer that is above Antarctica. In Punta Arenas the population receives 40 percent more ultraviolet radiation than is judged to be normal or healthy. There are whole days in Chile when the population is told it is not safe to exit their homes during daylight hours. Some self-serving politicians and business leaders may still debate the causes of ozone depletion and global warming, but everywhere one looks, signs are apparent that something is terribly wrong.

I was not certain that people could be as blind to environmental reality as some seem to be until I read a report written in 2001 by a man named Hugh Morgan who was a spokesman for the Western Mining Corporation of Australia. He suggested, in his report, that those concerned about the environment are nothing but "communists who have been reinvented as 'born again environmentalists.'" To Mr. Morgan they represent "a radical and uncompromising attack on Western traditions."[8] I was fascinated to notice that in this report, Mr. Morgan buttressed his argument by saying that what was at risk from the environmentalists was the Western tradition of building things which, he argued, was in response to the biblical injunction to "be fruitful and multiply and subdue the earth." Mr. Morgan does not yet seem to understand that the earth is now fighting back against human abuse, the most serious form of which is overpopulation. The first major battlefield in the war between overbreeding human beings and the environment we share with all other creatures appears to be occurring in the ozone layer of the southern hemisphere.

The ozone layer is a band that varies between six and thirty miles up within the earth's middle atmosphere. It is that shield which has made life possible on this planet. It both traps warmth and protects us from the killing rays of the sun.

The first warning about the thinning of this protective covering came as recently as 1974, when scientists discovered the effect of chlorofluorocarbons (CFCs), wonder compounds that were being used in refrigeration and in aerosol spray cans, among other things. Millions of tons of these chlorofluorocarbons had been sold and incorporated into products before the environmental danger was recognized. The fact that the thinning had become so noticeable that it is referred to as a "hole" in the Antarctica ozone layer became apparent in 1985. The finger of blame was soon thereafter, in 1994 to be specific, pointed exclusively at human beings. A NASA satellite provided the compelling evidence when it detected hydrogen chloride, a byproduct of chlorofluorocarbon decomposition, in the stratosphere. This charge became formal and official when a United Nations panel made up of twenty-five hundred of the world's leading climate scientists from one hundred countries stated in 1995 that "discernible human influence" could now be documented in the global climate. This conclusion was based on the fact that hydrogen chloride came not only from the breakdown of the chlorofluorocarbons, which only humans can create, but also from the production of such things as aluminum, halogens, halons and the nitrogen used in fertilizers, all of which bear a uniquely human stamp. Chlorofluorocarbons have long lifetimes, ranging from fifty to several hundred years. They rise in the atmosphere until they, along with other human-produced chemicals, are broken down by ultraviolet radiation into chlorine and bromine, both of which have the capacity and the appetite to eat the ozone. Though minuscule when compared with the vastness of the ozone, a single chlorine atom can destroy up to one hundred thousand ozone molecules.[9] It is not a fair fight.

In September of 2000 the "hole" in the ozone over Antarctica was said to have reached the size of eighteen million square miles, or six hundred thousand square miles bigger than it was two years earlier. To give my readers a point of reference to embrace this enormous number, the United States measures three and a half million square miles. Though there has been some evidence that the rate of the thinning of this "hole" has actually slowed down since 2000, there is no evidence that any recovery has begun. A thinning of the ozone layer over the Arctic is also visible but has not yet reached crisis proportions.

Nothing reveals better than this ozone problem the pressure of human population expansion together with the interdependence of our common environment. It also makes clear that in environmental degradation this world sometimes punishes the innocent rather than the guilty. The fact is that up to 90 percent of the human production of chlorofluorocarbons occurs in the northern hemisphere. Even more specifically, it occurs in a familiar band of latitude that encompasses the industrialized world, from Japan westward across Europe and into North America. These chlorofluorocarbons, once loosed in this industrial belt, travel toward the polar regions of our globe and sit within each polar vortex. The Arctic polar vortex is not as strong as the Antarctica vortex, since the atmosphere is warmer in the north because of heavier industrialization, so the Arctic region neither gets as cold nor stays cold as long as Antarctica. For that reason there is less ozone depletion in the Arctic. So while the industrial nations of the northern hemisphere are the prime polluters, the largest amount of ozone destruction takes place in the South Pole region! Another result of this same process is that every few years a chunk of Antarctica, typically the size of Rhode Island or Delaware, breaks off and floats away. The people who are first paying the price in this impending ecological disaster are the inhabitants of the southern hemisphere, particularly those nations that are nearest Antarctica. So children in Australia and New Zealand, Chile and Argentina receive regular instructions on how to survive an ozone "hole." It is not exactly fair. The wealthy, developed nations of the northern hemisphere create for their people comfort and a standard of living known nowhere else in the world, and the citizens of the poorer nations of the southern hemisphere develop the skin cancers, the melanomas and the other results of our environmental excesses.[10]

This ozone thinning is not the only place where the price exacted for the rapid proliferation of the human species and the incessant desire on the part of the ever-larger numbers of people to wrest the good life from the created world is visible. Plankton, probably the most basic item in the food chain of animate creatures, has already been depleted by 6 to 12 percent in the waters off Antarctica and that rate appears to be accelerating.

Mount Kilimanjaro in Tanzania is experiencing the shrinking of its ice cap at such a rate that it will disappear, except on older postcards, within fifteen years, says an environmentalist writer for the Reuters News Agency.[11] It has already lost 80 percent of its ice cap since it was first surveyed in 1912. The glaciers around the world are also shrinking. It is estimated that by 2025 glaciers will have lost 90 percent of the volume they possessed a century ago. The largest glacier in Peru retreated fourteen feet a year twenty years ago. Today it retreats ninety-nine feet a year. In Austria the ski slopes in the Alps are closing due to the bareness of that country's peaks. Melting in the Arctic region is so severe that the mythical Northwest Passage might become a reality. The Canadian government recently sent a military expedition into the Arctic to make sure that the nations of the world recognized Canada's ownership of that area just in case a trade route someday opens through Arctic waters.

Ocean temperatures the world over are rising, ocean water is expanding, sea levels are rising and evaporation is accelerating. This means that more water enters the atmosphere, which in turn traps more heat, which means that the surface temperatures on the earth are also increasing. Since 1980 ten of the hottest years in recorded history have occurred, with the years 1997 and 1998 being the hottest on record. The heat wave that Europe endured in the summer of 2003 was so severe that thousands died from it. People in the midwestern part of the United States report that the annual tornado count in 1980 was between two hundred and three hundred a year. Today that count reaches a thousand per year and is regularly reported on television. The amount of carbon dioxide in the atmosphere prior to the Industrial Revolution in the nineteenth century was 275 parts per million. Today it is 360 parts per million. It is expected to be over 700 parts per million by 2050.

In the northern hemisphere spring now arrives a week earlier than it did just twenty years ago. The migratory patterns of birds and animals have begun to change. Eighty percent of the species, from tropical butterflies to arctic foxes, are forging new migration patterns that take them farther north. In Richmond, Virginia, the first sign of spring used to be the welcome return of the robins in late February or early March. In the year 2002, the robins did not leave Richmond at all, and by overstaying their welcome and wintering there, they created a pest problem for many residents. According to a Queensland, Australia, museum arachnologist, spiders in that area that normally breed once a year are now breeding three or four times a year and some are doubling their size and their life span. Banana trees are now known to flourish as far north as Boston, Massachusetts.

There will be effects of global warming on all life everywhere. No one will escape it. The Intergovernmental Panel on Climate Change (IPCC) of the United Nations has warned that rising global temperatures "will disrupt fishing, farming and forestry." Global warming will "kill the coral reefs" found in the seas. It will cause ocean water levels to rise, "flooding coastal areas in China, Bangladesh, Egypt, the Gulf of Mexico and the Chesapeake Bay area."[12] Yet because these results do not come within the time frame of the next election, no political consensus builds in the developed nations of the world to force a preemptive strike against what increasingly looks like a coming disaster. Human beings seem to need a calamity of some sort to occur before they recognize the inescapable conclusion that overbreeding is not just an individual tragedy; it is a human tragedy and global warming is its first offspring.

Political leaders of the northern hemisphere's industrial nations have been forced to admit this reality, in response to massive amounts of data, but they have now shifted their line of defense. They cite the swings in the earth's temperature over the centuries that once gave us the Ice Age and suggest that we might be experiencing nothing more than a normal cycle of global warming and cooling that this planet has known before. It is interesting that no one in the southern hemisphere has been known to endorse this ostrichlike argument. In 2001, when President George W. Bush of the United States withdrew unilaterally from the Kyoto Treaty on the environment because it was not good for American business, he sent shock waves across the southern hemisphere. For this nation, which makes up 5 percent of the world's population but uses 25 percent of the world's resources and produces more trash and pollution than any other nation in the world, to take this stand was seen by the rest of the world as an act of arrogant irresponsibility. The fact that it was one of the first acts of his administration made it seem all the more pointed and all the more ominous. Mr. Bush was followed in this action by the head of the Russian government, Vladimir Putin, making the old Cold War competitor-nations new partners in the pending global disaster.[13]

Environmental arrogance seems to be higher among those who are the developed and thus the chief polluting nations of the world. Is it only a coincidence that they are also the nations most deeply shaped by the Christian re-

ligion? If these two things are related, can they also be unhooked? That will
not be easy, for traditional attitudes within Christianity must clearly be countered before progress in this area can be made. We have cited the various
texts in the biblical story that seem to validate exploitation, but can we go behind those texts and delineate the origins of those attitudes that came to be
reflected in the texts? I think we can, but it will mean a journey far back into
our religious history to a time before the Bible began to be written.

Somewhere around the middle of the thirteenth century before the Common Era, our ancestors in faith, the Hebrews, were a nomadic group of wan-
derers in the wilderness. The Bible, which did not begin to be written until
about the tenth century BCE, illumines that prebiblical time by telling us
that these Hebrews wandered in that wilderness for forty years between their
days as slaves in Egypt and their conquest of Canaan, which they regarded as
their Promised Land. In those wilderness years these Hebrews transformed
the monotheistic God they had met in Egypt into a powerful male deity, who
ruled the wilderness even though this deity was thought to live above the sky.
This God was interpreted as analogous to the wind—that is, operating on the
earth but never identified with the earth in any way. This God might periodically invade the earth from on high, but the earth was not the divine abode.
This God seemed to live in history, not in the cycles of the earth.

In the land of Canaan, however, which these Hebrews would invade and
settle, they were destined to confront an agricultural society with a religious
system closely associated with the earth. The ancient deity of these Canaanites was a fertility goddess named Astarte, who would later have a better-
known male consort named Baal, who had risen to prominence by the time
the Jews arrived. In the ensuing battle between these two competing world-
views the Jews were ultimately successful. They then interpreted their victory
to be the conquest by their God from the sky of the earth goddess and her
male consort, worshiped by the Canaanites. So conquering the earth was
considered to be a divine virtue. These people then built into the heart of
their religion, which later came to be called Judaism, a denigration of the sacredness of the earth that was destined to become an operative assumption in
their understanding of life.

Christianity, because it grew out of Judaism, almost inevitably carried this
"anti-earth" attitude with it. Its Jesus was understood as one who had invaded

the earth on behalf of or at the behest of the Father God from the sky. The religion that developed into Christianity encouraged its worshipers to dream of and to anticipate the real life that would occur in heaven and thus not to focus their attention on this earth or to have any responsibility for its care, its nurture or its transformation. Salvation was portrayed as escaping the earth, which was somehow evil. It was a human-centered but heavenward-bound religious emphasis. Ecological disaster was all but inevitable.

Lynn White has described Christianity as the "most anthropocentric religion in the world."[14] Heaven, not earth, was assumed to be the real home of the adherents of this religion. Charles Birch, an Australian biologist, took a similar tack when he wrote that "Christian monotheism" had, perhaps inadvertently, "denied the reality of the gods, spirits and demons that, in the belief of many religions, inhabit the world" and that, therefore, tend to make the world appear holy in these religious systems. Thus he suggested that Christianity had in effect "secularized the world" by stripping it of any sense of its intrinsic holiness.[15]

Maybe that is part of the reason why it has taken so long for a global consciousness to develop in the world and why when that consciousness did emerge it came from sources outside the Christian religion and was actually in conflict with Western views.

Many would suggest that the birth of this consciousness occurred in 1945, when atomic bombs fell on Japan from U.S. planes but radioactive dust was carried around the world. Our fledgling global consciousness gained maturity in 1962, when Rachel Carson published her book *Silent Spring*.[16] Carson's book opened the eyes of many to look anew at the environment and, particularly, at the effect human beings were having on that environment. Next came the space probe, led by Neil Armstrong, also in 1962, which gave us that indelible photograph of the planet earth seen from space. The globe was green and blue, distant and isolated, and all human beings began to embrace its smallness, its finitude, its unity and its fragility. The phrase "our island home" entered our vocabulary and even made its way into some of the Christian church's liturgies.[17]

Then came environmental disasters like the accidents at Three Mile Island in the United States in 1979 and Chernobyl in the Soviet Union in 1986, which forced human beings to embrace the terrifying reality that what happens anywhere will inevitably affect people everywhere. The rising tide of world opinion against atomic bomb testing by the superpowers and the proliferation of atomic weapons to such nations as Pakistan and India was another step in developing a world consciousness. Next came the realization and the fear that these weapons had found their way to rogue states like North Korea and from them perhaps into terrorist groups, which made every nation vulnerable, and once again a sense of the commonality of our humanity in facing our fears was born. All of these were signs of the death of both individual thinking and even Western arrogance. Wendell L. Willkie, Republican nominee for president of the United States in 1940, had reminded us that we are all citizens of "one world,"[18] but it was life's experiences that finally put substance into Willkie's concept.

The development of treaties establishing regional trading consortiums, like the European Common Market, the North Atlantic Free Trade Association (NAFTA) and the Trade Alliance developed by the nations of the Pacific Rim, also began to lead human beings beyond the individual and tribal thinking of their ancient past and into a new global, interdependent perspective. The European Common Market has developed political and economic power that is transnational. Standards for the workplace, the mutual recognition of passports and the initiation of a common currency (the euro) are but a few illustrations of this.

A new consciousness is being born. It is challenging ancient tribal and religious assumptions. It is opening us all to new understandings of life and new possibilities for future living. It is destined to change our values, to challenge our human-centered mind-set and to call into question those religious ideas that support that mind-set. It is calling us to a new reformation that will not be comfortable.

Mother Earth is fighting back. Mother Earth is rebelling against the way she has been treated by a single species which acts as if the whole world exists to provide comfort and wealth for that species.

This planet gives powerful evidence that it will no longer tolerate exploitation without killing, in some ultimate sense, the exploiters. It may not happen suddenly, but there is a point of exploitation beyond which there is no possibility of recovery. We do not know where that point is, but few doubt its reality and some environmentalists warn that it may already have been passed. This interdependent world does not exist to provide comfort, wealth, profits and dividends for the privileged few.

Christians facing the impending ecological disaster are like Pogo when he said: "We have met the enemy and he is us." Christian thinking based on what was said to be the divine command to "be fruitful and multiply and sub-due the earth" has got to be countered.

Any Christian church that continues to oppose birth control and family planning must be confronted by the fact that it is on the wrong side of the bat-tle for survival and must be called to accountability. Moreover, Christian eth-ical teaching that does not serve the purpose of enhancing human life but rather continues to trap its constituents in patterns of hopelessness, poverty and despair must be confronted with the fact that its operating principles are now nothing less than immoral. That is not a modest shot fired across the bow of ecclesiastical intransigence, but it is an inescapable one. It forces us to start on an irrevocable path toward a reformation that is destined to be so rad-ical it will not end until the idea of God that stands at the center of the Chris-tian faith has been redefined in the light of a new consciousness. Such a reformation will call the very essence of the Judeo-Christian faith system into question. Many wonder if this can occur without Christianity either dying or being changed so dramatically as to have no continuity with its own history. Those are the challenges to which the biblical attitudes of the past have driven us. I will walk next into both arenas.

6

BAD THEOLOGY CREATES BAD ECOLOGY

The rise of Dominant Society, the desacralization of Nature, and the complicity of institutions and religion speak clearly to the most urgent needs of our time. If we hope to address these needs successfully, we need to sound a call for spiritual awakening. To create a new global culture based not on dominance over Nature for economic and political gain, but on values that endure for all times and all people.

Ed McGaa, Eagle Man[19]

*I*deas Have Consequences was the title of a book I had to read when a young theological student. I recall today nothing but the title, which captures for me an elementary truth. Ideas are not disincarnate from history. Adolf Hitler had ideas that he expressed in a book entitled *Mein Kampf*. Karl Marx had ideas that he expressed in *Das Kapital*. Both sets of ideas have had enormous consequences for human history.

I would like to suggest that the way the Judeo-Christian faith has conceived of God is an idea that has had enormous ecological consequences, and that one of the reasons the Christian church has never really embraced environmental concerns is that the church has seen God as external to life and life itself as sinful and fallen, in need of rescue by our external deity. That being so, I now believe it will be impossible to save our world from human destruction unless we abandon that traditional understanding of God. We already have noted the enmity between large parts of the Christian church and the radical necessity to limit the human birthrate. Perhaps we are ready now to expose an even deeper point of conflict. To state it boldly and in a straightforward manner, the way the Judeo-Christian tradition has conceptualized God is a primary factor in the destruction of our ecosystem and ultimately of our world. I hope you recognize that those are strong words to come from a bishop of the Christian church. I recognize that they will not be happily received in many church circles. I have a deep wish that I did not have to say them, but I do, because I believe they are true. I also wish that I did not feel compelled to act upon them. But I do. I cannot be silent, nor can I retreat from their consequences. Let me hasten to put some flesh on these provocative thoughts.

In the biblical tradition, and consequently in Christian theology, which is largely based on the way the Bible has been interpreted, the claim is made that God is known primarily through divine revelation. That is, God is a divine being who comes to us from outside life. This means that God is thought to rule this world from a position outside this world. It is only because this deity is not part of this world that the divine command could be given to the single creature who was said to be made in the divine image, to subdue the world as if that creature were not himself or herself a part of it. One does not view the earth as an enemy unless one is alienated from it.

This understanding of God is called "theism" in theological circles. It assumes that God is a supernatural being who lives outside this world, but who periodically invades this world in a miraculous way. There is no question but that this is the popular and the majority view of the God that one meets in the pages of scripture. This God of the Bible can control the weather so as to send forty days and forty nights of rain to achieve the divine purpose of punishing a sinful world by destroying it with a flood, according to the story of Noah. This God is pictured as entering history to engage in a political conflict by slamming the Egyptians with plague after plague after plague, all in the service of this God's chosen people, according to the book of Exodus. This God can shape the norms for both worship and ethics by dictating the law at Mount Sinai.

This theistically understood deity was also said to have entered the world in the "fullness of time" in the form of a human life known as Jesus of

Nazareth. That is the central image upon which the traditional Christian faith story is built. So powerful was this theistic definition of God that it dominated the way people told the Jesus story. Ultimately it was this definition that prevented people from seeing Jesus as a God-infused human being and forced them rather to perceive him as a divine visitor who came from heaven. As a divine visitor Jesus needed a mythological landing field, which is what caused the tradition of the miraculous virgin birth to enter Christianity in the ninth decade of the Common Era (see Matt. 1:18–25, Luke 1:26–2:7). At the end of his earthly life he also needed a launching pad to propel him back to his "external to the world" home above the sky, which is why the story of his cosmic ascension entered the Christian tradition in the late ninth or early tenth decade (see Luke 24:50–53 and Acts 1:1–11). Between his miraculous entry and his miraculous exit, Jesus was said to have done other supernatural, godlike things that showed his dominance over the world of nature. He could walk on water (Mark 6:48, Matt. 14:25), still the storm (Mark 4:39, Matt. 8:18–27, Luke 8:22–25) and expand the food supply to enable crowds that numbered in the thousands to have their stomachs filled from just a few loaves and fishes (Mark 6:37ff., Matt. 14:16ff., Luke 9:13ff., John 6:9ff.). Christian theology developed through history in such a way that the humanity of this Jesus was radically diminished and his divine-visitor status was greatly enhanced. This trend reached its crescendo in 1739, when Charles Wesley penned his popular Christmas carol "Hark the Herald Angels Sing," which portrayed Jesus as not human at all, but one "veiled in flesh," through which only the godhead was seen.

The second element in the theistic definition of God was that it spoke to people's security needs in a way that nothing else could. That sense of safety has been a bulwark against raising any alternatives in theological development, and enormous fear is loosed when theism is challenged. Human beings like to pretend that there is a supernatural, all-powerful God who can and will take care of them. We like to believe that there is a miracle worker in the sky who can come to our aid, a divine parent figure to whom we can appeal when all seems to be collapsing around us. We take comfort in living in the delusion of a continuing childhood of dependency.

But this theistic God died long before the ecological crisis overtook us, and despite great efforts at denial by fundamentalists, those who embrace the modern world recognize that this is so. There is no theistic God who exists to take care of you or me. There is no God who stands ready to set aside the laws by which this universe operates to come to our aid in time of need. There are no everlasting arms underneath us to catch us when we fall. Ask the people who were the hapless passengers on those hijacked airplanes as they were hurtling toward the World Trade Center or the Pentagon on September 11, 2001. No divine hand reached down to save them. Ask the families and friends of the crew on the spacecraft *Challenger* as it exploded shortly after lift-off in 1986. No protecting deity embraced them. Ask the children, spouses or parents of service personnel during the various Iraqi wars where this supernatural God was when they received the official message from their government which began, "We regret to inform you . . ." Ask the Jews where the God who could split the Red Sea was when they were being marched into Hitler's crematoriums during the Holocaust. Ask the children who are born with the HIV virus or the parents of an only child who is killed by a drunk driver. The God that we presume lives above the sky, whose primary vocation is to watch over, guard and protect vulnerable human beings, somehow appears to be frequently off-duty.

When people question this theistic God in the light of the constant pain and trauma found in the normal course of human life, the pious rhetoric of theism's defenders becomes almost incoherent. One hears hysterical talk about free will, about how God allows us to bring pain upon ourselves and even about how God never asks us to bear more than we can endure. Sometimes religious spokespersons explain that we actually *deserve* the pain and trauma of life. How very trite these explanations are! Does a soldier, of his own free will, decide to walk into the line of fire, or does the theistic God finger a particular person for punishment? Does a baby choose, of its own free will, to be born to an HIV-infected mother or are only those babies who are particularly evil infected with this virus? Does God designate those who are to be executed in any religious or ethnic cleansing operation or in any mob activity? Are not these divine definitions little more than the pitiful pleas of human beings who prefer to live in a world of make-believe, human beings who want never to grow up? Is there some hidden hope, deep inside us, that manifests itself in our attempt to define God theistically so we might not have to alter our lives dramatically to save our environment? After all, if the theistic God can control the weather patterns, bring the rain and stop the hurricanes, could this deity not also vacuum the atmosphere to remove our pollutants and thus restore this external world to ecological balance? How many people really believe that this could happen? How many believe that the theistic God really exists?

Christian evangelicals like to use the term "born again." It is an interesting choice of words, for when one is "born again," one is newly a child. It represents a second return to a state of chronic dependency. Perhaps what we specifically need is not to be "born again," but to grow up and become mature adults. Until we recognize that this understanding of God is no more, that the theistic God has either died or that such a God never existed, we will fail to reach the maturity that enables us to recognize that we have to be responsible for ourselves—for our own breeding habits and for our constant violation of the earth that is our home. We human beings are not some alien visitors who happen to be on the planet earth. Our human life is *part* of this planet. We have evolved like every other creature into our present stage of life. We share a common environment and a common world with plants and animals to which we are related more closely than we have ever imagined. We breathe the same common air and drink the same common water. We can no longer sing, as one evangelical hymn suggests, "I'm but a stranger here, heaven is my home," with any integrity. Heaven is *not* our home. This planet earth is. That is the first realization we must embrace when theism dies.

Once we accept the fact that there is no theistic God who will come to our aid, religious authority crumbles. For it is the claim to be able either to speak for God or to explain divine behavior that is the source of religious authority. Part of the reason believers let church leaders get away with excessive claims of infallibility and inerrancy is that this kind of certainty keeps human fears in check. When theism dies, those fears become manifest. But theism is not God; it is nothing but a human definition of God—and a radically inadequate one at that. When theism dies God does not die, but a human definition of God does. That is an enormous difference that needs to be grasped. Our job is not to recreate God but to seek a more adequate, new definition of our experience of God.

To begin that task I turn to the minority voices of the Bible that speak of a different understanding of the God experience that might make more sense in our time. On the other, less frequently read pages of our sacred text one can also discover a God who is not an external supernatural being, but who is perceived as the life force that flows through all that is. Sometimes this God is called Spirit and is identified with the wind that vitalizes and animates the forests. Sometimes this God is identified with our very breath as an indwelling presence. When this divine life force comes upon us, it does not lift us out of the world. Rather, it brings life out of death (see Ezek. 37:1–15) or it calls us into a new state of living. The classic biblical story indicating this is the account of Pentecost (Acts 2), which suggests that Spirit-filled people can step beyond tribal boundaries and speak the language of their hearers and thus respond to a call to a new humanity because God is no longer external but internal.

Another minority voice in the Bible defines God simply as the power of love. If you abide in love, says one writer, you abide in God (1 John 4:16). Love is the power that somehow expands our sense of freedom and thus enables us to enter life deeply by giving ourselves away.

Still another image of God is found in the poetic language of the book of Psalms, where God is likened to a rock, that firmness underneath one's feet that is real (Ps. 18:2, 19:14, 31:2, 42:9, 62:2, 71:3). When the Bible is read carefully, we discover that the image of God as a supernatural invading external deity that has dominated Western religion is not the only way our spiritual ancestors perceived God. Why then should we be bound to an image, or to the religion based on that image, which has left a trail of pain across human history? Even today, as a direct result of our theology, people are still able to believe that God has commanded us to multiply and to do violent things both to our environment and to one another. It is in obedience to that dominant biblical understanding that we are today at the point of destroying the ability of this planet to sustain any life at all.

Returning to the concept of Spirit for a moment, I find a slightly different nuanced understanding in the creation story that deserves at least a mention. In the first chapter of Genesis, God is portrayed as a presence "moving over the face of the waters" (Gen. 1:2). A study of this text suggests the analogy of a mother hen brooding over her nest to bring forth life. A God who is understood after the analogy of a mother hen is not something external to this world. It makes a vast difference to our sense of responsibility to our world if we redefine God, not as the external deity who calls the world into being by divine command, but as the power that emerges within all of life.

We know from our study of evolution that life is a single whole. All life has developed from that first cell of living matter that was born in the sea some four billion years ago. Life moved from that single cell into clusters of cells over hundreds of millions of years, allowing in those clusters the beginning of cell differentiation and therefore organic complexity. Hundreds of millions of years later, this seamless source of life split, with one strand producing plant life and the other animal life, but both were deeply interdependent. Each was a source of life to the other. Hundreds of millions of years later, life left the oceans and moved into estuaries and riverbeds and it kept evolving and adapting. When the land finally became hospitable to life, these living specimens climbed out of the riverbeds in both plant and animal forms and began to live in the unique land environment, always changing and adapting, but still deeply related. No more than one to two million years ago, this process finally evolved into our earliest recognizable human ancestors. Perhaps no more than fifty thousand to one hundred thousand years ago, self-consciousness and the ability to create symbols, called words, to convey abstract ideas combined to make us uniquely human. Human beings were not created in the image of some external deity; we developed out of the evolutionary soup as part of the fabric of life itself. DNA evidence today demonstrates that we are kin not only to apes, but also to cabbages. We are part of an emerging life force sharing a common environment with every other living thing. No creature can dominate the world, as those called Homo sapiens have sought to do, because all life is radically interdependent. God's spirit, which brooded over the waters to call life into being, is not an external, but an emerging presence. It is not a theistic, supernatural, alien-to-our-world deity, but the source of our common life.

Even when the Bible moves on to a second story of creation, the portrait is still of a deity who is not really external. God breathes into Adam, says the ancient Hebrew legend. Adam becomes a living creature because the breath of God becomes his breath. God then creates the animals to alleviate the man's loneliness. All living things share that divine life. In Hebrew the word for breath is *nephesh,* and it is related to the wind, which was thought to be the breath of God. Nephesh, however, is present in all creation. It is the prophet Jeremiah who says that the animals too are the creation of God and must therefore be regarded as holy (Jer. 27:5). It is the Psalmist who asserts that all creatures look to God for their sustenance and that even the creatures are dismayed when God hides the divine face. When God removes the divine breath, says the Psalmist, even the creatures die (Ps. 124:29). God is *not* external to life. God is to be identified with the life present in all living things. The Psalmist goes on to say that God's springs quench the thirst of the beasts. God caused grass to grow for the cattle, cedars for the birds, fir trees for the storks, high mountains for the goats, rocks for the badgers. God even made the darkness so that creatures may seek their prey in it just as God made the day so that human beings could earn their livelihood (Ps. 124:10–30).

In the Noah story saving the animals was part of the plan of salvation (Gen. 6:20). In Ecclesiastes, Qoheleth, the Preacher, reminds his readers that "the fate of the sons of men and the fate of beasts is the same. . . . They all have the same breath, and man has no advantage over the beasts." In contemplating death this writer asks, "Who knows whether the spirit of man goes upward and the spirit of the beast goes down to the earth?" (Eccles. 3:19, 21). This is not the portrait of a supreme being living beyond the sky, separate from the earth; this is the portrait of a divine presence that permeates all of life, that binds all creatures into the mutuality of interdependency. These images are beyond theism, but they are not beyond God. Surely we can now see that we have created the theistic God in our image, even as we asserted that it was the other way around. We then used this God to justify the dreadful things we were and are doing to our world. Theism is a false notion, a human idol that must die, and when it does, God—seen as the sacred dimension in all of life—must replace it. The minority voices in our religious past must become the majority voices of our religious future.

So who is God? No one can finally say. That is not within human competence. All we can ever say is how we believe we have experienced God, doing our best to dispel our human delusions. Let me try to do just that. I experience God as the source of life calling me to live fully and thus to respect life in every form as embodying the holy. I experience God as the source of love calling me to love wastefully all that God has made, including the earth with its plants and animals. I experience God, in the words of Paul Tillich, as the "Ground of Being" calling me to be all that I can be and to affirm the sacred being of all that is. The worship of such a God could never result in the destruction of the planet that has produced us.

We have looked upward for a God above the sky for centuries, but we now know that this infinite universe is empty of supernatural invasive deities. We need to shift our vision to look within—at life, at love, at being.

The theologian Jürgen Moltmann wrote that the "alienation of nature brought about by human beings can never be overcome until men [and women] find a new understanding of themselves and a new interpretation of their world in the framework of nature."[20] That will occur, I believe, only when a new understanding of God is achieved. Good ecology requires good theology, and good theology alone will guarantee our very survival.

THE BIBLE AND WOMEN

THE TERRIBLE TEXTS

Then the Lord God said: "It is not good that the man should be alone. I will make him a helper fit for him." So out of the ground the Lord God formed every beast of the field and every bird of the air, and brought them to the man to see what he would call them; and whatever the man called every living creature, that was its name. . . . But for the man there was not found a helper fit for him. So the Lord God caused a deep sleep to fall upon the man, and while he slept took one of his ribs and closed up its place with flesh; and the rib which the Lord God had taken from the man he made into a woman and brought her to the man. Then the man said, "This at last is bone of my bones and flesh of my flesh; she shall be called Woman, because she was taken out of man."

Genesis 2:18–23

For man was not made from woman, but woman from man. Neither was man created for woman, but woman for man.

1 Corinthians 11:8–9

7

CREATION

THE WOMAN IS NOT MADE
IN THE IMAGE OF GOD

You [woman] destroyed so easily God's Image [man].

Tertullian¹

Patriarchy and sexism are certainly not limited to our own Judeo-Christian heritage, though that is the channel through which these evils have entered most of us in the Western world. It is also through that particular lens that I will seek to trace their ramifications. Before beginning that, however, I need to note the all but universal quality among human beings of a pro-male, anti-female bias.

This realization points us, I believe, to the fact that there is something deep in the human psyche that fuels an anti-female bias. If it is not a human phenomenon, it is at least present in the depths of the male psyche, and since prejudice is always a reaction to fear, it must, therefore, be assumed that men's hostility toward women expresses a primal threat that needs to be addressed. One has only to examine quotations from pre-Christian philosophers and from the sacred writings of each of the world's great religions to glimpse the universalism of a patriarchal understanding of life.

Plato, in *The Republic*, recorded Socrates as saying, "Do you know anything at all practiced among mankind in which the male sex is not far better than the female?"

Xenophon stated, "The ideal woman should see as little as possible, hear as little as possible and ask as little as possible."

In the sacred texts of the Hindus, we learn, "It is the highest duty of a woman to immolate herself after her husband's death." In another part of the Hindu tradition, we read, "Women are to be debarred from being competent students of the Vedas." The Hindu laws of Manu state, "In childhood a female is subject to her father. In youth a female is subject to her husband. When her lord is dead, she shall be subject to her sons. A woman must never be independent."

In Buddhism one is reborn a woman because of one's bad karma. Buddhist prayers include: "I pray that I may be reborn as a male in a future existence."

Jewish men are taught, in a book of Jewish prayers, to say, "Blessed be the God who has not created me a heathen, a slave or a woman." Talmudic writers added: "It would be better to burn the words of Torah than to entrust them to a woman."

In the Muslim Qur'an (Koran) we learn that the woman is regarded as "half a man" and that "forgetfulness overcomes the woman. They are inherently weaker in rational judgment."[2]

The reasons for this overwhelming negativity toward the woman are varied, but its reality is consistent. One reason, in early human history, was that the woman generally did not grow to be as large as the man and her ability to run and to compete in various tests of strength, upon which the survival of the tribe depended, were obviously limited. She was thus determined to be something of a second-class human being. The vulnerability of the childbirth process and the necessary dependency the woman exhibited in the later stages of pregnancy and while nursing helped cast her in the role of "the weaker sex."

The mother and the child were seemingly connected to each other in such a way as to put both out of circulation for long periods of time, causing women and children to be thought of as inextricably bound together in weakness. The phrase "women and children first," associated in our own folklore with the sinking of the great ship *Titanic*, captured this ancient attitude that defined both females and children as the helpless and dependent ones of society, people quite obviously not to be treated as equals. The children, at least the male children, might grow out of this second-class status, but women, it was thought, could never escape their destiny.

The study of ancient human traditions has uncovered other sources of fear that illumine this inquiry. Anthropologists and mythologists, such as Joseph Campbell, suggest that there was a time in human history when the feminine was the analogy by which God was defined.[3] The fertility cults of prehistory were dedicated to the Earth Mother, who was seen as the source and sustainer of tribal life. In time the male deity who lived beyond the sky and who impregnated the passive Mother Earth with the rains of his divine semen replaced her. This powerful sky deity was modeled after the tribal chief, whose strength led the tribe both in battle and in the hunt.

This shift from the earth goddess to the sky god can also be discovered in the lingering tension that existed in the ancient world between nomadic people and agricultural people. The former were always seeking food and water for their herds, which tended to produce a male deity who governed the wind and the rain. The settled agricultural people were more intent on causing the earth to bring forth a sufficient amount of food to sustain their life, which tended to produce a female deity of fertility.

In the nomadic societies better weapons were developed to fight off predators, both human and animal. It was not enough to hurl rocks and fight assailants with sticks. Long-range projectiles like spears, or even arrows sent forth from primitive bows, were better guarantors of success. These weapons served to remind ancient warriors, albeit subconsciously, of their own thrusting male power. After all, these weapons were so obviously phallic symbols and they would be developed into more and more overtly phallic forms as the years went by. Guns, rifles and artillery were simply erect rods which exploded, hurling their payload at their enemies. On psychic levels surely this identification was clear. The analogy of the male organ being thrust into one's female partner encouraged, I believe, the increasingly hostile male definition of a woman. Some of our slang words for sexual intercourse reveal enormous hostility even today. Words like "make," "screw," and "f——k" are not gentle, loving words. When males refer to lovemaking as a conquest, both the hostility and the military connections are overt and clear. More than we seem able to recognize, women historically came to be thought of as the enemy of men.

There is also a sense in which women were treated in earlier male-dominated societies almost as "prisoners of war." They had few rights. Their freedom was curtailed, both by social pressure and by male power. Their mobility was compromised, sometimes by a cruel but culturally approved method, such as binding their feet. The power they had to change their surroundings was minimal, resulting in their acceptance of abuse as both their fate and their due. The woman's inability to talk back without punishment, her general vulnerability and the fact that men had legal protection no matter how they treated their wives became cultural patterns in the West and even found their way into the common laws. Men claimed the "God-given right" to exercise authority over both the bodies and the lives of women. The woman's only real power was found in her feminine charms, her ability to attract, to seduce and to create in the male a desire and yearning for her body, a desire that rendered him powerless in relation to her, at least momentarily. This power, which also threatened the male sense of independence, was both enjoyed and resented by those against whom it was wielded. Those feminine wiles were techniques learned by women in the school of hard knocks. While the sources of the hostility that men have expressed toward women over the centuries can be debated, there is no debate about the fact that this hostility is real. There is also no doubt that this hostility has been justified as a virtue in religious circles. It has been claimed over the centuries that the all-powerful God of the universe, who was (and is) predominantly male, at least in the religions of the Western world, *meant* for life to be organized in this male-dominant way.

If an attitude finds expression in every prevailing religious system in the world, and in almost every society, one begins to suspect that this attitude has its roots in something very basic in our humanity. Religion incorporates and explains human content far more than it creates human content. Therefore, religion becomes the place where we begin to search for answers to the sin of patriarchy, and when we do so the sins of scripture in the form of the terrible texts about women in the Bible come into view. Read again the words with which this section of this book began, but this time in the older language of the King James Version, and judge for yourself their holiness:

> And the Lord God said, "It is not good that the man should be alone; I will make him an help meet for him." And out of the ground the Lord God formed every beast of the field, and every fowl of the air; and brought them unto Adam to see what he would call them: and what-

ever Adam called every living creature, that was the name thereof. (Gen. 2:18–19, KJV)

But for Adam there was not found an help meet for him. And the Lord God caused a deep sleep to fall upon Adam, and he slept: and [God] took one of his ribs, and closed up the flesh instead thereof; and the rib, which the Lord God had taken from man, made he a woman, and brought her unto the man. And Adam said, . . . "She shall be called Woman, because she was taken out of Man." (Gen. 2:20b–23, KJV)

Can anyone seriously argue today that these words are the "Word of God"? Are they not little more than texts of oppression? Centuries after they were written, Paul quoted the words from this ancient Hebrew source to support his negative view of women, and through Paul these words formed the dominant New Testament understanding of a woman. She was not made in the image of God. She was designed to be a male helpmeet, not an independent person. Since this story has been so influential in defining the sexes to this day, it is worth retelling, especially if it can be distanced from the stained-glass accents and pious sounds of scripture and understood not as literal history but as an ancient Hebrew myth. So gather with me around the campfire, where the wisdom of the past was recited for the education of those present in each generation, and allow me to transform this ancient tale—the tale out of which our major definition of a woman has come—into the story that it originally was. In that process we can begin to see how it came to be assumed that patriarchy was the will of God, a system created and blessed by a male deity.

Once upon a time, this myth tells us, before there were any people on planet earth, the Lord God decided to make a creature called a man and to place him in God's beautiful world to tend that world as God's steward. So it was that God came down from the sky and began to shape the dust of the earth into a human form as a child would make a mud pie. But when this creature was fully formed, he was still inert. So the Lord God swooped down upon this lifeless form in order to give this dirt creature mouth-to-mouth resuscitation, except that God breathed the living Spirit into the man through his nostrils.

When the breath of God entered this lifeless form, the creature came alive and God called his name Adam, which means "humankind." The fact that God named Adam meant that Adam was known by God and was subservient to God. God then set Adam to work in a place called the Garden of Eden, where plants, vegetables, fruit trees and shade trees were plentiful. Adam accepted this God-given vocation to be in charge of the world and tended this garden and so time went by. After some days or even months or years, Adam became dissatisfied. Perhaps he was lonely, and so the Lord God, perceiving this need in the first human being, decided to make a friend for Adam, for as God said, "It is not good for the man to dwell alone." So the Lord God got busy and made the first polar bear. Bringing this animal to Adam with some pride of creation, God presented it to him. "It is a very nice polar bear," said Adam, "but it is not the kind of friend that I seek." Adam, however, demonstrated his superiority over this animal by the act of naming the creature.

So God tried again. In turn, God made the cat, the horse, the camel, the cow, the pig and even the kangaroo for the people of Australia and God brought each animal in turn before Adam. Adam did not want to discourage God—these creatures were lovely and unique, after all—so Adam dutifully named each one, securing his position as the top of the pyramid of God's creation, dominant over all other forms of life.

When none of these special creatures satisfied Adam, God became a bit distraught. "Adam," he said, "I have now created all the animals of the world, looking for a helpmeet for you and you are telling me that none of them satisfies you!"

This ancient tale offers a marvelous picture of a trial-and-error deity who was clearly not omniscient or omnipotent, but was rather actively engaged in the world, responding and reacting to each event. It continues:

God shaped each creature individually and differently. Some had horns, some had tails—and some tails were curly and others straight. Some creatures produced milk, some had long trunks, some had humps on their backs, some were mammoth in size and some were tiny. Some carried their young in pouches, some could go for days without water, some loved the Arctic regions and others were at home in the heat of the equatorial forest. Some could fly, some could climb trees and some could sit on top of the water for hours, barely paddling their weblike feet. It was

soon a marvelously diverse world, but no matter how hard God tried,
nothing—absolutely nothing—seemed to satisfy Adam.

God was not quite sure what to do next. Since God did not know any
better than Adam what God was seeking to make, God said to Adam a
bit testily, "Adam, you are very hard to please."

In that day of intimate conversations between God and the first
man, Adam simply pled ignorance: "I would like to help you out, God,"
Adam said, "but how can I describe to you what I've never seen! It's one
of those intuitive things, God. I think I'll know it the first time I see it,
but not before."

So God decided to try a new approach. This time God put Adam to
sleep, and while Adam was sleeping (God must have used an anesthesia
that was not yet commonly known), God opened Adam's chest and re-
moved a rib from Adam's side. Then God closed Adam up again. From
that rib, God fashioned a new creature—like Adam, but not quite in
God's image. This creature was more human than the animals, but not
quite as human as the man. (This is an interesting picture of the first
human birth. One female theologian described it in my hearing as
"childbirth as only a man, who had never had a baby, could have con-
ceived of it.")

With this creature now shaped as only God could shape a creature,
with curves and lines that Adam had never seen before, God stood this
creature before Adam and gently wakened him from sleep. And sure
enough, Adam knew immediately that this was his helpmeet—and a
very satisfactory one too! Adam's eyes bulged out of their sockets about
three inches when he saw God's newest initiative. It was as if his eyes
were on coiled springs: boing! In response Adam said (according to the
King James Version translators), "This is now bone of my bones, and
flesh of my flesh: she shall be called Woman, because she was taken out
of Man." When one reads the original Hebrew of this verse, however, it
is a bit more effusive. Adam used a slang expression that might be trans-
lated thus: "Hot diggity, Lord; you finally did it!"

So the biblical writers said, "This is how the first woman was created." She,
like the animals, was made by God, but she, like the animals, was also subject
to Adam. He named her, as he had named all of the animals. She did not

share his status, his glory or his divine image. He was made by God. She was taken out of his body. She was kin to him in a way that the animals were not, but she was to be subservient, obedient and aware of her second-class status. Her chief role in life was to be the male's helpmeet, to bring him pleasure, to relieve his need for sex and companionship. Sex, incidentally, was originally meant for recreation, not procreation. The story hints that childbirth, with its resultant pain, was punishment handed out after the fall, not something that was part of the original intention in creation.

So in this way, according to this dominant biblical narrative, the sexes—male and female—came into being. Theirs was to be the relationship of the superior to the inferior, of the lordly male to the submissive female, of the master to the servant. No one could argue with this order since this story taught all who read it that this was God's very purpose. To argue was to violate or to subvert God's plan. One *relates* to this ultimate truth. One does not try to *change* it. So it was that the religious system called Christianity, which grew out of the Jewish womb that birthed this story, carried with it this God-given definition of female inferiority and installed it in our civilization as one of its unchallenged suppositions. Women were taught that they fulfilled their purpose by accepting this divinely imposed understanding. If they rebelled, the superior men in their lives could punish them, divorce them and even kill them without any fear of any other authority. Women were defined as less intelligent than men and therefore incapable of being educated, entering the professions or voting.

Long after this story was abandoned as literal history, the implications in this narrative continued to hold sway. This is true even today as these definitions splinter and break apart under the impact of our secular society. "Holy men" still quote these verses to keep intact the operative principle of male superiority and female oppression. In the name of God, women are still told that their sole purpose in life is to satisfy the man. They are told to obey their husbands in all things. Slowly but surely patriarchy turned into misogyny, and we are still dealing with the effects. Can Christianity in particular, or any religious system in general, continue to define any human being as subhuman or second class by nature and expect to be taken seriously by anyone?

The biblical story, however, went on. It was through the subhuman woman that evil entered the goodness of God's creation and subverted it. So the woman is to blame for sin. That is the next story that I must tell in order to expose these sins of the scriptures in all of their perversion.

8

SEXISM IN CHRISTIAN HISTORY

The Feminist agenda is not about equal rights for women. It is about a socialist, anti-family political movement that encourages women to leave their husbands, kill their children, practice witchcraft, destroy capitalism, and become lesbians.

Pat Robertson[4]

One of the most sexist institutions in the Western world is the Christian church. Its sexism is deep, pervasive and quite destructive. What makes this negativity doubly tragic is that the Christian church has wrapped this evil inside the rhetoric of sweet piety. For centuries this overt prejudice against women has been called "the sacred tradition of the church." It has been attributed to God and is an expression of the divine will from which there is supposedly no appeal. It has been justified by quotations from the Bible that the church calls the "Word of God" and for which excessive claims for truth have been made. In the Western world it is not easy to escape this systemic sexism. The church's powerful influence has shaped the stereotypes, definitions and role models of what a woman is or can be that permeate not only the religious institutions but the whole culture of our civilization. It has set the limits within which women have been forced to operate. It has introduced responses of both violence and rejection when those limits have been transgressed. It has claimed that to oppose the church's

views on human sexuality, and especially the sexuality of a woman, is to oppose God, the Bible and human decency. For these reasons the emancipation of women has been a gift won by women and for women, in spite of the
consistent opposition of institutional forms of religion. It has been the specifically nonreligious, secular society that has been the champion and chief ally
of women in their quest for equality.

No one can doubt the progress women have made toward full humanity
in recent times. They won the right to vote in 1920 in the United States.
They entered the cabinet of the president of the United States in 1932. They
flocked to coeducational private and public universities following World War
II. They entered the U.S. Supreme Court with a Ronald Reagan appointee,
Sandra Day O'Connor, in 1981. Today in the United States there are woman
governors, senators and representatives and their numbers are rising in all
three categories. Women have been heads of state in Great Britain, Norway,
Israel, Pakistan, India, Argentina, the Philippines and New Zealand.

Following World War II the professions began to open up to women. The
hiring was tokenism at first, but the trickle has since become a steady stream.
Law schools today have student bodies that boast 50 percent female students.
The sexes are also relatively even in schools of medicine and dentistry. Wall
Street and its various outlets today have so many bright female analysts and
stock managers that some of their names have become household words.
Large Fortune 500 corporations today have female chief executive officers
and few boards in corporate America fail to advertise the presence of women
in what was once thought to be an exclusively male preserve.

In almost every instance of this cultural redefinition process, however, the
Christian church has been on the wrong side of the debate, bitterly resisting
what the secular society has acted to empower. Even today as the progress of
women in every walk of life continues at a lively and brisk pace, the leaders of
the Christian church persist in pontificating about women, using archaic
words to make indefensible pronouncements clearly belonging to a world
that no longer exists. Many of us who still call ourselves Christians find these
ecclesiastical spokespersons an embarrassment. If one has to cling to antiquated definitions of the past as the price of religious devotion, that price becomes too expensive.

Among the images from the church that modern women have to confront is a gathering of pious, all-male Roman Catholic Church leaders,

clothed in their ecclesiastical dresses, pronouncing in the name of a God called "Father" what a woman can and cannot do with her own body. It should not be surprising how few women, including Roman Catholic women, either listen any longer to that message or care what their leaders say. Not to be outdone in irrelevance by the Roman Catholics, the Southern Baptist Convention—America's largest Protestant decision-making body—recently added to the core teaching of that church the idea that a woman must be subject to her husband in all things, for that, convention leaders said, was God's plan in creation. Women can be pastors, this convention stated a year later in a tip of the hat to a changing reality that they cannot control, but they are not to be *senior* pastors, for that would require a man to be submissive to a woman, which is a power equation specifically ruled out, they claim, by the "Word of God."[5]

These ecclesiastical attitudes enrage and alienate the people who still attribute some authority to the teaching of their churches, but in the secular society they are viewed as quaint glimpses into a past that is gone and will never return. They are but echoes from a world from which they have escaped and into which they have no desire to return.

On the first Sunday in Lent of the year 2000, Pope John Paul II issued a widely publicized apology to those people who had been hurt by the "sons and daughters" of the church. It was an interesting choice of words. It was not the Catholic Church, which by definition cannot be in error, but the "sons and daughters" of that church who can be, are and have been sources of both hurt and error. Among the Roman Catholic Church's victims, to whom this apology was addressed, were women. An apology implies that something wrong has been done. It is an admission of fault and normally carries with it a promise to make amends and to see that the hurting pattern is not repeated. But can this church's apology to women represent anything other than a fond hope or pious dream? Sexism runs so deep in Christianity that a change in the perpetuation of the hurt that it has caused women in particular would constitute a radical redefinition of everything from God to priesthood—a redefinition that this church shows no eagerness to encourage or to engage. As the necessary changes inevitably occur, they will be forced on a reluctant and resisting church by a secular mentality that will no longer tolerate the definitions of the past, no matter how ancient or how holy they are thought to be by the institution that promulgates them.

I think it is fair to say that every American man in my generation, raised in what people would call a Christian tradition, was infected with a deeply patriarchal mind-set, which institutional Christianity in all its forms clearly undergirded and enforced. That mind-set was not always conscious, but it was inescapable. It permeated the very air we breathed. It was incorporated into our rules of etiquette and our most intimate sense of the way things were and even ought to be. Since the men of my generation, certainly including me, were by and large beneficiaries of this patriarchal system, we could hardly have been expected to seek its overturn. Vested self-interest does not respond that way, unless something forces a reevaluation.

I was, for example, the first member of my family to receive a university degree. I have an older sister, but no one ever thought of encouraging her to enter a university. She was a woman. Her role in life, overtly stated and clearly understood even by her, was to get married and to have a family. Until she was married she might be gainfully employed in one of the underpaid, secondary positions of secretary, nurse or teacher, but no woman in that era was thought competent to reach a higher level of accomplishment.

My childhood ambition was always to be a priest, an ambition that was nurtured and encouraged by both my family and my church. My sister, however, could not even imagine that possibility for herself. It was not spelled out overtly in some set of rules. It was simply assumed.

By its deeds, my church, locally and nationally, made it quite clear that in regard to the teachings of God, women were disqualified for church service and need not apply. I was an acolyte who could live into the status of being vested in a distinctive garment and invited, after training, to serve at the altar during the sacred liturgy. As such, I was allowed to enter into holy space that women were prohibited from entering, except as they served in the necessary but menial details of the preparation and clean-up before and after divine worship.

The governance of my church was exclusively male. Women were, both by definition and by common consent, not included in the ranks of the eligible. My church even referred to the organization for women as "the Auxiliary." Only men could be readers or occupy the other nonpriestly roles in the Sunday services. Only men could serve as ushers. Only men could be elected to the vestry, or governing body, of the church. Only men could represent our church at regional, diocesan and national gatherings where all the decisions that governed our church were made. Obviously only men could be ordained. All of these prohibitions against women were based on the biblical idea that only the man was made in God's image. The woman's role was secondary, dependent and supportive. That had been the way God created things to be. It said so in clear and unambiguous detail in the sacred scriptures. We were bound by those definitions since that book was the "Word of God."

If that were not power enough, the history of the Christian church revealed its portrait of the ideal woman against which all women were to be measured. This ideal woman happened to be a "virgin mother." Since it is quite impossible in the normal course of events for a woman to be both a virgin and a mother, every other woman was immediately, by definition, assumed to be less than the ideal. Women could aspire to be virgins and enter the convent to serve the male God in poverty, chastity and obedience. That life choice was a way of holiness, but it was still short of the ideal for which their bodies were especially crafted. Women could also be mothers, the bearers of sons and daughters, thus fulfilling their God-given, biological necessity. That too was a way of holiness, but it was also not ideal. The mother had to engage the world of the flesh in order to bear children, which meant that her virginal purity had to be destroyed. Motherhood was nonetheless redemptive—but only if no barrier between sexual practice and procreation was erected, since the only redeeming feature to sexual practice was procreation. With the virgin mother as the ideal woman, all other women were reduced to a state of chronic unfulfillment. The very definition of a woman was now filled with the guilt of inadequacy by a church bent on keeping women in their place. The pain the church has inflicted on women, however, does not stop there.

Look next at the way the virgin myth developed in Christianity as it journeyed through Western history. Mary did not become the virgin mother of Jesus until the ninth decade, when Matthew first, then Luke, introduced that idea into the Christian tradition. Once introduced, however, it quickly swept all other ideas from its path. The virgin birth entered the creeds in the third and fourth centuries and became the chief bulwark in the battles that engaged the church in later centuries as that body sought to define the divinity of Jesus and to spell out the central doctrine of the Trinity.

As the church moved out of Judea and increasingly into the Mediterranean world, dominated as that area was by the dualistic thinking of the

Platonists and the Neoplatonists, it denigrated bodies, flesh and sexuality it-self—especially the body, flesh and sexuality of the woman. In response to this prevailing mentality, the church's depiction of Mary, the virgin mother of Jesus, evolved into Mary, the perpetual virgin. The holy womb, which bore the Christ child, could not have been contaminated later by other babies. Suddenly the brothers and sisters of Jesus, mentioned in Galatians (1:19) and Mark (6:3), had to be reconfigured: they became half-siblings, cousins or perhaps Joseph's children by a prior marriage and thus no kin at all, since Joseph was not really, it was said, related to Jesus. As the flesh of the Virgin Mary became more holy, so in an exact but reverse sequence the flesh of ordinary women became more evil.

Next, in the common devotion of the people, it began to be asserted that even when Mary bore Jesus, her virginity had been preserved both during (inpartu) and after (postpartum) the birth of the holy child. Tales actually began to circulate about Jesus being born out of Mary's ear! The church fathers (there were no mothers, of course) rushed to the scriptures to find validation for this new idea. The scriptures yielded the reward they sought. The prophet Ezekiel had written in the sixth century BCE that "this gate shall remain shut; it shall not be opened, and no one shall enter by it; for the LORD, the God of Israel, has entered by it; therefore it shall remain shut" (44:2). Without so much as an apology to Ezekiel, they leaped upon this text to prove that even the prophets had foretold the postpartum virginity of the Blessed Virgin. Later they saw in the Johannine story of the resurrection an account in which Jesus came into a room even though the windows were shut and the door locked, another indication of the ability of Jesus to pass through the birth canal without destroying the virginal hymen. With each new step Mary was desexed in order to emphasize her holiness, but in that process women in general were both consciously and unconsciously denigrated and their bodies were increasingly treated as base, sinful and evil.

The next step in the development of the virgin myth was to proclaim that Mary herself had had an extraordinary birth. Such a miracle was necessitated by the need to protect the Blessed Virgin, who as the child of Adam must also have been tainted by Adam's original sin which plunged the world into a fallen state. This explanation of her special birth, escaping the stain of sin, came to be called the Immaculate Conception. This addition to the Mary myth became official dogma in the Roman Catholic Church on December 8,

1854, in a proclamation issued by Pope Pius IX. In this step Mary was officially decreed not to have been born like an ordinary person, and thus she could no longer be thought of as human in an ordinary sense.[6]

Almost one hundred years later Pope Pius XII took the next step in Mary's evolution by pronouncing, on November 1, 1950, the doctrine of the bodily assumption of the Blessed Virgin into heaven. In other words, the church concluded that Mary did not actually *die*. Death, you see, was the punishment for the fall meted out by God to all creatures in the Garden of Eden. By her immaculate conception, Mary had been lifted out of the fallen human enterprise; likewise, by her bodily assumption she escaped the punishment of that sin.

Many people, including the world-famous psychoanalyst Carl Jung, rejoiced at the psychological implications of this latter doctrine. For the first time in Western history, Dr. Jung observed, the feminine had been lifted into heaven to become part of what God is. He regarded this pronouncement as a major moment in the religious history of the Western world.[7]

But is it?

Is it not strange that before the feminine symbol could be called holy and lifted into God by the Western Catholic tradition, it had to be first desexed and then dehumanized? That is what the symbol of the Virgin Mary has come to mean. She was systematically desexed, becoming first a virgin mother, then a permanent virgin and finally a postpartum virgin. Then she was dehumanized by attributing to her a miraculous birth and a miraculous assumption into heaven. The Blessed Virgin thus escaped both the trauma of a real birth into humanity and the trauma of a real death by her translation into heaven.

The question that this analysis begs is, What is there about women that caused the dominant strand of Western Christianity to state that before a woman could be envisioned as divine, she had to be desexed and dehumanized? This hostility toward women is not subtle in the Christian church. It is, in fact, pervasive. Even the acts of devotion to the Virgin Mary carry with them the baggage of the denigration of femininity.

Sexism is indelible and all but inevitable in Christianity. That is undeniable. How it got there, what it means and how it can be removed are the questions before us as the sinful texts regarding women in the Bible are brought front and center.

9

THE WOMAN AS
THE SOURCE OF EVIL

When a woman wishes to serve Christ more than the world,
then she will cease to be a woman and will be called man.

St. Jerome[8]

The ancient Hebrew myths with which the book of Genesis opens describe the biblical understanding of many things. Their purpose was to explain what is. It was men who undoubtedly framed these legends and eventually recorded them, since women in that society had no access to the power that explained God or to the ability to write. Furthermore, women were assumed to have no interest in, or understanding of, the realities of human life. Women thus neither influenced cultural assumptions directly nor shaped primal decisions about the nature of anything, nor were they engaged in any decision-making processes. So it should come as no surprise that when this male-written and male-shaped biblical narrative seeks to explain how evil entered into God's good creation, it does so by declaring it to be the fault of that subhuman creature created by God to be the man's helpmeet. Her name was Eve.

In a man's world women have been blamed for many things from that day to this. If a man rapes a woman, it is because she has tempted him with a provocatively appealing dress. If a man abuses a woman, it is because she irritated him. If a man divorces a woman, it is because she became one with whom he found it no longer tolerable to live. If a woman is competent at playing the man's game, she is put down with the suggestion that at best she is a hussy and at worst a bitch. If she resorts to feminine wiles to achieve her goal, she is playing "the female thing" for all she is worth. These assumptions continue the pattern established in this story told about the Garden of Eden. Eve was the reason for the man's downfall. She was responsible for the introduction of evil into the world. It is a wonderful story, but it is just that: a story. It is the narrative through which our ancestors tried to capture the "truth" of their existence. Let me continue the storytelling process begun in the previous chapter, separating the myth from the holy sounds of biblical language.

> In the beginning, said this ancient Hebrew legend, God created a perfect world. It was a world upon which the creating deity could look with a sense of satisfaction and pronounce all things good. It was also a finished world, so complete that God could take a day off to rest from the divine labors. It was in this way, this particular narrative suggested, that the Sabbath was established.
>
> Into that perfect world in the Garden of Eden God placed a perfect man, Adam, and his perfect helpmeet, Eve, to be the stewards of God's bounty. In this garden was all that they could desire. There was ample water since four rivers ran through it. Those rivers were named the Pishon, the Gihon, the Hiddekel (sometimes called the Tigris) and the Euphrates. The latter two rivers are today identified with the country of Iraq and were known in ancient history as forming "the Fertile Crescent" or the "Cradle of Civilization." There were also ample supplies of gold and onyx. The myth made no mention of how this first family would use these symbols of wealth, but whoever wrote the story understood their value and decided to include them in this first human dwelling place. There were also vegetables, fruit trees and all the other sources of food that human beings could want. It was a perfect world and the perfect man and the perfect woman who inhabited it had access to it all.
>
> God and the man and the woman lived in a perfect relationship, symbolized in the story by the fact that God walked with Adam and Eve each day in the cool of the evening. Air-conditioning had not yet been developed and God knew better than to come out in the heat of the day. That kind of behavior was to be reserved in history for mad dogs and Englishmen!
>
> There was but one rule in this original world. A tree stood in the midst of the garden, the fruit of which was forbidden to human beings. It was

called the Tree of the Knowledge of Good and Evil. It was not an apple tree. It did not become an apple tree until Jerome translated the scriptures into Latin in the fourth century of this Common Era.

Jerome's clever designation has enriched our language by entitling the cartilage that nervously vibrates in the throat of some men as the "Adam's apple." Apparently, the forbidden fruit stuck permanently in the throats of some of the sons of Adam!

So Adam and Eve settled happily into their life in this garden, enjoying it all while abiding by that single prohibition against eating the fruit of the Tree of the Knowledge of Good and Evil. Forbidden fruit, however, casts a peculiar kind of spell. It enters the fantasies. It creates wonder. One gets the impression that this tree was the subject of much conversation in the first family and even much mouth-watering anticipation. Nonetheless, Adam and Eve remained faithful to the divine command; at least they did so until one day when the woman was circling the tree alone. The story suggests that her fantasies simply overwhelmed her.

As Eve stared at that fruit, we are told, a serpent walked up to her on two legs, for that was the way snakes walked in those days. The snake spoke, probably in perfect Hebrew, since that surely was the only language Eve understood: "Miss Eve, did God really say you could not eat the fruit of this tree?"

"Yes, Mr. Snake," Eve responded. "God said that if we eat the fruit of this tree, we will surely die!"

"You won't die, Miss Eve," said the snake. "God knows that if you eat of this tree, you will be as wise as God. God doesn't want human creatures to compete with the Holy One! You, Eve," the serpent suggested, "can be as wise as God!" That was a new idea for this woman. It presented her with a vision of transcending the limits of her humanity; it offered her a way to become something more than any of her dreams or fantasies had suggested; it freed her imagination.

The story suggests that this new idea constituted an irresistible and therefore a determinative temptation.

Eve succumbed and ate the fruit. Then she called the innocent Adam over and urged him to try it. He did. The deed was done. God's perfect creation was wrecked. Disobedience had entered the human arena through the woman, who was clearly the weak link in God's creation. After Adam and Eve ate, the story tells us, their eyes were opened and they discovered that they were naked. Presumably they had been naked all along, but it appears that they had not noticed. Now, aware of their bodies, they experienced shame. They scurried to cover their nakedness with fig leaf aprons.

Suddenly they realized it was nearing the time for God's evening stroll through the garden. Before their disobedience, God had been thought of as their friend and as one whose presence they anticipated with pleasure. After their disobedience, however, God was perceived as their judge, the elicitor of their guilt, a presence to be feared and avoided. They decided that they could no longer endure the company of the divine one, so in an act of wonderful theological naïveté, they invented a human game called "hide-and-seek." God was to be "it." It was a primitive conception that seemed to assume it really was possible to hide from God in the bushes. So it was done.

This strangely human deity, who was clearly without the divine quality of being all-seeing, began the stroll through the garden, only to discover that it was empty. The astounded God could not find the man and the woman. So God called out for the senior member of the human family: "Adam, Adam, where are you?"

Since this was the first time the game of hide-and-seek had ever been played in human history, Adam did not quite understand the rules. If God called, he had to answer, so Adam responded, "Here we are, God, hiding in the bushes."

"What in the world are you doing in the bushes?" God asked. But then it suddenly dawned on the divine consciousness, which apparently did not know all things in advance, just what this behavior meant. So God asked, "Have you eaten of that tree?"

"It was not I," said Adam. "It was that woman. You remember, that woman you made."

"It was not I," said the woman. "It was that snake." So the process of blame and rationalization began.

Then the punishments were handed out. In an earlier chapter, when looking at the church's negativity toward the environment, I noted that the punishment for Adam in the Garden of Eden was that he must scratch his living from a hostile earth. The woman Eve would have to endure pain in childbirth, the serpent would be condemned to slither on its belly through all eternity and all living creatures would have to leave the garden. From that moment on, human life would be lived not in Eden, but "east of Eden," to borrow a phrase from John Steinbeck. Finally, all living creatures and their progeny were programmed to die. Mortality was their destiny. The universality of death would demonstrate, for all to see, the universality of that original sin, which brought death to God's world. That sin was to be the defining characteristic of humanity, corrupting every person and making it impossible for human life to restore its relationship with God.

All of this, the story suggested, entered human history through the weakness of the woman. She was made to bear the blame and the guilt. She was the source of death, which was inescapable. It was a terrifying charge to lay at the feet of the female, but that is what this primal myth does. It states that the reason evil and death are the most distinguishing marks of our humanity is the woman's disobedience. The apostle Paul certainly contributed to that definition. So did Augustine, the bishop of Hippo, in the fifth century. He made it the keystone of his thinking, and through him it was destined to dominate Christian thought for a thousand years. To this day this negativity toward women and sex is a major, if subliminal, feature of our religious life.

A whole theological system has been built on this story. We still refer to women as the "temptresses" of noble men. Women are still called the "forbidden fruit" for which male bodies yearn. Women are still defined as the corrupters and polluters of human holiness. They are still blamed for male powerlessness. Because of this story, holiness in Western Christian civilization came to be associated with avoiding women—that is, with sexlessness. Virginity in women and celibacy in men were established as the "higher way." Even marriage was defined as a compromise with sin, as we saw earlier, an option available primarily for the weak. Jerome, that great translator of the scriptures, who would be better remembered if he had stuck to translating, once observed that the only redemptive aspect of marriage was that it "produced more virgins."[9] That statement still makes me blink with incredulity. Women were indeed evil to their core. That was the message of the Christian church and it was built quite specifically on the story of Eve.

This is how a "terrible text" works. It is born in a patriarchal myth. That myth eventually loses its original power. No one today, outside the most rabid fundamentalists, thinks of Adam and Eve as real people. But the poisonous assumptions that were loosed into the bloodstream of Western civilization through the myth continue to live, to grow and to victimize anew in every century. Indeed it was relatively recently that this evil was challenged in the secular society and not surprisingly that challenge was resisted by the church as an act of "godlessness."

In 1873, in Illinois, a woman named Myra Bradford sued the state for the right to be given a license to practice law. There were no legal prohibitions to this possibility, since no one had entertained the idea that a woman would ever want to practice law. That was outside the boundaries of how the culture defined a woman and thus beyond people's imagining. No society ever prohibits something of which its members cannot conceive. Yet although Ms. Bradford had passed the bar examination and met all the other clearly defined prerequisites of her state, still Illinois would not confer on her the license required to practice law. When the local court denied her suit, she appealed to the Supreme Court of the United States, which ultimately upheld the decision of the state of Illinois not to grant the legal license. Justice Joseph Bradley, writing for the eight-to-one majority of the court in that decision, said:

> Man is or should be woman's protector and defender. The natural and proper timidity and delicacy which belongs to the female sex evidently unfits it for many of the occupations of civil life. The constitution of the family organization, which is founded in the divine ordinance, as well as in the nature of things, indicates the domestic sphere as that which properly belongs to the domain and function of womanhood. The paramount destiny and mission of women are to fulfill the noble and benign office of wife and mother. This is the law of the Creator. And the rules of civil society must be adapted to the general constitution and cannot be based on exceptional cases.[10]

But hostility and blame reveal threat and fear. What is it about a woman that causes such animosity? Is there something beyond the level of the conscious that might give us insights? Can that be identified? Where do we go to discover it?

One doorway into the patterns of the past, and into the unconscious fears and desires that underlie those patterns, is to examine the taboos that human beings set up to protect themselves from things they fear or do not understand. We find taboos in the prohibitions that people adopt—especially the irrational prohibitions. We also find them in the irrational negativities that people practice. To that discussion we turn next.

10

MENSTRUATION AND THE MALE FEAR OF BLOOD

Nothing is so unclean as a woman in her periods; what she touches she causes to become unclean.

St. Jerome[11]

Menstruous women ought not to come to the Holy Table or touch the Holy of Holies, nor to churches, but pray elsewhere.

Dionysius[12]

If a woman conceives and bears a male child, she shall be ceremonially unclean seven days; as at the time of her menstruation, she shall be unclean. . . . If she bears a female child, she shall be unclean two weeks, as in her menstruation; her time of blood purification shall be sixty-six days.

Leviticus 12:2, 5

When a woman has a discharge of blood that is her regular discharge from her body, she shall be in her impurity for seven days, and whoever touches her shall be unclean until the evening. Everything upon which she lies during her impurity shall be unclean; everything also upon which she sits shall be unclean. Whoever touches her bed shall wash his clothes, and bathe in water, and be unclean until the evening.

Leviticus 15:19–24

You shall not approach a woman to uncover her nakedness
while she is in her menstrual uncleanness.

Leviticus 18:19

Isn't it true that a woman can neither pray nor fast during her
menses?

An oft-quoted phrase in Islam[13]

s the male need to dominate the woman, and even to disparage her, a
rational response, or is it based on some subliminal fear? One can
certainly demonstrate that this need is universal, crossing all boundaries. Patriarchy's near universality forces us to view it as a response to a human need,
not a particular cultural response to a perceived cultural need or a particular
religious response to a perceived religious need. Given the depth and scope
of patriarchy in human history, we need to entertain the possibility that the
negative attitude toward women in the Bible is symptomatic of something far
deeper. That realization forces us to enter the realm of the unspoken and perhaps the unconscious, for that is where taboos are born.

A possible starting place would be to ask questions about unusual religious
practices. Why was it, for example, that early religions almost universally required rites of purification for a woman after childbirth? What is unclean
about having a baby? Why was it thought to be dangerous to bring a new
mother back into the life of the clan, family or church until she had undergone some cleansing rite? Likewise, why was menstruation feared in primitive societies? Why were women isolated from the tribe during the days of
their menstrual flow and in some times and places made to undergo cleansing rites before returning? Why were menstruating women thought to be so
dangerous that it was said of them that they polluted the water, killed the fish,
damaged the life of the clan and affected men adversely? Why is menstruation *still* covered with guilt or shame for many? What is the underlying
source that explains this prejudice? How did this perfectly natural part of
human life come to be called "the curse"?

One of the early church fathers explained menstruation by suggesting that
women were really castrated males and that the menstrual cycle was the way

the female body, once each month, mourned its lost organ. This seemed to him a perfectly reasonable explanation. Other equally bizarre explanations abounded in antiquity. When these practices and explanations are gathered together, a mammoth body of evidence is created that appears to point to the existence of irrational male fears that have come to be associated with menstruation. Our task is to determine the content of those fears, to raise these issues to consciousness, to confront them openly and then banish them. If we fail to do this, we must live forever under their power. I believe that the latent and still largely unconscious threat that men feel from women resides in this hidden area of life. It is out of this threat, I am convinced, that the hostility of patriarchy and acts of misogyny arise.

There has always been something mysterious and powerful about blood. Our language reflects this ancient attitude. Blood and life have been so deeply coupled in the human psyche that to "shed blood" has become a synonym for dying. In times of national crisis, the state still asks its sons and daughters to give their "blood"—that is, their lives—to protect their nation. Our breath was primarily identified in the ancient world with the spirit within, but our blood was the place where life itself resided.

Given that perspective, menstruation had to have been a profound mystery to early human beings. The woman could and did bleed from her most secretive and intimate opening on a regular basis. Yet despite that shedding of blood, the woman did not die. It was an almost incomprehensible experience. This was interpreted to mean, the taboos tell us, that every woman possessed some magical power—perhaps the power of life itself—that had to be respected and feared.

When these interpretive assumptions were combined with childbirth, the mysteries were only enhanced. Pregnancy stopped the menstrual cycle for nine months. Then, when the baby was born, the menstrual blood seemed to flow incessantly for days. Somehow, these two things were combined in the ancient mind. Prior to menopause the cessation of menstruation meant that life was being produced. The baby's birth then inaugurated an uncontrollable flow. Perhaps the menses actually worked *against* life, since the woman was incapable of producing life until they ceased. Perhaps when the baby was expelled, the unclean anti-life substance that had been contained by this new life was finally allowed to flow freely, a sure sign that the woman's body was once more unclean. If that was their understanding, purification rites were a necessity lest this latent death force be loosed publicly upon the clan. So myths grew about menstruation, myths that included such things as the assumption that a woman's hair would not curl during the menstrual cycle and the fear that the male organ might actually break off or become inoperative if intercourse took place during menstruation.

The only thing certain about these mysteries was that the woman possessed a power that was a threat and a thing to be feared. Women could lose their blood and not die; they could also produce a new life and, in the process, stop the menstrual flow. Men envied this power and sought some means whereby they could capture it. Sigmund Freud, that brilliant product of an extremely patriarchal mentality, once suggested that women suffered from what he called "penis envy." That was nothing more than a twentieth-century Freudian version of the myth that women were castrated males. They unconsciously yearned, suggested Freud, to have their penises restored, and thus to become whole again. Freud concluded that since this restoration could never happen physiologically, women reduced their anxiety by addressing this need psychologically. Though I have great admiration for Freud's enormous intellect, this is one place, I suggest, where Freud could not overcome his German predilection for male supremacy. Far from women suffering from "penis envy," I think a case can be made for the fact that men suffer from menstruation envy. Through the ages men have yearned to capture that female life power that enables women to bleed from their genitals and not die. That is, I believe, how circumcision entered the human and religious arena.

There is something quite irrational about circumcision. The body of the male is mutilated and religious reasons are given to support that mutilation. Circumcision was originally a male puberty rite. It was not practiced on infants until much later in history. Attempts to defend this practice on the basis of some presumed health value are so fanciful as to be amusing. These explanations suggest that because the foreskin is difficult to clean, it subjects the penis to potential infection. In other words, circumcision was designed to be a preemptive strike, a preventive measure. Does that not sound irrational? Ears are difficult to clean and become infected easily, yet no one that I know of has suggested that they be cut off to prevent those possibilities. It seems there is a better solution; namely, to wash them. Why was that procedure not applied to the foreskin?

As an alternative justification, it has been and in some places still is suggested that circumcision protects one's wife or partner from various genital infections. Once again, a good bath (even in the river) before sex would be equally as effective and much less traumatic. Have we gotten to the place where we think surgery improves on creation? Did the foreskin, like the appendix, originally have some purpose that has now become lost? If so, and the foreskin is rendered redundant, is life actually improved when the foreskin is removed? What utter nonsense! The foreskin was designed to roll back during sexual excitement and thus to provide a ridge of flesh that enhances sexual pleasure. Both the men who have been circumcised and their partners have had their pleasure diminished by this essentially barbaric practice, perpetrated first in the name of religion and now widely practiced for its "health benefits"—and perhaps for the extra fee the doctor earns for performing this surgical procedure today, primarily on newborn baby boys. Does not this inexplicable habit cry out for deeper understanding? How did this strange and irrational mutilation practice enter the human experience so deeply as to become commonplace?

My suggestion is that circumcision began in a male attempt to capture the woman's menstrual power. Circumcision enabled the man, just like the woman, to bleed from the genitals at puberty and not die. It became an initiation into manhood, a rite of passage. It was both feared and anticipated equally, the pain being offset by the expectation of adult sexual activity.

These thoughts were, as all irrational fear-related ideas are at their inception, quite unacceptable to the conscious mind and so they were pushed deep into the realm of the unconscious. That does not make them any less real, just more difficult to contemplate. What was not suppressed, however, was the fear of women's power—a fear that manifested itself in unrelenting male oppression of women, pejorative male definitions imposed upon women and the long and brutal patriarchal abuse of women. When one quotes God to justify prejudices and to uphold definitions of inferiority and inadequacy in 50 percent of the human race, one should look beneath the level of rationality to search for the reason why.

The woman's presumed inability to function fully during the days of her menstrual flow was used, in our patriarchal history, to keep her in protected domestic roles, rather than in vulnerable roles reserved for men. This, in turn, was used to enhance her servitude. This "protection" certainly played a major role in the way both the early church and the traditional, church-infused society understood and reacted to the cultural definition of a woman.

To bring this forward to our own day, we need to face the fact that a major part of the Christian church's historical negativity to the ordination of women has been the fear that this would admit polluting—that is, menstruating— women into the sacred sanctuaries of church life.[14] Behind the medieval practice of limiting church choirs to men and boys was the need to guarantee that holy places would not be corrupted by the presence of menstruating women. There was a time in church history when only prepubescent girls and postmenopausal women were allowed to enter the holy space around the altar, even to prepare that space for worship. Is it not time to force these insights into consciousness and to purge this ancient ignorance and this patriarchal fear from our lives? One place to start this process is by challenging those texts of the Bible that have presumed to define both women and menstruation as unclean. It is also time to redefine the claim made for the Bible that somehow it contains the very "Word of God." This book must be removed from its position of power, a lofty position that has allowed irrational ignorance to flow from its religious pipelines into the corporate life of our society, where the damage it has caused is still beyond measure. How to find an answer to this evil is now my task.

Denouncing a scriptural tradition that sees women as both corrupt and corrupting must be the operative principle of a religious system that quotes Jesus as saying: "I came that they might have life, and have it abundantly" (John 10:10). If the Christian scriptures have been a primary source of negativity toward women throughout history, then those scriptures have to be either jettisoned or reinterpreted. Perhaps parts of them might even need to be *discovered*! My suggestion is that in the scriptures themselves there is an antidote to the evils of patriarchy and misogyny. To that search I now turn.

11

RECASTING
THE NEGATIVITY

In Christ . . . there is neither male nor female.

Galatians 3:26–28

My right to speak my mind, to have a voice, to be what some
have called "opinionated" is a right I deeply and profoundly
cherish. My only hope is that, one day soon, women who have
all earned the right to their opinions—instead of being called
"opinionated" will be called smart and well-informed, just like
men.

Teresa Heinz Kerry[15]

C an the Bible, the source of so many texts that have produced unspeakable horrors, at one and the same time also be a resource to
articulate the hopes for human life that have not even yet been fully embraced? I believe it can. That is why I cherish the Bible, why I fight publicly
with those who misuse it and why I refuse to abandon this religious institution called the Christian church that has, more often than it is willing to
admit even now, been a killing, diminishing presence in the lives of many
people throughout history. So I turn now to discover again the minority
voices of holy people in the past who saw beyond the boundaries of human
security needs and whose words were included as nuggets of hope in a book
that for many has been the sentence of death. My search begins with words
that I suspect were originally a part of a baptism formula. Paul recorded them

when he wrote in what was probably his second epistle to the church in Gala-tia, "In Christ . . . there is neither male nor female" (Gal.3:26–28).

Paul, as an author, was a man of great ability, great passion, great energy and, let it never be forgotten, great conflict. His writings reveal his turmoil again and again. He came out of a rigid and traditional patriarchal back-ground that he reflected over and over when giving instructions to his churches. Women were to keep quiet in church (1 Cor. 14:34). Men were not to marry unless they could not control their passion (1 Cor. 7:9). Women had to have their heads covered as a sign of respect (1 Cor. 11:5ff.). A disciple of Paul's, writing in the name of his master, extended Paul's patriarchy when he wrote, "I permit no woman to teach or to have authority over a man" (1 Tim. 2:12, NRSV). As women have increasingly come into leadership roles in Christianity, they have vented their pent-up anger at Paul, who they believe was the original person to shape a misogynist church. I know women clergy today who choose to ignore Paul as the only alternative to loathing him. They dismiss Paul as an enemy who must be defeated, knowing that otherwise they will never be allowed to take their places in the life of the church as full and equal human beings.

Paul, however, was not single-minded on this subject or any other. In every area of his life this man lived in conflict. In the person Paul there was a strange combination. He is defined both by the prejudices he possessed, the rigorous training he had undergone and the binding rigidity of his pious prac-tices; but he is also defined by the freedom and love that he discovered in his conversion experience. The two sides of this man were never to live in recon-ciliation. Together they created for Paul a state of perpetual turmoil. It was as if Paul's very identity was at stake at every moment of his existence. There was a war, he said, going on in him between his mind and his body (Rom. 7:23ff.), between his past and his present, between his tradition and his eyes, from which Luke said "scales" had fallen at the time of his meeting with the figure, the memory or even the vision of Jesus (Acts 9:18). Thus we see two sides of Paul, and one of them is quite contrary to the anti-female bias that has become his major legacy. This other Paul is reflected primarily in the book of Acts in his appreciation of the women who were his co-workers and colleagues—for example, Priscilla, the wife of Aquila (Acts 18:2, 26), Lydia (Acts 16:14, 40) and Chloe (1 Cor. 1:11). One listens with wonder to the list of women to whom Paul sends his personal greeting in various epistles (Rom. 16:3, 6, 7, 13, 15; Col. 4:15).

The most overt countering text to Paul's perceived negativity toward women, however, occurs in Galatians, which is probably Paul's most passionate and therefore most revelatory epistle. Dated around 50–51 CE, it may reveal the real Paul because he is so angry he does not take time to think about what he is saying and edit his words. His Christ experience, he ecstatically proclaims, is so powerful that the barriers erected to keep human beings secure in their self-knowledge, their prejudices and their perennial struggle to survive their evolutionary history can be transcended. He lists those barriers as tribe, gender and economic bondage. The words "In Christ . . . there is neither male nor female" are the part of that text that I want to lift now into our full consciousness. As a result of the Christ experience, Paul says, the power equation between men and women—an equation presumed in the past to have been built on the will of God as expressed in the story of creation and used as the basis to impose second-class citizenship—has now been irrevocably broken.

Think about how entrenched was the view of women that Paul encountered. For long periods of history women were considered to be property, owned first by their fathers and second by their husbands. Recall, for example, that the last commandment orders men not to covet other men's wives or their oxen (Exod. 20:17). Upon that tradition were built laws that enabled polygamy to become a way of life, for if a wife was property, a man could have as many wives as he could afford. These laws refused to allow divorce as an option for women, no matter how abusive the husband was. They fed a tradition that defined women as not educable—not intelligent enough to vote, to own property, to enter the professions or to be part of the armed forces. This is what must be set aside, Paul stated in his revolutionary language to the Galatians, for in Christ there is neither male nor female, nor is there superiority or inferiority. Paul was articulating a startling, powerful new reality that exploded into this world in the Christ experience. Paul was suggesting that this is the vision, the experience, the reality that we must recover if the power of anti-female prejudice in Christian history is to be broken.

We move on to the gospels in our quest for other evidence of the fact that this new and profound equality was present before the authority attributed to the patriarchal texts of the Bible began to be used in Christian history to suppress it. In the first of the gospels to be written, Mark tells the story of a woman who, in the last week of Jesus' earthly life, broke in upon him at a dinner in Bethany, at the home of a man called Simon the leper. Simon was presumably a cured leper who would have a greater sensitivity toward anyone who might be an outcast. The woman's purpose in interrupting the dinner was to perform an act of devotion. She poured upon Jesus' head and feet a perfume known as nard, imported from India. Her act was a violation of every Jewish patriarchal custom, every defining patriarchal norm, and the men at the banquet moved to condemn her behavior. If such exceptions were allowed, the prevailing norms would no longer be norms. It was a potentially revolutionary moment. But Jesus is portrayed by Mark as rebuking her tormentors and affirming her right to be present, her actions and her motives. "She has done a beautiful thing," Jesus is quoted as saying. "She has anointed my body beforehand for burying" (Mark 14:3–9).

That same story echoes three more times in the canonical gospels, with interesting variations. In Matthew the events are recounted almost identically: they occur at the same time, in the same place, and with the same result (Matt. 26:6–13). In Luke, however, there is a dramatic shift. The episode does not occur in the last week of Jesus' life, and it is not a prelude to his burial; rather, it is located by Luke in the early Galilean phase of Jesus' ministry (Luke 7:36–50). The setting is not the home of Simon the leper, but the home of Simon the Pharisee; that is, one who is known for upholding the moral norms and cultural taboos of the tradition.

The intruding woman likewise has been heightened in very negative ways in Luke. She is "a woman of the city"—quite clearly, a prostitute. She is unclean and unacceptable. Her actions are much more bizarre, highly sensual and they violate significantly the norms for a woman in her day. Only in Luke does she wash Jesus' feet with her tears and dry them with her hair. This highly erotic act in a society where a woman would never touch a man in public is a dramatic challenge to the imposed sexual roles of the day. As in the other accounts, the value systems of the past emerge in the language employed by the male dinner guests to condemn her behavior roundly. They also condemn Jesus for allowing such provocative sexual actions to be done to him. "If this man were a prophet, he would have known who and what manner of woman this is." Because he does not condemn her, his credentials as a holy man are compromised in the eyes of the upholders of the moral laws. Because this is an unclean woman who has touched him, he is now, according to the Torah, a ceremonially unclean person in need of purification. But Jesus sets aside these patriarchal rules with their doctrines of cleanliness, and in an act of startling freedom he affirms the woman, accepts her action and tears down the barrier that would cause her to be rejected. He is acting in a way consistent with the Pauline insight that in Christ there is neither male nor female. A new humanity, Paul proclaims, has come into being in Christ. This new humanity transcends every ancient definition, every ancient rule and every ancient religious barrier. Something new is being born. A new consciousness is being formed. The texts of the past, which held people inside their defining prejudices, are being set aside.

This same story, in yet another variation, is told a fourth time in the gospel of John (12:1–8). This time the anointing of Jesus' feet takes place in the home of Mary and Martha. This means it is again in Bethany, but not in the home of one called Simon, whether he be the leper or the Pharisee. All of Jesus' disciples are present in this episode. So are the members of the family of Mary and Martha, which includes, this gospel alone asserts, a brother named Lazarus, recently raised from the dead (John 11:1–44). In this very public setting Mary, Martha's sister, is now said to be the one who does the anointing of his feet. She is neither a stranger, as Mark and Matthew have suggested, nor a woman of the city who was a sinner, as Luke has written. There is in this setting no sense of scandal and there is also no rebuke from anyone. The anointing is an act of which little or no notice is taken. How strange, one thinks, when these Johannine facts are absorbed. Where did the patriarchal rules, the sexual prohibitions go? Why did this act in this setting suddenly become acceptable?

The only thing I can think of that would have made such an act acceptable in the Bethany of Jesus' day is the knowledge, on the part of everyone at this gathering of intimate family and close disciples, that this woman was Jesus' wife. Nothing else could account for the response. Is this a new insight? Maybe. I suggest, however, that it is merely the lifting into consciousness of a repressed tradition that counters the teachings of the church, which has sought to portray Jesus as sharing in an anti-female bias that includes a commitment to celibacy. I do not draw that conclusion on this text alone, but this text is the one that first forced me to entertain this possibility.

One other story, taken again from Luke's gospel (10:38–42), adds to this speculative conclusion about Jesus and Mary. It also, once more, illumines Jesus' enormous power to break the negative definitions that have surrounded women in the Judeo-Christian tradition. This episode occurs, not coincidentally I believe, once again in the home of Mary and Martha in Bethany, where Jesus is now portrayed as being a guest for dinner. Martha is bearing the burden of the preparation of that meal. Mary, her sister, is sitting at Jesus' feet listening to him teach. This is the picture of a woman cast in the role of a learner, a pupil, even a rabbinic student. Quite obviously this is a prohibited role for women in those days and in that culture. Yet Jesus affirms Mary in that role. Martha, however, rebukes her. Martha demands that Jesus order Mary to abandon the pupil role for the more acceptable domestic role of assisting with the dinner preparations. Jesus supports Mary and defends her consciousness-raising act by stating that she has elected a higher choice. Jesus is asserting a revolutionary idea: a woman is educable; she can be a learner. Nothing in the new order that he has come to establish rules out this possibility, because in Christ there is neither male nor female. The divine barriers of power and pejorative definitions are simply transcended.

I see one other repressed truth in this story that once again causes me to suggest that Mary was Jesus' wife. Martha, according to this narrative, asks Jesus to order her sister, Mary, to help in the kitchen. Why did Martha not speak directly to her sister? Would that not be the norm in most homes? But suppose the sister was a married woman? Could it be that Martha understood that in Jewish society a woman's husband had the power to command and the wife had the duty to obey? Is that why Martha appealed to the one who was her guest to give a directive to her sister? This passage suggests that Jesus had a wife, a fact that apparently was once acknowledged! This is a hint that did not get repressed by biblical redactors.

Moving on in this attempt to read the nuances of the gospel texts, let me postulate the possibility that Mary, the sister of Martha, was the same Mary who later came to be called Magdalene. Magdalene is portrayed in the gospels as the leader of the female disciples who followed Jesus all the way from Galilee.[16] What kind of women follow an itinerant band of men? Are they not either wives or prostitutes? This was the same Mary who was the flesh-and-blood woman at his side during his life and the chief mourner at the tomb in his death. That would make her the same Mary who is portrayed in the tomb scene of the Fourth Gospel as calling him "my lord" and "rab-boni," titles appropriate in Jewish society only for a wife to use in addressing her rabbi husband. She would also be the same Mary who demanded access to his deceased body from the one she thought was the gardener, an act appropriate only for the deceased's nearest of kin.

Finally, let me suggest that the word "Magdalene" has no reference whatsoever to a village of Magdala, as many have suggested with the translation "Mary of Magdala." No one has ever been able to locate an ancient village of Magdala or any Jewish or Roman record that mentions such a village. A new Magdala has been built to attract modern tourist dollars, but it is not authentic.

Once we dismiss the possibility that Magdalene referred to a place, then other possibilities are allowed to surface. There is a Hebrew word, *migdal*, which has the same consonants as Magdala. Could Magdalene be a play on that word? *Migdal* originally referred to a tower (a *migdal edor*) from which shepherds could view the fields in which their flocks grazed. Such a tower—tall, large and of great significance—is mentioned twice in the Hebrew scriptures (Gen. 35:21, Mic. 4:8). A play on that word would suggest that the early church, by calling Mary "Magdalene," was asserting that she was a tall, large or great figure—that she was "Mary the great" or "the great Mary." If Jesus' mother was another Mary, not "the great Mary," could the great Mary have been anything except his wife? Jesus, I believe, had a female partner, a wife, to whom he gave a dignity and an honor that broke the barriers of the sexist definitions of the past. She was Mary—the Magdalene.

If this reconstruction could be sustained, would we not then have an ancient, nonsexist tradition to reclaim, one on which we could rebuild our sexual value system? The new values in that system, values of radical equality, would become the mark of the church of the future. In that church there would be no barrier erected against women, no attempt to define their worth as second-class citizens. That new church would adhere to the belief that in Christ "there is neither male nor female."

As we work toward that radical equality, the victory for women that has come through the secular society and against the entrenched patriarchy of the church will find a new ally in the Jesus who destroyed power boundaries and power definitions. This Jesus, who related to the primary woman in his life with the power of equal dignity, appears to have called women into a new being, to have enabled them to experience a new humanity.

It is a shame that by denigrating the woman called Magdalene during Christian history, the church destroyed the healthiest female symbol in ancient Christianity. There is no evidence in the Bible to support the familiar claim that Magdalene was a prostitute. That charge was fabricated beginning in the second century of the Common Era, when Greek dualism portrayed flesh as evil. This flesh-and-blood woman at Jesus' side was perceived by the dualists as a threat to his holiness. So the church set about trashing her reputation. Church leaders began to identify her with the woman taken in adultery in John's gospel (8:1–11), though there is not a shred of evidence to support this identification. Just to be safe, they also identified her with that previously mentioned but still unnamed woman of the city in Luke's gospel (7:36–50), though once again there is not a shred of evidence to support this identification. With her character in tatters, Mary Magdalene was left to play the role of the harlot in Christian history. In her place at Jesus' side, the church installed the sexless, and therefore unthreatening, virgin mother, who was docile, dependent and passive. With the two major female figures in the Christ story relegated to the classical roles in male fantasy of virgin and whore, there was no viable female role model left in the Christian story.

It is interesting to note that when the rise of women in the secular West began to break into consciousness, women adopted a fictional role model, a comic strip character created by William Molton Marstan, the pseudonym for psychologist Charles Moulton, as their inspiration. This character was called Wonder Woman, and her adventures captured the imagination of girls and women from 1941, when the strip was born, into the 1960s. When Gloria Steinem launched Ms. magazine in 1971, the cover featured a picture of Wonder Woman, who by this time had become the patron saint of the feminist movement.

Wonder Woman's secret was that she could do anything that men could do, and do it even better. She stood for strength, self-reliance, sisterhood and mutual support among women. Her body was an identifiable and well-proportioned female body. There was no mistaking her for either a man or a sexless figure. If history does not give us the defining models that we need when our perception of reality begins to change and the old models no longer work, then we create make-believe role models. I regard Wonder Woman as a necessary figure in the human story, since the one vibrant and whole woman in the Christian story, Magdalene, was obliterated by the keepers of the historic prejudices of patriarchy and misogyny, the hierarchy of the Christian church.

A new day is dawning in the lives of 50 percent of the human race. The church that was once the enemy of this new day, quoting and acting upon the basis of biblical texts born in patriarchy, could become both the ally of these oppressed ones and the place where a new humanity in which there is neither male nor female can finally be acted out. That is my vision. Magdalene is my role model. The church that adopts this vision will change radically. The church that does not adopt this vision will die! There is no other possibility! Now do you still want to waste your time arguing that the full inclusion of women in the power positions of church leadership violates scripture, overturns sacred tradition and threatens the unity of the church? That is the height of suicidal irrelevance for the Christian church.

I prefer to grasp the new day, to expose the "sins of the scriptures" and to claim the Jesus seen in the often hidden texts of the New Testament as the ally of a new humanity in every form. To follow that Jesus is to know that in Christ, humanity in all its fullness is what counts. Whether that humanity is male or female might determine biological functions, but it must never determine human worth or divine value.

THE BIBLE AND HOMOSEXUALITY

THE TERRIBLE TEXTS

But before they lay down, the men of the city, the men of Sodom, both young and old, all the people to the last man, surrounded the house; and they called to Lot, "Where are the men who came to you tonight? Bring them out to us, that we may know them."

Genesis 19:4–5

You shall not lie with a male as with a woman; it is an abomination.

Leviticus 18:22

If a man lies with a male as with a woman, both of them have committed an abomination; they shall be put to death; their blood is upon them.

Leviticus 20:13

So they are without excuse; for although they knew God, they did not honor him as God or give thanks to him, but they became futile in their thinking and their senseless minds were darkened. Claiming to be wise, they became fools and exchanged the glory of the immortal God for images resembling mortal men or birds or animals or reptiles. Therefore God gave them up in the lusts of their hearts to impurity, to the dishonoring of their bodies among themselves. For this reason God gave them up to dishonorable passions. Their women exchanged natural relations for unnatural, and the men likewise gave up natural relations with women and were consumed with passion for one another, men committing shameless acts with men and receiving in their own persons the due penalty for their errors.

Romans 1:22–27

12

THE ECCLESIASTICAL BATTLE OVER HOMOSEXUALITY

INTENSE, IRRATIONAL, THREATENING AND HYSTERICAL

This acceptance of homosexuality is the last step in the decline of Gentile Christianity.

Pat Robertson[1]

I t has all of the intensity of the final battle of Armageddon that is supposed to mark the end of the world. The opposing forces consider each other to be mortal enemies. There is no room for compromise between them, no middle ground, just mutually exclusive points of view. Threats and even violence are readily employed as the tactics of intimidation. Both sides appeal to God and claim that this fight is waged in the name of all that is deemed holy. The stakes are thought to be so high that many people on both sides assert that Christianity itself will die if the other side prevails.

What I am describing, however, is neither the end of the world nor the end of Christianity. It is rather a collision between a new consciousness based on new data and an old definition that has informed our cultural value system for at least two thousand years. Welcome to the church's battle over homosexuality, which today is in its final stages and marks the life of every part of this faith system the world over.

Each side in this conflict seems to understand that both the future and the integrity of this faith system are at stake in this conflict. People who stand outside the Christian faith are amazed at the passion, the rhetoric and the hyperbole, but those engaged in the issue believe that all those emotions are justified in what is to them a life-and-death struggle. If gay and lesbian people are not welcomed and accepted just as they are, many Christians believe, then the Christian church becomes nothing more than a sectarian movement that has no future. If gay and lesbian people are welcomed and accepted just as they are, many Christians believe, then morality itself collapses and the system of authority that has marked the Christian past will collapse. What emerges from that collapse will be something quite different, indeed unrecognizable from anything that has been called Christian in the past. At the center of the debate is the claim historically made for the truth of the scriptures. The sins of scripture with its terrible texts strike yet again.

Examine first just how the threat posed by the acceptance of gay and lesbian people has changed the guidelines which usually mark church debate. Pope John Paul II, who still maintains the traditional Roman Catholic position that there is only one true church, and it is constituted by those who accept the authority of and remain in communion with the bishop of Rome, has begun to court the support of those parts of the non–Roman Catholic Christian world that share his point of view that homosexuality is unnatural and deviant behavior. He has sent messages of support to fragmentary groups within other ecclesiastical traditions, tacitly recognizing both their existence and their validity. He has lectured Archbishop of Canterbury Rowan Williams openly and even rudely, as an angry schoolmaster might do, in an attempt to influence the direction of the worldwide Anglican communion at whose altars he still forbids Roman Catholics to worship. He has issued warnings to national and provincial or state governments not to move toward a new acceptance of homosexuality, maintaining his working definition that it is "an affliction" that needs to be cured, if possible, or endured without giving in, if cure is not possible. He has warned Roman Catholic legislators that they risk excommunication unless they stand firm on the official teaching of this church. One does not go to these lengths unless the issue is assumed to be a matter of life or death, or the threat posed by this new consciousness is deemed to be so dangerous that it might destroy all that he thinks is holy.

What makes this papal and Roman Catholic negativity so strange is that the hierarchy of the Catholic Church knows full well that its ordained ranks are liberally populated with gay persons. They know as a matter of fact that its priesthood has, for most of Christian history, either encouraged or required an unmarried status as a prerequisite for ordination. It has thus provided a safe haven in which gay men could escape the social pressure of marrying while being able to suggest by implication that they are motivated only by virtue and the sacrifice of answering a "higher calling." They also recognize, even if they do not admit it, that one of the major reasons for the incredible shortage of priests in that church today is that gay people, living as they do in a far more open society, do not need the church for a cover as they once did. Anecdotal evidence is always dangerous, but I could not help finding it compelling when I talked to a man who told me he had given up his ambition to join the Roman Catholic priesthood because he was the only heterosexual student in his place of theological training!

When the leadership of the Roman Catholic Church condemns homosexuality with the vehement public rhetoric we have become accustomed to hearing from its leaders, one has to realize that there is some hysteria present. Their cover is not holding, and they are condemning what they know to be true about themselves. There is no health in such a tactic. Rather, fear is rampant, honesty is a casualty and integrity is missing in action.

This behavior is quite frankly an acknowledgment that anxiety at the threat of exposure is very near the surface. It is a tacit recognition that the power of the teaching magisterium can no longer hold back reality. It is the dawning awareness that the authority system that undergirds its doctrines, dogmas and ethical pronouncements is becoming something other than self-evident truth. A new consciousness is in fact challenging their presuppositions. It is no wonder that this church has become so defensive.

While the Bible has never been for Roman Catholics the same kind of "Maginot" or defense line that it has been for Protestants, it is nonetheless always lurking in the background. One certainly cannot trace the rise of creedal theology in the first six hundred years of Western Christian history without becoming aware that quotations from the scriptures, which were assumed to be vested with the power of divine revelation, were essential in the development of such doctrines as The Incarnation, The Atonement and The Holy Trinity. Only when one realizes that these are the foundations that are shaking underneath the battle about homosexuality do the strange reactions and visceral intensity exhibited by Catholic religious leaders, who are presumably rational people, become at least comprehensible.

While denial and repression are both visible and obvious in Roman Catholicism, there is no part of the Christian church that has escaped this kind of conflicted debate over homosexuality, and the resulting behavior is highly revelatory. In the Church of England, for example, in 2003 an openly gay man, Jeffrey John, was nominated and approved at each level in that church's rather cumbersome decision-making process to serve as a bishop in the diocese of Oxford. This approval process included the imprimaturs of the appointing bishop of Oxford, Richard Harries, Archbishop of Canterbury Rowan Williams, Prime Minister Tony Blair and Queen Elizabeth II herself. Yet John was forced to step aside at the last minute when traditionalists mounted a campaign of incredible hostility that included the threat of violence and murder if this man were to become a bishop. This was not a debate on competence, for no one could doubt this man's qualifications. He was a greatly admired New Testament scholar with an earned Oxford PhD. His position at the time of his selection was that of overseeing the training of candidates for the priesthood in a major diocese. That is hardly a position into which one is placed without impressive credentials. He had previously served as vicar of a parish church, as well as dean of Magdalene College, Oxford.[2]

The startling, duplicity-dripping message that the Church of England was proclaiming was that it was okay to be gay in a low-profile church position, but not in a high-profile position. That is hardly a stance that many will salute.

In the American Episcopal Church, a Florida bishop wrote an open letter to the presiding bishop of his own church demanding that he step down from his position, since his pro-homosexual stand was, in the opinion of this Florida prelate, "outside the boundaries of Christian practice."[3] But it was the presiding bishop's position and not that of the offended Floridian that was supported by the highest-ranking decision-making body of the Episcopal Church. This suggests that the Florida bishop now sees the majority of his own church as violating the Christian faith so deeply that it is fatally flawed and can no longer claim to be Christian. Tacit excommunication is what this letter was about. That presents a very new idea. The defeated minority is now calling the majority schismatic!

In American Methodism's national conference, a body in which the traditional position is still in the majority, those who called for changes to enable the full acceptance of gay people were not just defeated in the assembly vote; they were arrested and jailed when they demonstrated against the winning majority.

Splinter bodies have sprung up in the various Christian denominations, claiming that all who do not agree with them are both faithless and no longer Christians. Vigilante groups within these several traditions go so far as to articulate their venom at the funerals of homosexual persons who have been killed in prejudice-driven hate crimes. One side views these victims as martyrs, while the other will actually say that their murders are the express will of God.

Some third world bishops, especially in Africa, feel so deeply about this issue that they are willing to sacrifice their sources of economic support rather than align themselves as part of a church that supports this "condition" they believe to be evil. But even in Africa the debate rages. The world-renowned Desmond Tutu, who prior to his retirement was both the Anglican Archbishop of Capetown in South Africa and a winner of the Nobel Peace Prize, has offered unflinching and even breathtaking support for the cause of full inclusion of homosexual persons in the body of Christ. It is quite difficult for African Christians of any stripe to maintain that this gentle and saintly man has stepped outside the boundaries of the Christian faith.

Astonishingly judgmental and hostile statements are made in this conflict by those who are publicly identified as Christians—statements that so deeply violate the Christian call to love that their witness becomes destructive. One American television evangelist suggested that homosexuals were behind the violence that marked the rule of Adolf Hitler and Nazi Germany. Perhaps he did not know that Hitler also killed homosexuals along with six million Jews. This man went on to say that homosexuals ought to be quarantined and isolated from society lest they infect the masses. In an interesting revelation of his blatant anti-Semitism, this same public evangelist said that "the acceptance of homosexuality is the last step in the decline of Gentile Christianity," and he warned his listeners that the agenda of the gay community is "to take your children and grandchildren and turn them into homosexuals." Since these are his convictions, he urges the government of this nation to discriminate against homosexuals on the same basis that we "discriminate against kidnappers, murderers, and thieves," lest the homosexual agenda "destroy all Christians."[4]

Others in the world of American television and radio evangelism are no less robust in their negativity. Regularly they claim the authority to speak for God and justify their hatred of homosexual people on the basis of what they perceive to be God's hatred of homosexuality. The validating authority that maintains this evangelical furor for these people is found in the sacred texts of the Bible. The "Word of God" is clear, they say. The word of hate is in the Book!

Yet one fascinating fact needs to be recognized. This vehement rhetoric reveals quite overtly the frightening but real assessment that even with God and the Bible presumably on their side, they are still losing this fight! If one has identified both God and God's Word with a cause that is losing, then everything that person holds sacred is about to collapse. These people live, they believe, at the end of an era—perhaps even at the end of their world, which they mistakenly identify with *the* world. Their winning enemies are not just the secular humanists who long ago left the church; they are also fellow Christians. How can this be? The martyr complex rises. The paranoia increases. The sense of despair sets in. Their special hatred is reserved for those who claim to be themselves believers and yet who reject what they are sure is the "clear teaching of scripture" in regard to the evil of homosexuality.

When a Christian community elects an unashamed and openly gay man to be a bishop and consecrates him publicly to that role and office, then it is clear that the old definitions of what it means to be homosexual are no longer holding. That is what happened in the Episcopal Church in 2003.[5] Just as certain is the realization that the "clear teaching of the Word of God" has, as traditionalists understand it, been set aside. This means one of two things: either the teaching of the Bible is not as clear as its advocates have always claimed or the Bible is not the "Word of God" in any literal sense. It might even suggest that *both* are the case.

What is that clear teaching, and where is it found in the Bible? That is the subject to which this study of the homophobic texts of the Bible must now turn. One discovers first how few these texts really are and second how convoluted is the reasoning that has attempted to use the Bible as the enforcer of cultural prejudices.

To set aside the Bible's supposedly "clear teaching" about the evils of homosexuality—a teaching that is contained in no more than nine references found in sixty-six books, written over a period of about twelve hundred years—has proved to be far more difficult than other conflicts that have marked Christian history. Does that not suggest that something more than a proper reading of the Bible is at stake?

But since the defenders of the traditional condemnation of homosexuality depend so vehemently on this "clear teaching" from the "Word of God," I must enter their battlefield and confront these condemning texts. It is a way of removing from those staunch defenders the righteousness of their claims that the Bible supports their prejudice. That, quite frankly, is not a very difficult thing to do, as I hope to demonstrate in successive chapters in which I will examine in detail the texts found on the opening page of this section. I will begin with Leviticus, not because it is first, but because it is the most frequently cited.

13

THE HOLINESS CODE FROM THE BOOK OF LEVITICUS

You shall not lie with a male as with a woman; it is an abomination.

Leviticus 18:22

If a man lies with a male as with a woman, both of them have committed an abomination; they shall be put to death; their blood be upon them.

Leviticus 20:13

This is the Word of the Lord?

The book of Leviticus was composed during the Babylonian Exile in the latter years of the sixth century BCE primarily by a group of Jewish religious leaders who came to be known as "the priestly writers." It was a survival document, calling and shaping the Jewish people into a dedication strong enough to continue their existence as a people who were not only separated from their homeland, but who would probably never see Judah again. Leviticus cultivated the sense of Jewish separation from everyone else that was deemed to be necessary for the maintenance of the Jewish national identity during that exile.

In the heart of the book of Leviticus is a section now known as "the holiness code." It was written to assist the captive Jews to achieve their objective of keeping themselves apart from the people among whom they were forced to live. Such separation was the key to their survival in history. It was incumbent upon the Jews as exiles to define themselves as both holy and different. They did this in several ways.

First, they established the seventh day of each week as the Sabbath and commanded that it be observed not only with a refusal to work, but also with attendance in the synagogue. To make this tradition the very hallmark of Judaism, these exiles created the six-day creation story with which the Bible now opens, contending that God validated this Sabbath tradition at the beginning of time by resting from the divine labors on the seventh day of creation. God then blessed the seventh day, enjoining it on the Jewish people forever after as a means of proclaiming themselves to be both holy and different.

Second, the exiled Jews adopted the kosher dietary laws also found in Leviticus. If a religious system imposes a strict diet on its constituents, adherents of that system are not likely to eat outside the faith community. Since people eating together is the primary way relationships normally grow, having to eat kosher food prepared in a kosher kitchen went a long way toward creating separation and encouraging the call to holiness at every meal.

Third, the captive Jews elevated circumcision to be the very mark of Judaism. This revived practice, which had fallen into general disuse, had the effect of putting the mark of their religion and tribal identity on the body of Jewish males, creating a separation that could never be denied.

Serving a similar motive, the holiness code of the book of Leviticus was designed to show that the Jews were different and thus meant to be set apart from the Babylonians among whom they were now forced to live as conquered people in exile. The priestly writers were surely aware of a variety of sexual practices among their captors and decided to define themselves in terms of a strict moral code that reflected their sixth-century BCE sense of values based upon their knowledge and the popular prejudices of their day. The defining passages about homosexuality quoted at the beginning of this chapter are taken from this section of Leviticus. They are clearly homophobic, but they also served the cultic need to articulate the attitude of the religious leaders at that time and to call the Jewish people into a life of identifiable boundaries that set them apart from the non-Jewish Babylonians.

In time Leviticus took its place among the first five books of the Bible as the very heart of Jewish life. "The Torah," as these five books were called, was identified as the work of Moses, the "father" and founder of Judaism. In time the Torah was supplemented by the writings of the early and late prophets and other material to form the Hebrew Bible. Later Christians added what they called the New Testament to these Hebrew scriptures to create the Christian Bible. Finally, that Bible began to be called the "Word of God." In this moment the prejudices of the ages ultimately found expression in these books and thus began their role in legitimating the dehumanization process of those who by these ancient definitions were outside the bounds of holiness as the Jews then defined them.

Like all other people, the writers of these sacred scriptures could escape neither their limitations in knowledge nor their place in history. Because of the advance in scientific learning, however, the attitudes, prejudices and ignorances of the past tend to die out as new ideas challenge old practices. This very normal and constant process is much more difficult to accomplish, however, if a cultural assumption is made along the way that the words in this particular book cannot be wrong because God is their author. So the limitations and the uninformed ignorance of ancient biblical authors have been quoted to perpetuate, throughout the history of those who call these writings sacred, the prejudices of antiquity. It is an interesting but closed circle, and the pain that has arisen from these attitudes is both measurable and palpable.

The first line of defense used by those who want to condemn homosexuality appears now to be the Bible. It is evident in Western society today that the major negativity against gay and lesbian people emanates from conservative Christian churches, both Catholic and Protestant.

A Canadian Anglican priest, the Very Reverend Peter Moore, now working as the dean of an evangelical seminary in the United States, has written, "There is nothing more certain than that the Bible condemns homosexuality. If the homosexuals win this battle, then the Bible will have no moral authority in any area of life." He then continues with a long and convoluted argument in typical evangelical style. His argument hinges on some version of the old and discredited biblical argument that "God wrote it; I believe it; that does it." It does not work. The argument from scripture about homosexuals is frail, fragile and pitiful. Perhaps those who offer it realize this, and that accounts for the hysterical quality of their rhetoric.[6]

"Have you not read Leviticus?" That was a regular refrain in letters written to me by Bible quoters when this debate on homosexuality was raging in my church some years ago. By Leviticus they could have meant only the texts from Leviticus 18 and Leviticus 20 with which I opened this chapter. I doubt if they were referring to the injunction in Leviticus that warns, "You shall not round off the hair on your temples or mar the edges of your beard" (19:27). I do not believe that much heed is paid today to the Leviticus prohibition against letting "your animals breed with another kind" (19:19, NRSV). Scientists have done amazing things in the field of animal husbandry to improve the herds of livestock.

The fact is that almost the only thing the Bible quoters know about the book of Leviticus is contained in these verses, one of which declares homosexual activity of a man with a man to be a prohibited abomination (18:22) and the other which prescribes the death penalty for those who violate this rule (20:13). It is interesting to note that Leviticus says nothing about lesbian relationships. Perhaps the author of Leviticus did not know there was such a thing.

I found the Leviticus 20 text emblazoned on a placard that was carried by a counterdemonstrator in the New York Gay Pride Parade some years ago. His sign proclaimed, "God said fags should die (Leviticus 20)." A version of that same text was carried by an anti-homosexual fundamentalist group from Topeka, Kansas, as they demonstrated at the funeral of Matthew Shepard, a young, gay university student who was beaten into unconsciousness and left to die on a fence post in subfreezing weather in Wyoming a few years ago.

It was also the implication behind the actions of the parents of a gay man whose story, related to me by an institutional Methodist chaplain, was one of the most poignant I have ever heard. This young man grew up in a family where the father and mother both expressed vehement negativity about homosexuality. Both parents were frequently heard to say that they would rather see their son dead than to know he was gay. So their son, knowing himself to be homosexual, hid deeper and deeper in his closet of security. When the time came for him to enter a university, he chose an academic setting on the other side of the country. University activities crowded his summers and holidays so that he was able to return home for only brief visits. When he graduated, he took a position near his university. Contact with his family was minimal. He drifted into the gay ghetto and ultimately contracted AIDS. When it was finally diagnosed, he faced the fact that he would not live much longer.

His deepest hope was to reconcile himself with his parents before he died. The relationship was so estranged, however, that he did not know how to do it. That was when he sought the counsel of this Methodist chaplain. After some conversation they decided together that the best way to approach this young man's parents was through a letter that would tell them that he was gay and dying with AIDS and would convey his dying wish to visit them and seek reconciliation. The letter was carefully crafted, addressed and mailed. About ten days later, a reply was received. The young man did not want to open this letter alone, so back to the Methodist chaplain he went. When the envelope was opened they discovered that it contained a blank piece of paper that when unfolded revealed the torn pieces of a printed document. It was the remains of this young man's birth certificate. The Leviticus theme of "God says fags should die" had been lived out yet again. It is surely a terrible and terrifying text.

We are living in a time when a new consciousness is arising in which there is a growing recognition that for homosexual people their only "sin" seems to be that they were born with a sexual orientation different from that of the majority. Yet we now know that orientation to be perfectly normal. It is like other minority positions within the human family: left-handedness, red hair. Minority positions, when not understood, tend to frighten people, and in their fear people strike out to protect themselves by rejecting and sometimes killing the different ones. That is understandable; we know why it happens. But it is evil nonetheless, and when it is validated with appeals to God and "God's Word," its evil reaches demonic levels. That is where this debate now lies inside the religious institutions of the Western world. The entrenched fear is that if something the Bible calls an abomination becomes acceptable, then that which makes religious people different will disappear and the defining "Word of God" in the Bible will collapse, leaving believers unsure about who they are. The battle rages and ultimately the Bible quoters will lose. When they do, their religion will either change or it will die.

Overwhelming scientific and medical knowledge exists today pointing to an inescapable conclusion. Sexual orientation is not a moral choice. It is something to which people awaken. It is therefore not morally culpable. The texts in Leviticus 18 and 20 are simply wrong. They are morally incompetent because they are based on ignorance. They should be viewed, as should so much else in Leviticus and the rest of the Torah, as stages in human development that we have outgrown, that we have been educated beyond and have therefore abandoned. To quote these texts to justify our prejudices and even our violence destroys the very essence of what Christians say they believe about God. The God who is love, the God who is heard through the words of Jesus promising life more abundantly, the description of the way others will recognize our desire to follow Jesus "by our love," all are violated if the texts of Leviticus 18 and 20 are given legitimacy. The time has come for all Christians to decide whether a person can follow Christ and still maintain his or her homophobic prejudices. I do not believe that is possible. Deep down all of us know this to be true. The decision is not both/and; it is either/or. We can either follow Christ or maintain our prejudices. There can be no compromise. The contending positions are mutually exclusive. There must be no wavering. Leviticus 18 and 20 cannot be allowed to remain in the lexicon of Christian behavior.

It is also no longer a morally defensible argument for hierarchical figures to protect the destructive homophobia of some leaders and church members in order "to preserve the unity of the church." A church unified in prejudice cannot possibly be the Body of Christ. Can anyone imagine a church preserving its unity by tolerating slavery in its midst? Is there any difference between that situation and tolerating homophobia? Any prejudice based upon who a person is, his or her very being as a child of God, cannot be a part of the church's life. Quoting Leviticus to justify our prejudices is no longer an option.

"Those Leviticus verses do not stand alone in the Bible," my critics will say. "They are but a small part of the biblical condemnation of homosexuality!" Fair enough, so next I will turn to Genesis 19, the chapter that has given us the words "sodomy" and "sodomite," as our examination of the biblical texts regarding homosexuality continues.

14

THE STORY
OF SODOM

The men of the city, even the men of Sodom, compassed the house round, both old and young, all the people from every quarter: And they called unto Lot, and said unto him, "Where are the men which came in to thee this night? Bring them out unto us, that we may know them."

Genesis 19:4–5, KJV

And Lot . . . said, "I pray you, brethren, do not [act] so wickedly. Behold now, I have two daughters which have not known man; let me, I pray you, bring them out unto you, and do ye to them as is good in your eyes."

Genesis 19:6–8, KJV

A sodomite! That at one time meant simply a citizen of the city of Sodom. Today, "sodomite" has come to mean one who performs sexual acts on a person of the same sex, and the word "sodomy" is used to describe that activity. It also sometimes means both anal sex and the act of a sexual encounter with a subhuman creature. That is quite a journey for two words to take, as I shall seek to demonstrate by examining this biblical reference to homosexuality. It is a text that has been used, throughout the centuries, to justify human hostility toward those who either are or are thought to be homosexuals. I find it of signal interest to note that even though the story of Sodom and Gomorrah is regularly quoted in the debate about the church's full acceptance of homosexual people, this narrative itself is seldom, if ever, read in its entirety. That is the first fact I want to raise to consciousness, because it indicates once again that we are dealing with irrational prejudice and not reasoned argument.

I start, therefore, by relating the whole story of the city of Sodom. It begins in Genesis 18:1 and concludes in Genesis 19:38. That means it absorbs two entire chapters in the Torah.

The story opens by the oaks of Mamre with Abraham sitting at the door of his tent in the heat of the day. He lifts up his eyes and sees three men approaching. One is said in the text to be the Lord; the other two are later identified as angels. Abraham, in the custom of the Middle East, goes out to greet these visitors and to offer them the hospitality of his home. In a ritualistic fashion he offers to have their feet washed, to share his shade underneath the tree and to provide them with a "morsel of bread" (KJV) so that, refreshed, they can pass on.

It is not just a morsel, however, that Abraham prepares, but a full banquet of meal cakes, a roasted lamb, curds and milk. Sarah, Abraham's wife, helps in the preparation of this meal, but she does not eat with them, for after all she is merely a woman.

At dinner these visitors, who obviously have access to divine knowledge, discuss with Abraham the fact that Sarah, his wife, is to have a baby. This child will enable God's promise to Abraham to be fulfilled, that through his "seed" all the nations of the earth will be blessed. There is, however, a problem that seems insurmountable: Sarah is well advanced in years—or, as the King James text so delicately puts it, "it [had] ceased to be with Sarah after the manner of women." When she hears this plan Sarah, who is hiding behind the tent door where she hopes, in vain it now appears, to catch up on the dinner gossip without being discovered, laughs out loud. She then utters words that later Victorians would never have used or even understood. "After I have grown old, . . . shall I have pleasure?" The Lord hears this, however, and rebukes Sarah for thinking that anything is impossible with God. Embarrassed, she denies laughing, but the Lord says, "Oh yes, you did laugh."

Only then does the conversation turn to the city of Sodom. The Lord decides to share with Abraham, who is to be the father of a great and mighty nation, the divine plan for that city. Since God has chosen Abraham, then Abraham must be informed of God's plans! A report has come to the Lord suggesting that the cities of Sodom and Gomorrah are very sinful. The Lord has decided to check out this report by sending his own emissaries to these places to seek verification. This is not the picture of an all-knowing deity; God needs a firsthand, eyewitness account. The divine plan, as outlined to Abraham, is this: the Lord's two angelic companions are to be dispatched to Sodom, while the Lord will remain with Abraham. During the absence of these two companions, the Lord will fill Abraham in on the details for destroying the entire city, should the reports by the messengers justify such a response.

Abraham then engages the Lord in a bargaining or haggling session similar to those that regularly took place in the marketplaces of that region, when the seller sought to gain for his goods a price twice their value and the buyer sought to pay for them half of what they were worth. As in the market, before the final price is agreed to a vigorous debate takes place.

"Wilt thou," asks Abraham of the Lord, "also destroy the righteous with the wicked?" (KJV). That seems a rather ungodlike thing to do, as Abraham will try to convince the Lord. Abraham is also concerned, we soon learn, about his nephew Lot and his family, who are residents in the city of Sodom. "Peradventure," Abraham says as the bargaining begins, "there be fifty righteous [people] within the city: wilt thou also destroy and not spare the place for the fifty righteous that are therein?" (KJV). That would not be fair, argues Abraham, reminding God of the divine character: "Shall not the Judge of all the earth do right?" (KJV).

God agrees with Abraham's initial parry and so, recognizing weakness in his bargaining partner, Abraham presses his advantage. He first reminds God of God's greatness and of his own status as dust and ashes. It sounds much like the self-denigration that takes place on the first tee of a golf course before the bets are placed. Suppose you don't quite get to fifty, says Abraham. Say you fall short by five, will the shortfall of just five righteous people trigger the destruct button? God responds positively that the city will be spared if forty-five righteous people can be discovered there. Abraham continues the debate, reminding God that he knows full well how impertinent it is to confront the Holy One, but Abraham, nonetheless, presses the bargaining process down to forty righteous people, then thirty, then twenty and finally ten. At this point the Lord promises not to destroy the city of Sodom for the sake of ten righteous people. Then the Lord departs and Abraham returns to his tent.

The storyline shifts to the Lord's two angelic companions as they enter the city of Sodom just as dusk is descending.

There were no hotels or motels in the ancient world. Travel was hard and dangerous, so travelers were few. The operative code governing the rights of strangers in that region was straightforward and clear. Visitors to a city had no rights and no protection unless hospitality was offered and accorded to them by one who was a citizen of the city. If that hospitality was not offered, then the strangers became fair game for abuse, which usually took the form of ribald play in which the manhood (no women would ever have been travelers unless whole families were forced into migration) of the strangers was compromised. This meant forcing the unprotected visitor to play the role of a woman in a sexually abusive act. This kind of episode constituted an evening of entertainment for the male citizens of the city, breaking the monotony of their normal existence.

So when the men of Sodom see these two strangers appear near sundown, with little chance at that late hour of hospitality being offered, their hopes begin to rise in anticipation of a night of debauchery.

However, Abraham's nephew Lot at the very last moment takes these strangers into his home and thus thwarts the plans of his fellow citizens. Enraged at this lost opportunity, the men of Sodom, including, says this text, "young and old, all the people to the last man," surround Lot's house, demanding that these two visitors be surrendered to them for sexual sport. For Lot to do such a thing would be to violate not only his word, but also the hospitality code of the region, a code that was for travelers in that day the difference between life and death. Once the protection of a home had been offered, the honor of the whole household was at stake if this protection was compromised.

Lot refuses their demands, but the rage of the crowd is not lessened. Lot, after rebuking his fellow citizens by urging them not to act so wickedly, then makes a counteroffer. I will give you instead, he says, my two virgin daughters, and you may "do to them as you please." The implication here is that these two daughters, both of whom appear to be betrothed to young men who are part of the mob, are to be gang-raped for the evening's entertainment. That is exactly what happens in a similar story told in the book of Judges that follows the Sodom story very closely (see Judg. 19).

There is no indication in this biblical narrative that Lot's daughters are consulted about this offer, since they are, after all, only women and thus have no rights. Women were viewed in that period of time as the property of their father, who could do with them whatever he desired until they became the property of another man willing to pay the bride price to the father. At that point women simply became the property of their husbands. This is what the Bible overtly says.

The men of Sodom seem dissatisfied by Lot's offer of his daughters and begin to be violent, forcing their way into Lot's home. The two angelic visitors, using supernatural power, come to Lot's rescue, striking the men of the city with blindness. These angelic visitors then order Lot and his family to leave the city. Ten righteous people have not been discovered in the city of Sodom, so the Lord is primed to destroy it. Lot, his wife and his daughters are the only righteous people to be identified and now, in a divine act of mercy, these four people are to be allowed to escape. An offer of safety is also made to their potential husbands, who are invited to accompany them in their flight, but they decline the offer. Perhaps they are still recovering from their blindness. Lot and his family now flee the city and the divine destruction begins: fire and brimstone rain down and Sodom and all its citizens are destroyed.

Lot first plans to enter the city of Zoar, where he and his family will have the status of strangers. After second thoughts, however, knowing well what can happen to unprotected strangers in a foreign city, he opts not to run that risk and heads instead for the mountains. His wife, the story says, then makes the fatal mistake of looking back, as all of them have been warned not to do, and she is turned, immediately and magically, into a pillar of salt. At last only Lot and his two daughters are spared. This man who has offered his virgin daughters for gang rape is nonetheless judged by God to be righteous and worthy of deliverance!

The story does not end there. The "righteousness" of this group of three is destined to be compromised yet again. As the story continues, these two daughters slowly realize that they will never marry and bear children "after the manner of all the world," as the text says. Their purpose in life as women, according to the biblical definition, is therefore destined never to be fulfilled. They are now without either clan or tribe, which is where husbands would normally be found for them in that world. Their father is thus the only man available, so they conspire to get him drunk. They ply him with wine and then, while he is in a drunken stupor, turn him into their sexual partner and lover, with the older daughter lying with him on the first night and the younger daughter on the second night. Both daughters accomplish their purpose, even on these one-night stands, and become pregnant by their father. These incestuous acts bring into life two sons: Moab, who was said to have been the father of the Moabites, and Ammon, who was said to have been the father of the Ammonites. It is on this note that the story of Sodom and Gomorrah finally comes to an end.

This ancient biblical narrative features a view of God so primitive that this God does not know what is going on in the world and has to send divine emissaries to bring back firsthand intelligence. Yet this ancient story has been used to demonstrate God's negativity toward homosexual persons. This story that portrays all of the men of Sodom as eager to gang-rape two heavenly visitors, who have no rights in that city unless a citizen offers hospitality and protection, has been used to condemn faithful and loving homosexual relationships. This biblical narrative is one in which a father, in order to protect the Middle Eastern code of hospitality, can offer his virgin daughters to be gang-raped and still be regarded by both God and the author of this story as righteous and deserving of divine protection. Finally, a narrative that depicts scheming daughters, a drunken father and dual acts of incest has been turned by the prejudices of later interpreters into an anti-homosexual biblical text that feeds the basest side of our humanity. How is all of that possible unless prejudice overwhelms rationality and moral judgment?

Of course gang rape is wrong whether its style is homosexual or heterosexual. Of course the plot to commit incest is wrong. But what does that have to do with the hopes and aspirations of two women or two men in the twenty-first century who love each other, and who want to live for and with each other in a partnership of intimacy and faithfulness and with the blessing of God? How inappropriate can prejudice, wrapped in the authoritative blanket of scripture, become? On the basis of this narrative, the fear of something that seems odd and strange to heterosexuals has been combined with a perceived threat to their heterosexual identity posed by the presence of the reality of homosexuality in our world, to produce a bitter, hostile, destructive response that has victimized gay and lesbian people throughout the ages. This biblical story has been used for centuries to justify murders, oppression and gay persecution. People whose only crime—or "sin," if you prefer—is that they were born with a sexual orientation different from that of the majority have been victimized because of that difference. That victimization has been justified by appeals to ancient biblical texts like this one about the city of Sodom. That is so blatantly evil, so overtly ignorant and so violently prejudiced that it should be worthy of nothing but condemnation. If this is what traditionalists mean when they use the phrase "clear teaching of scripture," then let it be said that this use of the Bible has no place in our world unless ignorance is to be called knowledge and evil is to be called virtuous!

The Bible supports the prejudice of homophobia only by having its message twisted with a strange literalization, coupled with the ability to read ancient tribal history and practice as if it could be made holy by calling it the "Word of God." If that is what biblical morality is, I want none of it. For that reason I, for one, will no longer tolerate or respect anyone who quotes the Sodom story to justify this violent prejudice. This ancient and destructive text, now exposed, must never again be used in my hearing in the service of oppression.

When people seeking to use these texts from Genesis to defend their homophobic prejudice realize that they have come up against solid opposition, they do an interesting two-step. This story, they say, does have some weaknesses, since it is found in the Hebrew scriptures which in many of their details have not been adopted by Christianity. But the New Testament, they say with hopeful enthusiasm, *does* condemn homosexuality. Look at the writings of Paul, they say. Did Paul not condemn homosexual behavior? Is Paul not proclaiming the "Word of God" to which Christians must listen? To the homophobia of Paul I turn next.

15

THE HOMOPHOBIA OF PAUL

They glorified [God] not as God, neither were thankful; but became vain in their imaginations, and their foolish heart was darkened. . . .

For this cause God gave them up unto vile afflictions: for even their women did change the natural use into that which is against nature: And likewise also the men, leaving the natural use of the woman, burned in their lust one toward another; men with men working that which is unseemly, and receiving in themselves that recompense of their error which was meet.

Romans 1:21, 26–27, KJV

For although they knew God they did not honor . . . God or give thanks to [God], but they became futile in their thinking and their senseless minds were darkened. . . .

For this reason God gave them up to dishonorable passions. Their women exchanged natural relations for unnatural, and the men likewise gave up natural relations with women and were consumed with passion for one another, men committing shameless acts with men and receiving in their own persons the due penalty for their error.

Romans 1:21, 26–27

This is the most overt and, I might add, the strangest condemnation of homosexual acts in the New Testament. It is the only place in the Bible where there is a specific allusion to female homosexuality. It is a text frequently quoted to justify blatant homophobia. Yet its obvious meaning is simply ignored or dodged. Let me state that meaning boldly. Paul is asserting that homosexuality is the punishment given by God to those who fail to worship God properly! Homosexuality for Paul is not a sickness or the result of a choice which one has freely made; it is a punishment for the sin of not attending to the details and practices of proper worship. In other words, Paul is saying that God infects people with homosexual desire if they engage in improper worship or use improper images of God. It is both a startling and an ill-informed claim. Imagine what it must be like to live in fear that God will turn your sexual desire "from the natural use of a woman," making the recipient burn with lust toward one of his own gender! If God could or would do that, would God be worthy of anyone's worship? Would God not be an ogre, a demon or something worse? Could Paul really have believed such a thing? What in the world would be the experience of a human being like Paul that would cause him even to think in these strange explanatory terms? Is there any reason why anyone should believe that this convoluted and bizarre understanding of the tortured Pauline mind could ever be called the "Word of God"? Is it rational to think that these words would ever be used to condemn or to oppress those who awaken to the reality of their homosexual orientation?

The inability or the unwillingness to see this text for what it so overtly says is a powerful witness to the distorting lenses through which so many people read Holy Scripture.

Paul, as a rabbinical student who studied under Gamaliel (Acts 22:3), surely knew well the passages from Leviticus and Genesis to which I have previously referred. To be homosexual, or at least to act on one's homosexuality, was according to his religion to come under the condemnation of the Torah. It was a serious offense. Death was the penalty prescribed by the law for those who did not repress their homosexual orientation. Paul also in all probability knew the books of the Maccabees, found in the Apocrypha, which were incredibly popular in his time of Jewish history. These books recounted battles in the second century BCE between Jewish guerrilla fighters, led by Judas, who was given the nickname "the Hammer" or in Aramaic "Maccabeas," and the army of the Syrians. Paul would certainly have been aware of the injunction found in 4 Maccabees which suggested that if one were faithful and disciplined enough in the worship of God, all desires could be overcome (4 Macc. 2:2, 3:17).

Fortunately, we do not have to speculate on Paul's meaning in the absence of other firsthand data, since we have other works of Paul that we can search for additional clues. In the epistles to the Galatians (1:13–17) and to the Philippians (3:5–6) Paul relates some of his autobiographical history—his passion for the law, his willingness to work on his studies with zeal and his advancement in holiness beyond all of his fellows. Paul was quite clearly a religious zealot, perhaps a religious fanatic. This kind of behavior that we call either zealotry or fanaticism is always compensatory, always in the service of something unresolved and more pressing, perhaps more threatening. Fanaticism in religion is normally employed in the suppression of something deep within the person that is deemed unacceptable—indeed, is of such magnitude that it might not be admitted even by that person.

One of the marks of fanaticism is a tendency to erupt in rage whenever some of the protective layers in the fanatic's security system are challenged or exposed. We need only to recall Paul's days as a persecutor of the Christians, which both he (Gal. 1:13) and the book of Acts (Acts 9:1ff.) relate. He describes himself as violently trying to exterminate the Christian movement (Gal. 1:13). Luke says Paul sought authority from the high priest to arrest the Christians in Damascus and to bring them bound to Jerusalem for imprisonment (Acts 9:2). Luke even portrays him as participating in their executions (Acts 7:58, 8:1). I do not think we can be certain of the historicity of these details found in the book of Acts, but they are certainly consistent with everything else we know about Paul and about religious fanatics in general. Religious fanatics are deeply controlling people. The very nature of fanaticism is revealed in the inability on the part of the fanatic to deal with diversity or pluralism. Fanatics make constant attempts to silence their critics, to excommunicate them, sometimes to burn them at the stake. They are enraged when challenged. They are people who are clearly busy suppressing something inside themselves with which they feel they cannot cope. They attach themselves to the authority of religious rules and systems that become unbendable and self-defining. They see anyone who is against their security-producing rules as being against God. It is a typical pattern: fanatical rhetoric is indeed the same generation after generation.

The most rigid priest I have ever known personally lived this pattern out totally—and yet, I might add, he did it rather beautifully. He was the kind of priest who would never think of appearing in public without the proper uniform of a jet-black suit and clerical collar. He followed a rigid discipline of daily worship, including obligatory rites of matins and evening prayer. He celebrated or attended the Eucharist—he called it the Mass—each day of his life. He was deeply disturbed by changes in the liturgy and in the practices of the church. The idea that the liturgy might be modernized was anathema to him. The possibility that women might ever become priests was inconceivable to him, for in his mind it required that the church be willing to sacrifice everything that was holy.

When the bishop would come to the church served by this priest for the annual confirmation visit, it would create in this priest an anxiety level that was all but unmanageable. For weeks in advance he would choreograph that liturgy to make sure that the bishop did not violate his customs and rules and thereby suggest to the members of this congregation that this priest's patterns were not eternally binding on the faithful. This priest's anxiety clearly spilled over into the congregation, many of whom were attracted to that church out of deep needs for the security of certainty that this priest offered. The members of his church had bought into the rigidity of worship that this church offered and they felt a sense of comfort in their ability to master the magic of the details of their typical liturgy so that God would be pleased and, not coincidentally, so that God would bless them.

Ultimately, all of these control needs proved too much to be sustained, even for this priest, and he finally endured what was later called a nervous breakdown. He literally fell apart and for a period of time was absolutely out of control, unable to function in any area of his life. It was a classic meltdown of defenses. The dark specter of depression began to consume him as the unacceptable parts of his identity entered his consciousness. During this critical moment in his life, both suicide and a psychotic break that might have rendered him a mental patient for life were distinct possibilities.

Instead, like Paul as Luke describes him on the road to Damascus, this man saw a bright light and heard a heavenly voice call him by name and he allowed his deeply debilitating fear of what he thought of as a loathsome and unacceptable homosexuality to be set aside. He experienced, as Paul seems also to have done, a love that embraced him just as he was, an acceptance that swept over that part of his sexual identity that he had been certain was unacceptable. He discovered the courage to be himself, a self that was not rejectable either eternally or today. That was when the healing process began. Like a phoenix rising from the ashes, that priest started to live anew. To use the language of evangelical Christianity, he was "born again." He came to terms with his homosexual reality. He began to allow his heart and soul to accept what his mind and emotions had long been telling him he was, and he laid down both his rigidity and his fear. As he was restored to health, a person came into his life that he allowed himself to love. In time they became partners and lived with each other in life-giving faithfulness until age finally separated them with death. I learned much from this man.

"Paul is just like I was before I became honest with myself," he said to me. "He was rigid about all the rules, violent when challenged, a persecutor of those who suggested that the law with which Paul had bound himself was not itself ultimate, and that perhaps even that which was judged to be so totally unacceptable could be loved by the God who had made him." Under the tutelage of this priest I began to look again at Paul. It was for me a life-changing experience.

In Romans Paul described his inner struggle: "I see in my members another law at war with the law of my mind and making me captive to the law of sin which dwells in my members" (7:23). Paul's experience was that he followed one law with his mind, another with his body. This sin that he feels "dwells in my members" caused him to proclaim that "nothing good dwells within me, that is my flesh." He went on to say, "I do not do the good I want, but the evil I do not want is what I do." He concludes this interior lament by saying, "Wretched man that I am, who will deliver me from this body of death?" It was a plaintive cry reflecting a longstanding memory. That plea ultimately fades into an acclamation when he asserts that he has been given victory over the affliction. "Thanks be to God through Jesus Christ our Lord," he says (Rom. 7:18–19, 24–25). Paul culminates this section by stating that he is now persuaded that nothing will be able to separate us from the love of God in Christ Jesus our Lord (8:39), not even our "nakedness," he adds in a revealing choice of words in verse 35. It is a remarkable portrait of a remarkable man. Perhaps what is even more unusual is that the words of Paul are still quoted today to condemn the homosexuality that Paul surely knew was his own hidden secret.

Yes, I am convinced that Paul of Tarsus was a gay man, deeply repressed, self-loathing, rigid in denial, bound by the law that he hoped could keep this thing, that he judged to be so unacceptable, totally under control, a control so profound that even Paul did not have to face this fact about himself. But repression kills. It kills the repressed one and sometimes the defensive anger found in the repressed one also kills those who challenge, threaten or live out the thing that this repressed person so deeply fears.

Much of the persecution of gay and lesbian people both within the church and in the broader society has been carried out by self-rejecting, deeply closeted homosexual people. Frequently homophobic but homosexual clergy and bishops, together with their most loyal lay followers, have wrapped their externalized rage, their rejecting and sometimes killing fury, inside the security of some authoritative system. They quote either a hierarchy that claims infallibility or a sacred source from scripture that people have said is inerrant. That is how fanaticism works. That is certainly what is revealed in the Pauline tirade recorded in Romans 1—a frightened gay man condemning other gay people so that he can keep his own homosexuality inside the rigid discipline of his faith.

Paul sought throughout his pre-conversion life to worship properly, and thereby to banish his own unacceptable desires. His words have been used to do great harm to great numbers of people. The "Word of God" he uttered has become a weapon of oppression. This was and is a sinister, inaccurate and incompetent way to use the writings of Paul, but that has been the fate of this first chapter of Romans. I now seek to expose it for what it has always been with the hope that, weakened and revealed, it will no longer claim new victims in every age. It will be a "terrible text" or a sin of scripture no longer.

There are other places in the Pauline and pseudo-Pauline corpus that have also been used to hurt homosexual people. In 1 Corinthians 5:10 and 6:9 Paul uses the word *malekos*, which means "soft" or "lacking in self-control," and the word *arsenokoitis*, which means "a male lying" and is frequently used to refer to male prostitutes. The normal translation of these words has been "sexual perverts," by which most people mean homosexuals. There is much debate in New Testament circles as to whether this translation is accurate. If Paul is referring to male prostitutes or even to abusive homosexual relationships, then a word of condemnation might well be in order. For that condemnation to be extended to include faithful, loving, nonexploitive gay and lesbian partnerships would be to stretch the text to the breaking point in service to one's own prejudice.

There are three other frequently quoted New Testament texts used to buttress the "clear teaching of the Bible" against homosexuality. One of these, 1 Timothy 1:10, is sometimes attributed to Paul, but almost every New Testament scholar in the world acknowledges that Paul was not the author of 1 Timothy. In that epistle once again the word *arsenokoitis* is used. It is rendered "sodomites" in the Revised Standard Version of the Bible and "them that defile themselves with mankind" in the King James Version. Let me say that I regard any sex that is predatory or forced to be evil, whether it is homosexual or heterosexual. But to have that kind of behavior used to define all homosexual relationships makes as much sense to me as using the word "rape" to define all heterosexual relationships.

Finally, there are two texts, one in the epistle of Jude (1:7) and the other in 2 Peter (2:6), that are frequently used by Bible quoters seeking to justify biblical negativity toward homosexuality. These two references are related to each other. The verse in 2 Peter appears to be dependent on Jude. Both are related to the Sodom and Gomorrah story and both are designed to show how God will destroy those who do not believe (Jude) or those who teach heresy (2 Peter). As sources to be quoted to condemn homosexuality, they are simply not worthy of further comment.

That is all there is in the "clear teaching of the Bible" in regard to the condemning of homosexuality. No lawyer could win a court case with such flimsy evidence, but people have been exposed, tortured and killed in obedience to the understanding supposedly gleaned from the sacred scriptures that God hates homosexuality and, by implication, homosexuals (unless they repent of their evil being). This, in turn, has justified the religious hatred of homosexuality and created the cataclysmic battle that tears churches apart as the new consciousness of today collides with the old and dying definitions of the past. There is no doubt about how this debate will come out: the new consciousness will not be defeated.

In a *New York Times* magazine story[7] about a conservative southern bishop in the Episcopal Church named Peter Lee, who had finally voted to support a gay bishop elected to lead the diocese of New Hampshire, Bishop Lee's wife, Kristina, was quoted as saying to him, "Peter, do you want to be on the side of the future or of the past?" Bishop Lee voted for the future and received the predictable wrath of his Virginia constituents who, firmly rooted in the past, vowed to defend the "clear teaching of the Bible." They too will pass, and Peter Lee and others like him will discover that the debate is over and that, for all their struggles, they did finally come down on the side of life.

The Christian ethic is ultimately a life ethic. When behavior enhances life, expands love and calls all parties involved into the experience of a new being, then it must be called good. But when behavior denigrates, uses, violates or diminishes one or more of the parties involved, then it must be called evil. Furthermore, no text from the Bible can ever be used appropriately to validate the prejudiced behavior of homophobia, which is clearly evil. That kind of outcome can never be derived from the "Word of God."

THE BIBLE AND CHILDREN

THE TERRIBLE TEXTS

He who spares the rod hates his son, but he who loves him is diligent to discipline him.

Proverbs 13:24

Folly is bound up in the heart of a child, but the rod of discipline drives it far from him.

Proverbs 22:15

Do not withhold discipline from a child; if you beat him with a rod, he will not die. If you beat him with the rod, you will save his life from Sheol.

Proverbs 23:13–14

16

THE APPEAL
IN THE TEXT
"SPARE THE ROD"

The day my father caught me with a chaw [of tobacco] in my
cheek, I got a thrashing to remember. . . .

In the strictness of my upbringing there was no hint of child
abuse. While my parents were swift to punish when punishment
was deserved, they did not overload me with arbitrary
regulations that were impossible to respect.

I learned to obey without questioning.

Billy Graham[1]

Spare the rod and spoil the child" is typical of the way the biblical
texts on the opening page of this section are usually quoted. Most
people do not know either their source or their literal form. This shorthand
version instead has been passed on from generation to generation as a kind of
self-authenticating folk wisdom.

These texts are located in a seldom-read part of the Old Testament called
Proverbs, which is quite frankly a rather boring book. Thirty-one chapters in
length, it is located between the Psalms and Ecclesiastes. It is mostly ignored by the various ecclesiastical lectionaries,[2] so it is seldom heard in
churches. It is identified by scholars as part of the wisdom tradition of the
Jews, made popular in the fifth and sixth centuries BCE. It consists for the

most part of utterances designed to guide the routine activities of the daily Jewish culture. In Jewish piety this wisdom literature was attributed to King Solomon, building on his reputation as the wisest man in Jewish history. This attribution, however, has no basis in fact. Solomon had actually been dead for at least four hundred years before either Proverbs or the wisdom tradition itself ever came into being, although some of the original sayings may date back to as early as the latter years of the eighth century BCE.

In addition to the verses that underlie the "Spare the rod and spoil the child" dictum, there are a few sayings from the book of Proverbs that have entered our consciousness, though most people are not likely to know their source. Among them would be maxims like "The fear of the Lord is the beginning of wisdom" (Prov. 9:10) and "A soft answer turns away wrath" (Prov. 15:1) and the suggestion that a friend might be "closer than a brother" (Prov. 18:24).

When Paul wrote in his epistle to the Romans, "If your enemy is hungry, feed him; if he is thirsty, give him drink; for by so doing you will heap burning coals upon his head" (12:20), he was quoting Proverbs 25:21–22. In the opening hymn to the divine logos, or the "Word," in the first chapter of the Fourth Gospel, the author appears to be leaning on a text from the eighth chapter of Proverbs (vv. 22–31).

Although this book has had influence in Christian history, its impact has generally not been recognized by most people. Yet the words from this book suggesting that physical discipline of children is appropriate have played a major role in the history of childrearing and, I would argue, in the history of child abuse. The failure to include these texts in a book seeking to raise consciousness to the "sins of scripture" would be a major oversight.

Words that affirm the rightness of punishment seem to touch something in the human psyche and to illumine something deep in the human experience. If one is the *victim* of corporal punishment, these words suggest a sense of "deserving" and thereby play into a self-negativity that rises from a particular definition of humanity. If one is the *perpetrator* of corporal punishment, these words seem to feed a human need to control, to exercise authority or even to demonstrate that forced submission is a virtue. If our religious tradition suggests that a child is "born in sin," it is clearly the duty of that child's parents or their surrogates to curb that willfulness and to control with force that implantation of "the devil." When this understanding of human life is coupled with an attitude toward the Bible which suggests that its words are in fact holy and divine messages from God, then all criticism is muted. It matters not that child psychologists and child development experts generally condemn this style of parenting. They can be dismissed as "godless people who do not understand the nature of our humanity as the Bible portrays it." Their insights are also dismissed in the religious segments of our society as "new-fangled learning" that does not value the "traditions of God-fearing people."

Parents punishing their children for their misdeeds fits comfortably into the view of a God who is also perceived as a parental figure ready to punish sinful adults, or at least to punish the One who is said to be the vicarious substitute for all the people. Is it not of interest that Christians from the very beginning have applied the image of the "Suffering Servant" from Second Isaiah[3] to the story of Jesus, so that it is said of him, "With his stripes we are healed" (Isa. 53:5), and "the Lord has laid on him the iniquity of us all" (Isa. 53:6)? It sounds very much as if God has a heavenly woodshed reserved for the physical punishment of God's "wayward children," or their designated surrogate.

This kind of discipline has been supported through the centuries by a variety of pious claims, allowing it to wear the mask of intellectual and religious credibility. Only in recent decades has Western consciousness been raised on this subject and as that consciousness has risen corporal punishment has begun its inevitable retreat into the past. Yet the glorification of physical discipline for children still lingers in pockets of our culture that, not coincidentally, I believe, tend to be identified with conservative Christian churches. Parochial schools are notorious for their use of physical discipline. The nuns in yesterday's Catholic schools were in many instances quite clearly feared by the students. When that reality is augmented by the sexual abuse of children by Roman Catholic priests that now appears to have been present in shocking, almost epidemic proportions in recent decades, the sickness present in the attitude of the Catholic Church toward children becomes very clear.

Not to be outdone in this evil by the Roman Catholic tradition, in Protestant fundamentalist circles the exultation of corporal punishment is still defended today in the United States by such people as Dr. James Dobson and his "Focus on the Family" organization.[4] To press the connection one step further, Philip J. Greven, a Rutgers University professor, has written a book entitled *Spare the Child*, in which he seeks to demonstrate that, almost to a person, the well-known preachers in American history and the popular radio and television evangelists of today have revealed approvingly in their preaching or in autobiographies that they were physically punished regularly as children.[5] Dr. Greven has suggested that this life experience helped to shape their evangelical message, which portrays an angry God standing ready to punish sinful people through all eternity unless they repent.

During the late 1990s a task force on children in the Episcopal Diocese of Newark, where I was serving as the bishop, chaired by the Reverend Edward Hasse of Montvale, NJ, made a report to the Diocesan Convention. This report included the following resolution presented for debate: "Resolved, that there are no circumstances in which corporal punishment is appropriate as a method of disciplining children." Prior to the convention this report and its resolution were circulated at the pre-convention meetings, designed to inform delegates of the issues that would be coming before them. It was a normal part of our decision-making process. At this time we discovered that this report had titillated the secular press, which now began to follow this debate rather closely and quite enthusiastically.

When the resolution was ultimately placed before the assembly, the debate was quite revealing. It was for me, as the presiding officer, like watching some six hundred people engaging in a group therapy session. We had people justifying publicly their own behavior as parents by praising their methods of discipline and the ways their own parents had disciplined them. "My father beat me regularly," said one man well into his seventies, "and it made a man out of me." Another said, "My children have said to me that the physical discipline I meted out to them was the best thing I ever did for them." Still another used the old cliché that attempts to turn violence into virtue by insisting that "I did it for their own good and it always hurt me more than it hurt my children."

Other delegates to this convention, however, spoke in very different tones, as childhood memories emerged through adult voices. These men and women shared their sense of being violated and humiliated in ways that were so deep they had never spoken of it publicly until that very moment. They told of the psychic damage they had sustained, the rage they had felt and the residual anger they still felt as adults. They shared openly feelings of being humiliated anew when their parents would speak of a particular disciplining session to neighbors, friends or extended family in a casual manner as they sought to gain approval for their form of parenting.

The debate was interesting in one other detail and that was how the vote turned out. This was a relatively well educated, socially prominent assembly of approximately 150 clergy and 450 elected lay delegates. Yet no consensus ever emerged and they were not willing to vote the resolution up or down. Finally, in a face-saving leap toward easing the assembly out of this dilemma, the Reverend John Hartnett, a priest from Ridgewood, NJ, offered an amendment. For the words "corporal punishment" in the resolution, he moved to substitute the words "injurious or humiliating treatments" so that the resolution then read: "Resolved, that there are no circumstances in which injurious or humiliating treatments are appropriate as a method for disciplining children." No one thought their own use of corporal punishment was either "injurious" or "humiliating," so they leaped on this way of removing the subject from debate. The amendment passed almost unanimously, which in church gatherings means that it falls into the same category as resolutions opposing sin and extolling virtue, or what politicians call "God, motherhood and apple pie" resolutions. It committed no one to anything.

Yet the interest shown, the emotions expressed, the stories shared and the anguish revealed in this debate painted an unforgettable portrait that is still vivid in my mind, for it made clear the levels of inner conflict that still mark so many lives. It also made me wonder why it is that the physical punishment of children is apparently validated by a book called the "Word of God." More significantly, it caused me to wonder what there is about Christianity itself that has brought about its constant emphasis on God as a punishing deity, its concept of hell as a place of eternal punishment and its portrait of Jesus as the one who took our punishment for us. "Spare the rod and spoil the child" is one more biblical injunction that opens a doorway that needs to be entered. In this section of this book, that is exactly what I plan to do.

17

VIOLENCE IS ALWAYS VIOLENT, WHETHER THE VICTIM BE A CHILD OR AN ADULT

John Newman was a private in the Infantry of the United States army who joined me as a volunteer and entered into an enlistment in common with others by which he was held and mustered as one of the permanent party. In the course of the expedition, or shortly before we arrived at the Mandan villages he committed himself by using certain mutinous expressions which caused me to arrest him and to have him tried by a Court Martial formed of his peers; they finding him guilty, sentenced him to receive seventy-five lashes and to be discharged from the permanent party. This sentence was enforced by me, and the punishment took place. The conduct of this man previous to this period had been generally correct, and the zeal he afterwards displayed for the benefit of the service was highly meritorious.

The Journals of Merriwether Lewis and William Clark [6]

The physical abuse of children under the guise of "proper discipline" has been practiced in Western history for so long and so frequently that it has come to be thought of as normative. It has had the approval of our recognized sources of cultural values—tradition, Bible, church, school and family. It has found expression in popular novels written by such noteworthy nineteenth-century authors as Charles Dickens and Mark Twain and by the twentieth century's ultraconservative political pundit William F. Buckley, who also wrote detective stories when he was not otherwise stating his opinions on current events.[7] When some of these novels (not Buckley's, to be sure) were turned into motion pictures, the scenes in which corporal punishment was administered in school settings were often quite graphic. One thinks of the violence displayed in *Nicholas Nickleby*, for example. Every schoolboy and schoolgirl in my generation can recall the scene from the movie *Tom Sawyer* in which Tom volunteered to take the punishment about to be administered to his girlfriend, Becky, which won for him not just Becky's devotion, but her words, "Tom, how could you be so noble?"

In the schools of Western history—which were normally church-related, whether parochial or public, given the role of Christianity in Western civilization—corporal punishment was regularly employed until quite recently, certainly within my lifetime. Almost always such punishment was meted out with parental approval.

Reuters News Service in 2004 told the world of a Roman Catholic order of nuns in Ireland, known as the Congregation of the Sisters of Mercy, who had "apologized unconditionally for the physical and emotional trauma its nuns had inflicted on children raised in its orphanages and schools." This abuse had been uncovered in a television exposé of enormous maltreatment in Dublin in the 1950s and 1960s. An earlier apology that did not go far enough had been rejected by the victims.[8]

In boarding schools of the nineteenth and early twentieth centuries this disciplinary activity sometimes had about it a ritualistic quality and even came to be thought of as a kind of "liturgical observance."[9] That is, the act of discipline was carried out at a certain time. It was scheduled on a particular day for all offenders during a specified period of time for which the school staff prepared the instruments to be used, such as a bunch of bound switches or a freshly cut cane. It was followed through in a prescribed, unchanging and traditional manner. The intended victim or victims would have to wait in fearful anticipation until the proper moment when the price of their misbehavior was exacted. The disciplinary act clearly defined boundaries and made all aware of where authority resided.

In my own experience, as a public schoolboy growing up in the southern Bible Belt, corporal punishment was employed, but much less ritualistically. It was administered on the spot whenever it was deemed essential to control the classroom and as a response to a particular act of misbehavior.[10] Although not used frequently, it also followed a set form that we all recognized. I recall in my seventh-grade class, which was the last time I knew such discipline to take place, only two of my classmates were subjected to it during the entire year. The fact, however, that I can still recall both instances some sixty years later indicates that each of these occasions made an indelible, albeit not a positive, impression upon my young mind. Most of us who were not the actual recipients of the punishment were in fact intimidated by it.

The offending student, in both cases a boy twelve or thirteen years old, was asked to accompany the teacher with ruler in hand to the room adjacent to the principal's office, which was reserved solely for this purpose. That room also happened to be next door to our classroom, so even though we could not observe the act of discipline, we could not fail to hear it. The students remaining in the classroom sat in silence during the period of time it took the teacher and the pupil to reach the required location and to assume the proper positions for discipline. Then the noise of the ruler landing on its target resounded. No cries were ever heard, because proving that he "could take it" preserved the pupil's last shred of dignity. Finally the blows would cease and in a few minutes the chastened student would return to the class, followed by the teacher, still gripping her ruler. The student, taking his seat, would say something about it "not hurting at all," a brave attempt to reestablish his place in the social fabric of the class. It always seemed to me, though, that it took the disciplined child a day or so to absorb the humiliation before he began to ease back into the life of the school community.

The teacher used each such episode as a teaching moment, warning the other students that a similar fate awaited each of them if their behavior made it necessary. The ever-present threat that the ruler would be employed again instilled apprehension and fear and developed something of a herd instinct among us all. Instead of enhancing life, it seemed only to bruise fragile egos. It certainly taught by example that physical force was a proper way to deal with those who are smaller and weaker. It surely issued in a more controllable classroom, but it was never, in my opinion, a pathway into maturity.

It is interesting to note what classes of people, besides children, were subjected to corporal punishment during at least some part of the history of our Judeo-Christian world. There were basically four types of adults for whom corporal punishment was deemed, in years past, to be appropriate discipline. The one thing each of these four groups of people had in common was that they were thought to be deserving of the status of a child.

The first category was adult prisoners—those who had violated the rules of the society in such a way as to be judged a threat that must be removed, jailed and punished. I suppose the reasoning process was simple. If physical punishment made schoolchildren more pliable and obedient, to say nothing of being easier to control, then why should the same tactic not be used on those adults who consistently disrupted the well-being of society? So the right to use corporal punishment was written into the penal codes of most Western, and by implication Christian, nations.

The public whipping post was a regular feature in the criminal justice system in nations like Great Britain and the United States until the twentieth century. The last state to make it illegal in America was Delaware in the 1970s. It is still employed to this day in Singapore and in several Muslim nations, including Pakistan and Saudi Arabia. The familiar jail diet of "bread and water" was just another form of corporal punishment; that is, it was the physical punishment of the body.

By extension from the penal codes, physical discipline was used in situations where control was deemed essential to survival. It was a standard practice, for example, on the ships of the colonial powers in the eighteenth and nineteenth centuries. The whole world was shrunk to the dimensions of an individual boat, with the captain exercising the decision-making responsibility for discipline, indeed sometimes for life and death, with no further appeal. Physical discipline was also employed in the military expedition led by Lewis and Clark across the continental United States on their journey to open the West to the Pacific Ocean. As we saw in the epigraph to this chapter, the diaries from that journey describe what Lewis and Clark believed was the salutary effect of this discipline. There is a sense in which both ships at sea and military expeditions operated with prisonlike rules.

The second class of adults to be treated in this physically abusive manner during our history was slaves. Christians must never forget that even in the New Testament the institution of slavery was accepted as normal. Paul, in his epistle to Philemon, directs a runaway slave named Onesimus to return to his master Philemon, not with the request for his freedom, but with the request that he be treated kindly. In Paul's epistle to the Colossians, he orders slaves to "obey in everything those who are your earthly masters" (3:22) and urges masters to "treat your slaves justly and fairly, knowing that you also have a Master in heaven" (4:1). With no rights accruing to the slaves, who were defined as subhuman and therefore childlike, it followed that punishment for disobedience was to be administered to slaves in the same manner that it was deemed to be appropriate for children. It is worth noting, even if it is embarrassing, that many church officials including popes have historically been slaveholders.

No one can deny that slaves were lashed in the United States for everything from disobedience to running away. The records of this part of our history are indisputable. The master had the right to do to his property whatever he wished. Slaves had no rights, no legal protections. When slavery ended following the Civil War, these tactics of intimidation continued to be employed against powerless blacks in the South by quasi-religious organizations like the Ku Klux Klan. Even the murders of black people who were deemed to be "uppity," or who looked at a white woman in what whites considered an inappropriate or lecherous manner, were protected by racist police, courts and judges in the segregated South. It is not as large a step as people now think to move from the corporal punishment of a slave or former slave whose bare back absorbed the lash while the victim was tied to a tree, to the ultimate act of corporal punishment called lynching, in which the victim was hanged from that tree. That transition happened more frequently than anyone today is eager to admit. Both physical lashing and lynching were tactics of intimidation acted out on the body of the victim. Violence is always violent. The degree of violence is the only difference. I still carry in my mind's eye, with deep embarrassment and suppressed horror, the scenes of the beatings and lynchings of both slaves and freed African-Americans that were depicted in the serialized television presentation of the powerful book *Roots*.[11] What the inmate and the slave had in common was that neither had power and no vestige of adulthood accrued to their status, meaning that they could be treated like children who had no rights. If it was the proper thing to punish powerless children physically, it must also be appropriate treatment for powerless adults—so went the reasoning. Violence is never contained. It always seeks new victims. Corporal punishment was and is legalized violence.

In the most deeply patriarchal part of our male-dominant Western history, women became the third category of adults who were defined as fit subjects for corporal punishment—but at the hands of their husbands. This exercise of power was carried out with the full approval of both the state and the church. A husband could beat his wife whenever the husband deemed it beneficial or expedient to do so. She was, if not his property like a slave, at most his ward, with no more status than a dependent child. Physical abuse of one's spouse is not unknown today, but it is now called "domestic violence" and is recognized as a crime for which both arrest and incarceration are seen as appropriate.

That, however, has not always been the case. A book written by Suzanne Fonay Wemple, a medieval historian, made me aware for the first time that one of the primary functions of nunneries in the early Middle Ages was to be a safe haven to which an abused woman could retreat.[12] Not even the power of the male in a rigidly patriarchal society could invade the domain of the Mother Superior! Modern readers, both male and female, whose sense of history is rather short, blink in disbelief when reading of the accepted domestic violence during this period of history. Perhaps they need to be reminded that the word "obey," as a part of the bride's sacred vows to her husband, was in almost every wedding ceremony in every part of the Christian church until well into the twentieth century. The word "obey" implies dependent submission to the authority of the one who requires it, and it carries with it the implicit threat that the failure to obey will bring upon the disobedient one the power of enforcement. Society in that day deemed physical discipline the necessary means of enforcement. The word "obey" did not get removed from the wedding ceremony in the Episcopal Book of Common Prayer until 1928. It was mandated for the bride alone, of course. It was inconceivable that the groom would take a vow of obedience. The prevailing social system would never have approved that. Because the 1662 Prayer Book of the Church of England is still in use in England and throughout the nations that once constituted the British Empire, the word "obey" is still, to this day, required of the bride in many English-speaking marriage ceremonies the world over. Wherever it is used, wherever obedience is assumed to be appropriate, the subservient person is deemed to be dependent, childlike and by implication an appropriate recipient of the discipline of the authority figure. That was the fate of women for more centuries than most of us would be happy admitting today.

There is no question that the definition of a woman as a dependent child, subject to her husband's authority, is one of those legacies from the Christian past that has had to be challenged first and dismantled second. Perhaps that helps to explain why it was that the conservative parts of the Christian church resisted so deeply and so emotionally the women's liberation movement, with its goal of the total emancipation of women. Even today in the Catholic tradition women are in many ways still treated as second-class citizens. The embarrassment of this attitude in a world where consciousness has been raised on this issue has resulted in some rather convoluted rationalizations that hint at an ecclesiastical version of the old racist slogan "separate but equal" as this church seeks to defend continuing anti-female practices.

In the evangelical wing of Protestant Christianity leaders have accused the women's liberation movement of being home-breaking, family-violating, godless and lesbian assaults on traditional values.[13] At every stage along the way, from the suffrage movement that won for women the right to vote in 1920, to the battle to make birth control and abortion legal in the twentieth and twenty-first centuries, the Christian church has been a vigorous opponent.

The women's liberation movement declared that women are not children, that women are not dependent or subservient and that women are not designed to be submissive to men or to anyone else. The power to define oneself as adult, competent and independent became the ticket out of a world where discipline and physical abuse were considered to be appropriate patterns of interpersonal behavior.

The final category of adults who were subjected to corporal punishment during the earlier days of our Western and Christian history were members of religious orders. This violence was seen as appropriate inside the vows of the religious life, in which obedience joined poverty and chastity as sacred obligations. Obedience again and again lends itself to the creation of a childlike and dependent person, one who is subject to the discipline of his or her superiors (or God). It is that understanding of human life which has, time after time, led to the abuse of the bodies of those in religious orders in some form of corporal punishment.

In the fourteenth century, in response to the bubonic plague, a movement arose among Christians who called themselves "the flagellants." They walked through the streets of the cities of Europe, sometimes in numbers ten thousand strong, lashing themselves with whips in an act of public penitence. It was an age in which people knew nothing about viruses, germs or bacteria bringing sickness. They knew only that they were living through a fearful period of history in which massive numbers of the adult population were succumbing to this epidemic. The common religious explanation for this devastation was that God was angry with the people for some real or imagined sin. The hope of the flagellants was that by brutally lashing their own bodies with whips they could punish themselves so severely that God would withdraw the divine punishment of the plague that was decimating their families. It was a strange practice based on a faulty, but deeply believed, premise; namely, that punishing their bodies would somehow win for them divine approval. The idea was that if they punished themselves, God would not have to do it. Yet this practice grew out of and reflected that belief held so deeply in the Western Christian world, that God was a punishing deity and those who were disciplined by God deserved it because of their sinfulness. Beating the body as an act designed to please God was never far from the religious consciousness of the Western world.

When that understanding is combined with the religious sense of universal human sinfulness, then physical discipline is thought to offer a "therapy" for an evil situation. If God's revealed Word in the Bible called for such discipline to be administered to children and to those under authority as an act of love, and if this discipline was regarded both as a virtue and as a sacred obligation owed to one's religious superior, then all arguments against it were stifled. So corporal punishment has not infrequently marked the relationship of the religious superior to the monk, the nun or the penitent. Sometimes this punishment of the body was ordered by the superior but was inflicted by another, from time to time even by the penitent person himself or herself in an act designed to enhance contrition.

That was long ago, we think, until we read a more contemporary writer like Karen Armstrong.[14] This brilliant woman, who has authored such bestselling titles as *A History of God, One City, Three Faiths* and *The Battle for God,* spent the first years of her adulthood in a convent in England, leaving as recently as the late 1960s. In her autobiography she describes her experience as a sister. Confession and penance were a regular part of her life. On occasions as her penance she would be given a small whip and told to go to a private place and there to lash herself for her sins, if she deemed that appropriate. There is ample reason to suggest that corporal punishment was practiced in the religious life and that disciplining the body physically was taught by the church to be an act pleasing to God, since the body had been judged from the early years of Christianity to be carnal and sinful.

The path followed in our religious history started with a definition of human life as fallen or sinful. Step two involved developing the practice of combining that definition with the appropriateness of punishing the sinful body physically. Step three was to validate the practice by pointing to a text in a book called the "Word of God," demonstrating God's approval of these tactics. At least in the rearing of children, that grounding would make it an adult's solemn obligation to steer the sinful and wayward child from the paths of evil to which, because of the child's very distorted, sinful nature, the child was predisposed. Physical punishment thus even came to be seen as virtuous. Step four was to expand the definition of the child to include all the powerless and thus childlike adults: prisoners, whose behavior had caused society to strip from them adult rights and to relate to them as those in need of punishment; slaves, who had no rights at all and who by law and custom were required to be obedient to their masters; women, regarded as inferior, not fully human adults, who were so childlike and dependent and incapable of maturity that they had to pledge to be obedient to their husbands; and finally religious figures who lived under the authority of their superiors and who believed themselves deserving of physical discipline because of their own sins or in order to force God to withdraw the divine wrath that was believed to be causing their suffering.

So physical abuse was part of the story of the Christian West. God approved it and the church administered it. The then-current understanding of God required it. After all, the portrait of God as a punishing judge ready to discipline deserving sinners was deep in the Christian tradition.

It is a portrait of God that must now be lifted into full consciousness so that it can be banished along with those texts from the "Word of God" that have been used to justify abusive behavior for far too long.

18

GOD AS JUDGE

SEARCHING FOR THE SOURCE OF THE HUMAN NEED TO SUFFER

The Voice of Christ: My Child, I came down from heaven for your salvation and took upon Myself your miseries, not out of necessity but out of love, that you might learn to be patient and bear the sufferings of this life without repining. From the moment of My birth to My death on the cross, suffering did not leave Me. I suffered great want of temporal goods. Often I heard many complaints against Me. Disgrace and reviling I bore with patience. For My blessings I received ingratitude, for My miracles blasphemies and for My teaching scorn.

Thomas à Kempis[15]

Is it an accident, a coincidence or just fate that Christianity has managed to preside over centuries of Western history in which physical punishment has been the primary means of discipline in so many parts of our society, from children to prisoners to slaves to women and to those in religious orders? Or is there something within the Christian story itself that pushes us toward abusive behavior? These are the questions to which our study of biblically justified corporal punishment now drives us.

The idea of God as a punishing heavenly parent figure is certainly present in the heart of the Christian story, though originally it was not nearly so prevalent or rampant as church history and practice might lead us to believe. The picture of God as judge assigning people to the eternity of hell with its ever-burning flames is surely found in the gospels, but it was never a major theme. Mark, the earliest gospel writer, introduces this idea with one single reference by having Jesus say that if any part of one's body—the hand, the foot or the eye—causes that person to sin, then that body part must be removed lest the whole body go to the unquenchable fires of Gehenna, or hell (Mark 9:43–48). Paul, who wrote before Mark, is often quoted as having said that it is better to marry than to burn, but when the text is read in its entirety, it is clear that this warning had nothing to do with the fires of hell, a concept that Paul never mentions. What Paul says in this text is, "It is better to marry than to be aflame [or to burn] with passion" (1 Cor. 7:9). Mark's reference is therefore the first written reference to the flames of hell to appear in the Christian story. The gospel of Mark enters the Christian tradition in the eighth decade of the Common Era, more than forty years after the earthly life of Jesus came to an end. On the basis of this data it would be hard to maintain that punishment in eternal flames was an idea important to or perhaps ever even mentioned by Jesus.

The underlying assumption in Mark's reference is really strange. Mark is saying that some punishment is always deserved by fallen, sinful people, so self-inflicted punishment can serve to make it less necessary for God to mete out an even worse punishment later, a punishment that would last through all eternity. Maiming the body as the way to gain salvation is hardly a healthy message, as history has revealed. It is easy to understand, though, why literal-minded believers who see this injunction as coming directly from God have used this verse to do great harm to themselves or to encourage great harm in others. In the third century, a Christian theologian of enormous influence, a man named Origen, had himself castrated as a direct response to this text. Origen never revealed just how it was that his male organ caused him to sin. What we need to understand is that this is yet another rather extreme form of corporal punishment—one that Origen clearly believed he deserved. The fallen evil body must be disciplined.

Matthew's gospel (ca. 82–85 CE) contains more specific references to the fires of hell than the contributions of all of the other gospel writers combined. Matthew is also the author who gives us the very familiar story of the final judgment that is to come at the last day, when the Son of Man arrives in his glory to judge the nations by separating the sheep from the goats (25:31–46). The sheep are rewarded by this judge with entry into the kingdom of God, which was "prepared for you from the foundation of the world" (v. 34). The goats, on the other hand, are condemned to the eternal flames. It is interesting to note that the standard by which both are judged has nothing to do with proper believing or creedal orthodoxy. It has to do rather with how well or how poorly each nation, and by implication each person within that nation, perceives the presence of the "Son of Man" in the faces of the hungry, the thirsty, the stranger, the naked, the sick, the dispossessed and the imprisoned.

Luke, the third of the gospel writers (ca. 88–92 CE), has only a single reference to hell or Gehenna (12:5). It was included in a text warning his readers not to fear those who can kill only the body. The real one to fear is presumably God, who has the power to send a person, once deceased, to hell. John, the final gospel writer (ca. 95–100 CE), never refers to hell in his entire work and includes only one reference to fire, naming it as the fate for unproductive branches of the vine (15:6). Outside of Matthew, the fires of hell are a very minor note in the gospels.

Yet the uncontested idea that permeates the Christian story as it develops its creeds and doctrines and most especially its understanding of Jesus' role in the drama of salvation is that human beings are fallen, baseborn and in need of rescue. If there is no rescue, then they are doomed. How these doomed humans are to be properly punished in order to be saved becomes a major theme, perhaps *the* major theme, in Christian theology.

If one begins a faith journey with the definition of a human as a fallen creature who is deserving of punishment, then the faith system that grows out of that journey will surely develop a cure for the accepted diagnosis. That is what has happened in the way the Christian story has been told historically. That is also the doorway through which the human sense of guilt and its corresponding need for punishment entered the tradition and found therein a compatible dwelling place.

The way the Hebrew myth of creation with which the Bible opens was interpreted in early Christian history served to place this definition of human evil squarely in the Christian arena. That story was traditionally understood to say that we human beings are not what God intended us to be. We are fallen sinners, willfully disobedient creatures who have been banished from God's presence and who deserve thereby the divine wrath.

Human life, says the myth of the fall, had been endowed with the uniquely human qualities of freedom of choice and self-consciousness. Our original ancestors, using those gifts, disobeyed God and plunged God's perfect world into sin and evil. In the process of that fall, a definition of human life as distorted and depraved developed. Not only were we fallen, but we had no power to rescue ourselves from our self-inflicted wounds. Even when we tried very hard to be good, we only became self-righteous and thus judgmental of others. Attempts at virtue only served to exacerbate our sense of being separated. Angels with drawn swords, the legend said, guarded the gates of Eden so that we could never go back. As direct descendants of Adam and Eve, we would bear as our birthright the marks of that disobedience.

The sin of the fall was said to show up in the biblical narrative time after time. It was seen when Cain killed Abel (Gen. 4:8) and when sinful, prideful people decided to build a tower so high it could reach into heaven, where they might be restored to God (Gen. 11:1–9). It was acted out in the story of the flood in which God's punishing wrath was said to have destroyed every living creature on the earth except for the righteous Noah and his righteous family (Gen. 7–8). Presumably, given the sense that God is just, human beings must have merited that destruction. Yet even that divine effort to eradicate the evil so endemic to human life failed. The Bible suggests that the mark of sin was still manifested in Noah, for after he disembarked from his boat he became intoxicated (Gen. 9:21). Next the Bible says that God intervened to give people the law (Exod. 20ff.), a guide to lead them back to God. That also failed. Then God raised up prophets to recall these people to their original covenant, but the prophets were banished or killed. Finally, this storyline continues, God decided to enter human history in the person of Jesus, who was understood to be the divine life in whom the rescue from sin was finally accomplished. The price of salvation was, however, the death of the divine Son on the cross of Calvary. That is the way Christians have told their faith story. The operative assumption has been that human life is flawed; that this flaw is the source of evil; that only God can save so evil a creature; and that this salvation is costly indeed to God. Salvation always involves punishment, even if that punishment is accomplished vicariously. To know oneself, according to the way the Bible has generally been read, is to know one's own evil, to experience guilt and finally to stand in need of punishment.

Founding myths are always human attempts to provide answers for human questions and yearnings. Why am I not content to be who I am? Why do I seek more? Why am I inadequate? Why do I experience guilt and jealousy? Why am I separated from God? Why am I victimized by sickness and pain? Why am I mortal? Why do I die? Starting with the unchallenged assumption that human life was corrupted and has fallen from God's grace, religious leaders began to organize the world so that human beings would recognize the necessity for our punishment and the human need constantly to implore God to save us, to rescue and redeem us. The stated goal of the Christian life was to live forever in that divine presence from which our ancestors had been banished in the Garden of Eden. Proper punishment for our sins thus became the prerogative of the heavenly parent and was necessary if we hoped to achieve our goal. Moderate suffering here and now was a blessing to be endured as necessary, if sinful people wished to avoid eternal suffering in the world to come. To state it bluntly, human beings were taught to understand themselves as the children of God who deserved God's punishment. That is the diagnosis of the human situation against which the story of Jesus was destined to be told.

Though most educated people in the world today dismiss this biblical story of Adam, Eve and the Garden of Eden, with its interpretation of human origins, as a myth not to be literalized, that story has nonetheless continued to set the tone for the way our religious systems relate to human life in our world. Christianity, in both its Catholic and Protestant forms, was constructed around its presumed unique ability to deliver forgiveness and thus to rescue hopeless, lost sinners. Enhancing guilt therefore became a necessary prerequisite for the maintenance of institutional power. Once people accepted the diagnosis of themselves as fallen sinners, the church set about the task of convincing them that only through the channels of grace that the church controlled was forgiveness available. It served the church's power needs well. In the Catholic Church oral confession, required as one of the seven sacraments, kept guilt ever visible in each human life. An endless list of ecclesiastical rules, with their emphasis on such things as days of solemn obligation and a prescribed set of inescapable religious duties, made guilt inevitable and thus proper punishment from God, mediated through the church as penance, became necessary for salvation. The reenactment of the vicarious death of Jesus in the sacrifice of the Mass reminded sinners weekly of the price Jesus had to pay because of their sins. The Catholic Church's use of manipulative guilt is hard to overestimate.

In Protestant Christianity the sense of human depravity was portrayed perhaps even more graphically. Human life was denigrated by the revival preachers as wretched, miserable, wormlike and hopeless in order that the glorious grace of the rescuing deity could be more fully appreciated. The eighteenth-century Protestant revival known as the "Great Awakening," which swept across this continent led by the noted Massachusetts evangelist Jonathan Edwards, was ignited by Edwards' frightening portrait of God dangling sinners by the singed hairs of their heads over the fiery pits of hell. It was preaching designed to elicit a proper confession and to win a full pardon. It focused on human depravity.

That focus still characterizes much of evangelical Protestantism. The head of the evangelical Moody Bible Institute in Chicago repeated the mantra of his religious conversion in a radio broadcast with me some years ago, as he stated this theme of depravity over and over again: "The one thing I know is that I stand condemned before the throne of grace." The power found in the phrase "Jesus died for my sins" cannot be overestimated. It is used in some form almost every Sunday in evangelical circles. It elicits guilt and gratitude in its message that we, though the children of God, are disobedient beings who deserve to be punished and Jesus' death was the rescuing moment, since he is portrayed as absorbing our punishment for us. We are evil indeed if our sinfulness cost God the life of the divine Son as the price that had to be paid! That amount of guilt is unlimited. Yet this became the word that people heard coming from the church through the centuries.

In both Catholic and Protestant Christianity the picture was clear. Human beings were fallen sinners standing in need of punishment. A righteous heavenly parent figure called God was presented as the judge prepared to be the disciplinarian. That was the message at the heart of Christianity, which makes it easy to understand why the image of the disobedient child standing before the parent prepared to apply corporal punishment fits so neatly into Christian history. We were *all* adult children standing before our heavenly parent, who was also prepared to punish us. We raised our children with a style modeled after our understanding of how God was relating to us. That is also how violence and an unconscious sadomasochism entered the Christian story. That is why so much of our faith tradition borders on the neurotic need to suffer. If the portrait of human life that we paint is unhealthy, then the portrait of the God that this human life envisions will also be unhealthy. To that portrait of God we now turn.

19

GOD AS DIVINE
CHILD ABUSER

THE SADOMASOCHISM IN
THE HEART OF CHRISTIANITY

The place of Atonement or, rather, where atonement actually takes place—namely, where men and women, races, classes and nations are in fact made one, where reconciliation, release, renewal, the reunion of life with life are experienced. This, I believe, must be our starting point.

John A. T. Robinson[16]

Those whom I [God] love, I reprove and chasten; so be zealous and repent.

Revelation 3:19

Can you imagine that something so destructive and life-denying as sadomasochism has become overtly a part of the Christian story? Impossible, you say! Christianity is about life and love, not about pain and punishment. Well, before you dismiss this thesis, you might want to listen to the words from a hymn found in the Episcopal hymnal:

Before thy throne, O God, we kneel;
Give us a conscience quick to feel,
A ready mind to understand
The meaning of thy chastening hand;
Whate'er the pain and shame may be,
Bring us, O Father, nearer thee.

Search out our hearts and make us true,
Wishful to give to all their due;
From love of pleasure, lust of gold,
From sins which make the heart grow cold,
Wean us and train us with thy rod;
Teach us to know our faults, O God.[17]

Can you visualize the scene being depicted in this hymn? Is there no sadomasochism present here? Listen next to the self-deprecating words that punctuate the Christian liturgies: We were "born in sin"! We are "miserable offenders." There is "no health in us." We can do nothing good without you. "We are not worthy to gather up the crumbs" under the divine table. "Have mercy, O Lord, have mercy!"

Are these words not the picture of a quivering child before a punishing parent? Over and over again in the forms of our worship, we seem obsessed with guilt and penitence. Is this not an expression of the human need for punishment being drilled into believers by the church in multiple doses almost daily? Are these liturgical phrases not admissions that deep down we believe we deserve the wrath for which we are almost asking? These elements are deeply and intrinsically part of our faith story. During the season of Lent, church bulletins frequently feature the standard implements of torture— whips, nails and a crown of thorns. The Bible, again and again, portrays a wrathful God's intention to punish the chosen people. When the faithfulness of the Jews falters in the biblical story, God raises up enemies to defeat and punish them. When they are evil, God sends a pestilence or a plague. The Bible describes human beings as sheep gone astray; then it describes God as the heavenly parent whose divine righteousness must be vindicated. We tremble before the throne of this deity, knowing that if God gives us what we deserve, we are doomed to suffer forever. "If you, Lord, were to note what is done amiss, O Lord, who could stand?" (Ps. 130:2 BCP, 1979). Worshipers in church, hearing the above words, are pictured like schoolchildren waiting in quiet, anxious dependency for the moment to arrive when the price of their sinfulness will be exacted. Protestant churchgoers reveal their inner masochism when they say of the preacher, "He really laid it on us this morning." Catholics reveal it when they meditate on the wounds of Jesus as they have been taught.

On this diagnosis of the nature of our humanity, the entire Christian story tends to be based. Punishment is our due; we have earned it. We cover these neurotic aspects of our worship with layers of piety or with the smoke of incense, but they are always there just below the surface. If one were to take these words from our liturgies out of their sacred environments and read them in a secular setting—in Greenwich Village, New York, for example—those hearing them for the first time would tell us exactly what the words really say: "I am a bad boy. I deserve to be punished. Either God will give punishment to me directly, or God will give Jesus the punishment I deserve. That is how I am saved." Is that healthy? Does it enhance life? Does guilt enable growth to occur? Is watching Jesus die on the cross anything more than an act of sadomasochistic voyeurism? Is it not time that we raise these issues to consciousness?

If this focus on punishment, which seems to fit our theology, is not yet visible to all Christian people, it is because we do not yet want to see it. We will be forced, however, by this newly emerging awareness to look again and again. Perhaps the beating scenes or the sadism evidenced in the blood from the crown of thorns streaming down the face of Jesus in Mel Gibson's controversial motion picture *The Passion of the Christ* will finally be enough to make us see the violence that Christianity has fostered based upon the perceived human need to suffer.

The primary way in which the Jesus story has been traditionally and historically told portrays the holy God involved in a cruel act of divine child abuse that was said to have occurred on a hill called Calvary. We are told that there, instead of punishing *us* for our sins, God required the suffering and death of the divine Son. God's righteousness was restored when the Son of God was punished as a substitute for us. Does that not sound strange? The Christian church has invited the faithful to meditate on Jesus' pain, to revel in the blood that he shed. In the evangelical hymns of Protestantism it is said both that his blood is precious and that it has the power to wash us clean.

With so much sin to be washed away, Jesus must suffer and bleed excessively. In Catholic devotion it is the blood of Jesus that the church invites us to drink in the sacrament of the Eucharist. That blood is said to have the power to cleanse us from within. Either way, the blood of Jesus becomes a fetish, a grotesque image that rivets our attention on the trauma of the cross. We are taught that the suffering of Jesus was our fault, our responsibility. One of the Passiontide hymns states this quite overtly:

> Who was the guilty?
> Who brought this upon thee?
> Alas, my treason, Jesus, hath undone thee.
> 'Twas I, Lord Jesus,
> I it was denied thee:
> I crucified thee.[18]

Since Jesus is punished for our sins, we are left with a sense of heavy guilt that is all but unendurable. It is a timeless process, because our sins kill him anew each day. In that extension of the divine life that Jesus, understood as the second person of the Trinity, was said to represent, God is portrayed as eternally absorbing the punishment that was our due. God rescued us from sin by paying the price of our sin through Jesus.

That is the story scraped clean of its piety so that its horror can be viewed with full awareness. It is grotesque. It is barbaric. It creates a distorted, even a sick, humanity. It paints the portrait of a sadistic God served by masochistic children. How can that be good news? How can that lead to human wholeness? It is bad theology because it is bad psychology.

Perhaps that is why religious people have become more and more unloving, more and more judgmental and more and more eager to force others to stand where they stand. Misery loves company. Unrelieved guilt leads to the willingness to endure incredible pain—pain that is deemed to be necessary to satisfy our need to suffer.

That is the traditional way in which Christianity has prescribed the cure for human sin. It is obviously a nonstarter! Yet that picture still lies at the heart of our liturgy, our hymns and our theology. It validates violence because it attributes to God's punishment of Jesus salvific themes; and not surprisingly, it validates our own violence, since when we abuse others we are only acting after the example that God has set for us. The punishing God is thus replicated in the punishing parent, the punishing authority figure and the punishing nation. Violence is redemptive. War is justified. Bloodshed is the way of salvation. It all fits together so tightly, so neatly, and it justifies the most destructive and demeaning of human emotions. It is, however, neither true nor vaild.

Let me state this boldly and succinctly: Jesus did not die for your sins or my sins. That proclamation is theological nonsense. It only breeds more violence as we seek to justify the negativity that religious people dump on others because we can no longer carry its load. We must rid ourselves of it. One can hardly refrain from exhorting parents not to spare the rod lest they spoil their child if the portrait of God at the heart of the Christian story is that of an angry parent who punishes the divine Son because he can take it and we cannot.

This interpretation of Jesus as the sacrificed victim is a human creation, not a divine revelation. It was shaped in a first-century world by the disciples of Jesus, who drew on their Jewish liturgical symbols as a way the crucifixion of Jesus might be understood. They borrowed this understanding directly from the Jewish Day of Atonement, Yom Kippur, in which an innocent lamb was slaughtered to pay the price for the sins of the people. The sinful people then had the cleansing blood of that sacrificial lamb sprinkled on them so that they could experience what it meant to be cleansed—or as we say, "washed in the blood of the Lamb." In the second act of the Yom Kippur liturgy an innocent goat had the sins of the people ceremonially heaped upon its head. As the bearer of the people's sins, that goat became so evil that people were invited to curse it and to call for its death. But the goat, now the sin-bearer, was not killed; it was rather run out into the wilderness, carrying the sins of the people with it and thus leaving the people cleansed. This creature came to be known as the "scapegoat" and became, liturgically, "the Lamb of God who takes away the sins of the world." Yom Kippur was a worship-filled drama designed by the Jews to relieve at least symbolically their sense of human separation from God, a separation they understood to be the source of human guilt. Jesus was interpreted by his earlier disciples inside these Jewish liturgical images. They are all based, however, on an understanding of human life that is quite simply wrong.

We are not fallen, sinful people who deserve to be punished. We are frightened, insecure people who have achieved the enormous breakthrough into self-consciousness that marks no other creature that has yet emerged from the evolutionary cycle. We must not denigrate the human being who ate of the tree of knowledge in the Genesis story. We must learn rather to celebrate the creative leap into a higher humanity. Our sense of separation and aloneness is not a mark of our sin. It is a symbol of our glory. Our struggle to survive, which manifests itself in radical self-centeredness, is not the result of original sin. It is a sign of emerging consciousness. It should not be a source of guilt. It is a source of blessing. We do not need to be punished. We need to be called and empowered to be more deeply and fully human and to develop the godlike gift of being able to give ourselves away freely in the quest for an even deeper sense of what it means to live. Jesus did not die for our sins. Jesus demonstrated in an ultimate way that it is by giving that we receive and by loving that we enhance life.

Guilt, judgment, righteousness, orthodoxy, creedal purity: these are the products of a religion of control in which we hide in fear. They are attempts to build security. None of these boundary marks is life-giving. All are methods of seeking righteousness when that for which we yearn is love.

The angry deity who judges human life from some heavenly throne might make us feel safe, but this deity always shrinks life, for that is what guilt, fear and righteousness do. That is a god-image that must be broken; but when it is, the traditional way we have told the Jesus story will surely die with it. I believe it *must*. When it does, I think it will be good riddance, for with the death of that understanding of Christianity this faith may yet have a chance to be born again. To the possibility of that resurrection we turn next.

20

MOVING BEYOND
THE DEMEANING GOD
INTO THE GOD OF LIFE

The Incarnation is an act co-extensive with the duration of
the world.

Pierre Teilhard de Chardin[19]

O nce we step beyond the religious formulas of yesterday, questions
flood our minds. If God is not a punishing and rescuing deity, then
who or what is God? If the biblical explanation of the source of evil is no
longer operative, as I have now suggested, then from where does evil come?
What is its origin? How is it to be explained? Can the way evil is viewed be
changed, transformed or transcended? Can we human beings escape our
need to view ourselves negatively, which is the interior situation that makes
the punishing God necessary? If the task of the Christian faith is not about
rescuing and restoring the fallen sinner to wholeness, a task that was said to
justify the church's use of guilt, threat, fear and violence as tactics of control
and discipline, then what is the task of this religious system? Does it have
one? To this probing series of questions about God I believe Christians must
turn new attention. Not to face these issues is not to engage the most pressing
agenda before the religious establishment. That would be like casting a vote
in favor of total irrelevance.

That God probe, however, is still only the tip of the iceberg. If behavior
control is not the church's primary social agenda, and surely it is not, then we

are forced to conclude that so much of the way we portray the content of the Christian faith simply falls away. To focus this discussion quite specifically on traditional Christian doctrine, we need to raise the question as to whether Christianity as we know it can survive without its doctrines of atonement and incarnation, both of which hang on the sin and rescue themes we have discussed. Is there any way to see the divine presence of God in the life of Jesus other than to view Jesus as the incarnate sinless one who came from the realm of heaven to enter the arena of the fall to pay the price God required for our sins and thus to rescue us from that fall? What happens to this faith story if God can no longer be viewed as either the heavenly parent or the punishing judge? Does our understanding of the righteousness of God depend on this definition of the sinfulness of human life? Can we dismiss once and for all the ancient Christian symbol of Jesus as a blood offering, a human sacrifice required by God?

To all of these Christ inquiries I would answer not only that we *can*, but also that we *must*. The Christology of the past has rested on a false definition of human life and has helped us thereby to develop a false understanding of who God is. A true reformation must be radical indeed. It must rid the Christian tradition of both the current concept of human evil and the idea of a punishing God. At the same time this reformation will, I submit, cut the ground out from under the manner in which violence has been justified on the basis of this religious system. It is thus a reformation eagerly to be sought.

The deconstruction begins with the dismissal of the story with which the Bible opens. It has already moved from being thought of as literal history to being viewed as an interpretive myth. The next step is to dismiss it as not even an accurate interpreter of life. It is a bad myth, a false myth, a misleading myth. There never was a time, either literally or metaphorically, when there was a perfect and finished creation. That biblical idea is simply wrong. It is not even symbolically valid. It is an inaccurate idea that has helped to set the stage for the development of a guilt-producing, dependency-seeking neurotic religion. Nothing more!

Whatever else we know about creation, we are now certain that it is an ongoing, evolving and still-incomplete process. A further insight follows quickly from this: we can no longer properly conceive of God as resting from the divine labors of creation and pronouncing good all that God has made.

Since there was no perfect beginning, no Garden of Eden and no first man and woman who walked with God in perfect communion, there can also be no fall into sin and thus no act of disobedience that destroyed the perfection of God's world. These details cannot be true even as symbols. They constitute, rather, an inaccurate perception of human origins. We were created neither in the original goodness that Matthew Fox has proclaimed,[20] nor in the original sin that has been established as the primary understanding of human life inside which the Christians have traditionally told their story, at least from Augustine on. Since these understandings are basic to the whole superstructure of Christian creeds, doctrine, dogma and theology, this realization means that they will all eventually come crashing down.

Creation must now be seen as an unfinished process. God cannot accurately be portrayed as resting from divine labors which are unending. There was no original perfection from which human life could fall into sin. Life has always been evolving. The Psalmist was wrong: we were not created "a little lower than the angels" (Ps. 8:5, KJV). Rather, we have evolved into a status that we judge to be only a little higher than the ape's.

That is a very different perspective. There is a vast contrast between the definition of being fallen creatures and that of being incomplete creatures. Our humanity is not flawed by some real or mythical act of disobedience that resulted in our expulsion from some fanciful Garden of Eden. It is rather distorted by the unfinished nature of our humanity. The fact is we do not yet know what it means to be human, since that is a status we have not yet fully achieved. What human life needs, therefore, is to be called and empowered to enter a new being. We do not need some divine rescue accomplished by an invasive deity to lift us from a fall that never happened and to restore us to a status we have never possessed. The idea that Jesus had to pay the price of our sinfulness is an idea that is bankrupt. When that idea collapses, so do all of those violent, controlling and guilt-producing tactics that are so deeply part of traditional Christianity.

It is like an unstoppable waterfall. Baptism, understood as the sacramental act designed to wash from the newborn baby the stain of that original fall into sin, becomes inoperative. The Eucharist, developed as a liturgical attempt to reenact the sacrifice that Jesus made on the cross that paid the price of our sinfulness, becomes empty of meaning. Various disciplinary tactics, from not sparing the rod with our children to the use of shame, guilt and fear to control the behavior of childlike adults, become violations of life based on an inadequate knowledge of the nature of our humanity. They are the application of the wrong therapy designed to overcome a faulty diagnosis. Even the afterlife symbols of heaven and hell, designed to motivate behavior by promising either eternal reward or eternal punishment, now lose their credibility. A system of rewards and punishments, either in this life or beyond it, does not produce wholeness, nor does it issue in loving acts of a self-giving person. It produces rather a self-centered attempt at survival. It leads to behavior designed not to do good for good's sake, but to do good in order to win favor or to avoid punishment. When the plug is pulled on the definition of human life as something infected by the sin of the fall, then the mighty fortress of systematic beliefs that people think constitutes the Christian faith collapses like a house of cards. That is when reality erupts in our consciousness and forces upon us the inevitable conclusion that Christianity as we have known it cannot endure. It has two choices only: change or die!

If change is the tactic to be adopted, the change cannot be simply cosmetic, an adjustment around the edges of our faith story. It has to be so total and so radical that many will think such a change is either impossible or will result in the death of the patient. It would be easier, some say, to start over by building an entirely new religious system than it would be to seek to reform this one so totally that continuity might be strained to the breaking point. They may be right, but I am not yet convinced of that. The Christianity of the catacombs in the first century of the church's life could never in its wildest imagination have envisioned a future that was capable of producing the concept of Christendom, with its dominating cathedrals. Yet the Christianity of the thirteenth century could look back and see its ancestor in the church of the catacombs. Our task is thus not to build tomorrow's church. That is something into which we have to live one day at a time. Our task is rather to face the need for radical change and take the first, probably tiny, step necessary to erect a totally new foundation. That step is found, I believe, in acknowledging our evolutionary origins and dispensing with any suggestion that sin, inadequacy and guilt are the definitions into which we are born. This also means that we rid ourselves of the idea that the world was created for the benefit of human beings, or even that the planet earth is somehow different or special in the universe.

Anthropocentrism is a product of a pre-evolutionary mind-set. This planet is part of the whole universe and we human beings are simply the self-conscious form of life that has emerged out of the evolutionary soup. We are kin to both the plants and the animals. Homo sapiens were not made to dominate the world, but to enrich it by living out our role in a radically interdependent world. We might be a dead end in the evolutionary process, a creature like the dinosaur, destined for extinction. We might instead be the bridge to a brilliant future that none of us can yet imagine. Our task is first simply to be what we are, then to adapt and finally to be a link to that emerging new being. That is quite different from the role generally assigned to human beings in the ongoing story of our religious teachings.

From where does evil come? We cannot deny its presence. We see it every day. It is certainly not derived from a fall from perfection, as we were taught. It rises rather from the incompleteness of the evolutionary process. We are not fallen sinners who need to be rescued; we are incomplete creatures who need to be empowered to step into the new possibilities of an expanding life. It is not appropriate to wallow in our inadequacy or to accept as our due being denigrated by religion or having our behavior controlled or our guilt expanded. We do not need to be punished either in this life or in the life to come, nor do we need to have some mythical god figure take our punishment for us. What we need is the power to take the next step into a new and more complete humanity, to transcend our limits, to step across the self-erected boundaries of our insecure humanity. We need to face—no, even more proactively, to *embrace*—the trauma of self-consciousness, the self-centeredness of that hysterical struggle for survival that only self-conscious creatures can understand, which leads to the erection of security systems that finally destroy our emerging humanity. We need to see that the evil things we do to one another are the result of this incomplete humanity for which punishment is inappropriate. Evil cannot be controlled by threats or by discipline, parental or divine. Security can never finally be built on violence. To be "saved" does not mean to be rescued. It means to be empowered to be something we have not yet been able to be.

Is there any role for Jesus in this new vision of reality? Can the Christian story clamber out of this pit? I think so, but developing this idea fully is a task for a later day.[21] Suffice it for now to say that Jesus emerges as a symbol for a humanity that is not defined as fallen or sinful. It is a humanity that is portrayed as so whole and so complete that it is experienced as God-infused. Jesus cannot be a divine visitor from the heavenly realm. He cannot be, as

John A. T. Robinson said of him some fifty years ago, "a cuckoo inserted into the nest of humanity."[22] Jesus can only be a product of humanity, created out of its gene pool. If our ideas of divinity cannot be found in this pathway, then what most people regard as the essential tenets of traditional Christianity will have to be abandoned. Christianity may well not survive so radical a dismissal of its core doctrines. But if we can understand, as I believe that we are beginning to do, that divinity is a human concept that can be found only in humanity, then the link into a Christian future will be established. So I do not despair that the traditional understanding of the faith that has guided me for a lifetime is about to die. I see in Jesus one so radically human and free, so whole and complete, that the power of life, the force of the universe—that which I call God—becomes visible and operative in him and through him. It is a new way to travel theologically. It operates from a new angle of vision that has been built on a new premise about the origins of life itself, through which I now engage a primary Christian assertion. That assertion is that somehow, in some way, through some means, God was in this Christ and that this God presence can still be met in the depths of our humanity.

The doctrines of the incarnation, the atonement and the Trinity were necessitated in traditional Christianity by the premise of the fall. God alone could overcome the fall, and since Jesus was perceived as the rescuer, then Jesus had to be a divine visitor accomplishing this divine task. When the fall is dismissed, traditional Christology cannot help but go with it and a new Christology must emerge, as a phoenix rising from the ashes of the past. It will be a Christology based not on fall and rescue, sin and salvation or even guilt and forgiveness, but on the call to wholeness, the power of love and the enhancement of being. More work must be done here, for this is the doorway through which Christianity must walk if it is to live in tomorrow's world.

For now I am content only to take the first step, which is to expose the negativity in the terrible texts that have for so long fed the neurotic human need to justify both suffering and violence as our due, as something earned by the fall into sin over which we had no control.

There is surely a better way than this to love God with one's heart, soul, mind and strength and to love our neighbors as ourselves. There is also surely a better way to speak of Christ as the "human face of God,"[23] in whom we meet the source of life, the source of love and the ground of being. That is the Christ I seek and that is the Christ to whom I am still powerfully drawn.

THE BIBLE AND ANTI-SEMITISM

THE TERRIBLE TEXTS

So when Pilate saw that he was gaining nothing, but rather that a riot was beginning, he took water and washed his hands before the crowd, saying, "I am innocent of this man's blood; see to it yourselves." And all the people answered, "His blood be on us and on our children."

Matthew 27:24–25

If you were Abraham's children, you would do what Abraham did. You are of your Father, the devil, and your will is to do your father's desires.

John 8:39, 44

Israel failed to obtain what it sought . . . God gave them a spirit of stupor, eyes that should not see and ears that should not hear down to this very day.

Romans 11:7–8

21

SEARCHING FOR THE ORIGINS OF CHRISTIAN ANTI-SEMITISM

The Jews of Temple Beth Sholom are sinful, greedy, hell-bound, money-grubbing sodomites; and they have dedicated their synagogue to be a gay and lesbian propaganda mill and recruiting depot, so luring young people to sodomy.

Westboro Baptist Church, Topeka, Kansas[1]

The darkest and bleakest side of the Christian faith is revealed in the Christians' treatment of the Jews throughout history. Anti-Semitism is a terrifying prejudice that is rooted so deeply in the church's life that it has distorted our entire message.

Christianity was born in the womb of Judaism. Jesus was a Jew. Tradition tells us he was circumcised on the eighth day and presented in the temple on the fortieth day of life. The story of his journey to Jerusalem at age twelve has about it the marks of a bar mitzvah–type ceremony. The gospels refer to Jesus going to the synagogue "as was his custom." The picture drawn of Jesus was that of a devout and God-fearing Jew who was deeply engaged in the worship tradition of his people.

The earliest disciples, beginning with the twelve and expanding rapidly after the Easter experience, were Jews. They were not called Christians until the second or third generation of the movement. The book of Acts suggests that this name was first used in Antioch (11:26). The date for the adoption of this label is not easily established, but it could be no earlier than the 50s, or at least twenty years after the events of the first Good Friday, and was probably later than that. The book of Acts is normally dated in the mid-90s of the first century. Even then the title "Christian" was somewhat pejorative. The word "Christ" was derived from the attempt to translate the Hebrew word *mashiach,* which literally meant "the anointed one," into Greek. So "Christian" literally meant "follower of the anointed one," which lent itself to a negative second meaning of the oily ones or the greasy ones. One recalls the derogatory putdown "greaser" that teenagers once used for those they regarded as "nerds" or social misfits. The name the disciples of Jesus first called themselves was "followers of the way."

What is important, however, is that we recognize that these disciples of Jesus continued to be part of the worship life of the synagogue until well into the ninth decade of the Christian era. This becomes very obvious when we recognize how deeply Mark, Matthew and Luke, known as the synoptic gospels, were shaped by the liturgical life of the synagogue. The Christians told the Jesus story inside the context of the Hebrew scriptures. This demonstrates far more than we realize that it was inside the synagogue that the Jesus story unfolded, for that was the only place the Hebrew scriptures were read and expounded. Please recognize that the people in that day did not have their own copies of the scriptures. Books—and when we say that word we need to think ancient scrolls, not bound hard copies—were very rare and very expensive. Yet the Jesus story as revealed in the gospels is intimately bound up with the Hebrew scriptures. Even the heart of the Christian story, the passion narrative, which was probably the first part of the Jesus story to achieve written form, is deeply dependent on what were thought to be the validating texts from Isaiah 53 and Psalm 22. All of the titles that were used for Jesus—"Christ," "Lamb of God," "sin-bearer," "Son of Man," "Paschal Lamb"—came directly out of the liturgy of the synagogue. The synagogue is the place in which the Christian faith was born.

Yet something happened early on that poisoned the relationship between this Jesus movement and its Jewish place of birth, something that caused Christianity to become intensely hate-filled toward all things Jewish. That deeply destructive attitude continues to this day. Throughout the centuries the primary gifts that Christians have given to the Jews have been pain, death, ghettoization and unimaginable religious persecution. The words that were most frequently used to justify that negative behavior came time after time from the New Testament itself. The favorite text of anti-Semitism has been, historically, the words from Matthew's story of the cross. In this narrative the Jewish crowd, prior to the crucifixion, is portrayed as responding to Pilate's plea of innocence by saying, "His blood be on us and on our children" (Matt. 27:25).

I suspect that no other verse in all of Holy Scripture has been responsible for so much violence and so much bloodshed. People convinced that these words justified their hostility have killed millions of Jewish people over history. "The Jews asked for it," Christians have said. "The Jews acknowledged their responsibility for the death of Jesus and even requested that his blood be placed upon the backs of their children in every generation." In this way Christians have not only explained, but also made a virtue out of, their violent anti-Semitism. No other verse of the Bible reveals more tragically the "sins of scripture" or better earns for itself the designation of a "terrible text."

This Matthean verse is not the sole textual justifier of anti-Semitism, even if it is the one most quoted. The Jews are denigrated by polemical Christians time after time in the New Testament. Paul, quoting Isaiah (29:10), refers to the Jews as those to whom God has given "a spirit of stupor, eyes that should not see and ears that should not hear down to this very day (Rom. 11:7–8).

John's gospel quotes Jesus as saying that the Jews are "from your father the devil, and you choose to do your father's desires" (8:44). Whenever the phrase "the Jews" is used in John's gospel, there is a pejorative undertone. When John tells about the first Easter appearance of the risen Christ, he suggests that the disciples were in hiding behind locked doors, "for fear of the Jews" (20:19). The reason the tomb of Jesus had a detachment of temple guards placed around it, according to Matthew, was because the Jewish chief priests, together with the Pharisees, told Pilate that "this imposter" had predicted that "after three days, I will arise again" (Matt. 27:62ff.). The list could go on and on. The clear message portrayed in the gospels is that Jews are negative, sinister, anti-Christian characters who were responsible for the death of Jesus. That is the definition that has emerged from the Bible to infiltrate the minds of two thousand years of Christian history. Far more than Christians today seem to understand, to call the Bible the "Word of God" in any sense is to legitimize this systemic hatred reflected in its pages.

Anti-Semitism is not confined to the past. In this present century, called by many a "postmodern" and even a "post-Christian" world, the cancer of anti-Semitism is still spreading. Synagogues and Jewish gravesites and businesses are still defaced periodically with swastikas or hostile words. A noted American politician in the last decades of the twentieth century, seeking the Democratic presidential nomination, referred to New York City in a derogatory way as "Hymie Town."[2] Another presidential candidate, this time a Republican, just to be nonpartisan, openly expressed his admiration for Adolf Hitler.[3] A national leader of a Southeast Asian nation, speaking at the end of the twentieth century, referred to the Jews as the source of all the ills in the world.[4] It has not been an easy journey through history for those whose national rhetoric, as portrayed in their sacred scriptures, defined themselves as "God's chosen people."

Starting with this recent history, I want us to walk backward step by step toward the period of time in which the New Testament was written, when the "followers of the way" were still all synagogue-worshiping Jews. I hope to accomplish two things in this process: first, to make us aware of how consistent anti-Semitism has been throughout Western history, and second, to see if we can locate and understand its origins. Until we embrace the depth of the problem and identify what it is in the Christian faith itself that not only gave anti-Semitism its birth but also regularly sustains it, we will continue to violate the very people who gave us the Jesus we claim to serve.

The obvious place to start this backward journey is with the Holocaust. This emergence of inhumane horror in the third and fourth decades of the twentieth century occurred in Nazi Germany when Reichschancellor Adolf Hitler inaugurated what he called "the final solution of the Jewish problem." Its first eruption into public awareness in Germany came in the early thirties, but it was not until what came to be called Kristallnacht that the world took much notice. "Crystal Night" was a moment in 1938 when marauding bands of Nazi youth smashed windows in homes, shops and synagogues in Jewish communities throughout the Reich, terrorizing people and destroying property. It ended some six million deaths later in 1945 when the Nazi concentration camps in which Jews had been systematically exterminated were finally overrun by the Allied armed forces and the few remaining emaciated prisoners were set free. This tragedy occurred in a modern, well-educated, Western, ostensibly Christian nation with little protest from any branch of the church. Indeed, the Catholic Church's Pope Pius XII, referred to by one author as

"Hitler's pope," has been deeply implicated in these crimes.[5] He either actively supported the atrocities, if the worst-case scenario is correct, or simply acquiesced without opposition. Either way, it seems that Christian anti-Semitism played a huge role in the Holocaust.

Protestant Christian leaders did not cover themselves with glory either. The Protestant church within Germany accommodated itself to the Nazi agenda far more than anyone would like to believe. Those who spoke out were so few that their names are still remembered: Dietrich Bonhoeffer and Martin Niemöller come immediately to mind.

Revisionist historians like to suggest that this murderous prejudice was limited to Nazi Germany and did not affect the rest of the Christian world. However, the facts do not support this self-serving conclusion. The governments of Great Britain, Canada and the United States knew what was going on in Nazi Germany well before World War II began, yet none of them made efforts diplomatically or politically to bring pressure on the German nation to halt this violence, nor did they attempt military efforts such as bombing the rail lines that led to the extermination camps. They refused even to allow persecuted German or Polish Jews to enter their countries as political refugees. Anti-Semitism was strong enough in each of these nations that politicians were not willing to be perceived as pro-Jewish. This negative response to the greatest human tragedy in Christian history was one more manifestation of the underlying hostilities that had marked the relationship between Christians and Jews for two thousand years. Hitler was not an individual phenomenon that had no previous significant antecedents.

Part of what created Hitler and his regime was surely the work of Martin Luther in the sixteenth century. The great church reformer helped both to create the German nation and to advance the German language, yet he had a destructive, anti-Semitic blind spot. His rhetoric about Jews was unbelievably hostile. Jews were, for Luther, nothing short of evil by nature, lacking redeeming value and saving grace. He railed against them, publicly and privately, suggesting that they were, by their very being, demonic people who had compromised their right to live and so the world was well served by their deaths. Luther's followers felt free to act out their anti-Semitism, given the permission they had received from their leader.

The story does not get brighter as we continue this backward trek and find ourselves in the fourteenth century, when the Black Death was decimating the population to such an extent that people began to think the human race itself might actually die out. Death was so prevalent during that plague that the people's ability to bury the dead was strained to a breaking point and bodies were often left to rot in the streets. Disease at that time in history was both mysterious and fear-inducing. People knew nothing about the causative agents of sickness. The majority opinion, encouraged by the leaders of the church, was that illness was an expression of divine wrath. Something human beings were doing had infuriated God so deeply that God in this instance had sent the Black Death as God's divine scourge. Whatever this human evil was, it had to be something in which the entire human population shared, for the punishment was falling indiscriminately on faithful God-fearing worshipers as well as on godless renegades. Given this perspective, the religious leaders sought to understand the mind of God so that repentance, prayer and resolve could root out this sinfulness and thus bring an end to their peril. The questions they asked rose quite naturally inside their frame of reference: "What have we done to incur God's wrath that this plague has reached such unprecedented proportions?"—in other words, "What is our sin?"

It was in answer to that question that two movements developed in Christian Europe. The first, called "the flagellants," about which I have spoken already in another context, sought to purge their sin through self-inflicted pain. The second moved beyond self-punishment and thus became far more destructive and far more evil. An areawide plague, in the minds of this group of Christians, had to be caused by some kind of behavior that was systemic. At last, as with a flash of insight, the cause was identified and it fitted: Christian Europe had tolerated "infidels" in its midst, and this toleration of false believers had incurred unspeakable divine anger. If Christians would only begin to purge these infidels from the ranks of its world, the argument went, then the wrath of God might be withdrawn. It was an emotionally satisfying solution. Latent prejudices could be revived and justified. The anger present in every tragic death experience could be focused. The enemy could be identified and "virtuous" hatreds could flow freely.

Who were these infidels? Why they were the Jews, of course! Slowly, there was a shift from self-blaming to blaming the Jews, a prejudice-enhancing shift. The Jews must have poisoned the wells, infesting the drinking water, people said. That is why the plague was so rampant and so indiscriminate. Rationality was a casualty of the fear and hatred people felt, as it often is

when those emotions run rampant, and with its demise came the worst out-
break of anti-Semitic horror that the Christian world had yet seen. Jews were
murdered, beaten, kidnapped, forcibly baptized, robbed of their assets, expelled from their homes and ghettoized. Even those Jews who had converted
to Christianity were investigated and many were charged with continuing to
observe Jewish rites in private. Jews were among the most prominent victims
who faced the fires at the stake during the period of history we call the Inquisition. It was one more dark chapter in the continuing saga of anti-Semitism
in the Christian church.

Our journey backward in time tracing the history of this ever-spreading
anti-Semitism comes next to that bizarre period in our Western past that we
call the Crusades. The desire to win eternal reward and the need to oppress a
rising religious threat, combined with an obsession to free Christian holy
places from the control of infidels—not Jews this time, not yet—fueled centuries of crusading fervor. The holy city of Jerusalem, which included such
sites as the Mount of Olives, the Garden of Gethsemane, the hill of Calvary
and the place of Jesus' tomb in Joseph's garden, was being "defiled" by Muslim control. Six miles away lay the little town of Bethlehem, the sacred birthplace of Jesus, also under Islamic auspices. Encouraged by the Vatican, local
princes identified this external Muslim enemy and were easily able to rouse
the population of Europe into a frenzy. Eternal reward was promised to those
who led a contingent of followers to the Holy Land to kill the infidels and to
free the holy places. Some battalions of Christian crusaders were large, led by
the ruling kings of Europe. Some were smaller, led by a local duke or noble-
man. Others were organized by a single citizen who frequently had more enthusiasm than wisdom. Militarily, all of them were quite unsuccessful: the
Holy Land has generally remained under Muslim control until this day. However, the Crusades left a hatred deep inside the souls of the Islamic people and
nations that still plagues the Western world at this very moment.

Because this present search of our past is for the origins of anti-Semitism,
we need to note that most of these fervent Christian soldiers who set off on
their "romantic" Crusades never actually made it to the Holy Land. They
made it only to one or two villages or towns away from their homes, where in
their frustration they acted out their vehemence against the only "infidels"
they could find in these communities: these infidels were not Muslims but
Jews. "One infidel is as good as another," became the motto of the crusaders

as the Jews were killed in village after village. "They deserved it," the Christians said. "They not only killed Jesus, but they bragged about it and accepted the consequences for themselves and their children." That is what the "Word of God" had stated. The echoes from Matthew's words were never far from the minds of these Christian warriors.

This persecutory mentality had made itself obvious even earlier in European history after Christianity became the dominant religious expression in the empire. Heads of state, acting with papal authority, barred the Jews from owning land. To survive economically, Jews became bankers and jewelers. Christians, who were taught that usury was sinful, could not charge interest on loans, so banking was unprofitable for them. This opened a rich market that allowed Jews to become the dominant financiers of Europe. Kings borrowed money from Jewish bankers to underwrite their wars and even their Crusades. This enabled the Christians to feed stereotypical prejudices that portrayed Jews as money-grubbers. If there were any doubts about this, the story of Judas Iscariot was retold. Had he not betrayed the Lord for thirty pieces of silver? It all fit together. Christians needed the Jewish bankers, but they hated them simultaneously.

Banking time and again proved to be an unsafe haven for the Jews. Whenever a king's debts to Jewish financiers became excessive, it was easy for him to begin another round of persecutions in which Jewish property would be confiscated. That property frequently included those paper assets called bank loans and the king's debts disappeared into thin air! In time, the Christians would abandon their principles about the sinfulness of interest. Banking was too lucrative an enterprise to leave in Jewish hands. Another layer of anti-Semitism is thus laid bare.

Next we arrive at the period of Christian history in which the church celebrated its founding fathers—Polycarp, Irenaeus, Justin Martyr, Jerome, Tertullian and John Chrysostom, just to name a few. Not surprisingly, there were no founding mothers in this patriarchal world. These male figures were the key players as the church learned how to survive in a period of persecution and to prepare its faith tradition to become the dominant religion in the Roman Empire by the fourth century. It is fascinating to discover how deep and virulent the anti-Jewish rhetoric was in almost every one of these "fathers." Their words, when read today, are still chilling. Jews were called "evil," "vermin," and "unclean." They were said to be "unfit to live." Christians were taught that it was a virtue to hate Jews actively. These religious leaders castigated and caricatured the Jewish tradition in ways that would have made it impossible for a faithful Jew to recognize it as his or her own sacred story. Jews were not to be trusted, not to be allowed access to power, not to be considered as potential friends, not to be consorted with in any common meal.

When we arrive at the second century, still searching for the origins of this prejudice that seems to have infected Christians at a very early stage, we come to a man named Marcion, who did his work around 140 CE. Marcion regarded the God of the Jews as a demonic figure. He proposed that Christians dismiss the Old Testament from what they considered sacred scriptures. He and his followers even began to edit out of "Christian" books—those that would someday form the core of the New Testament—all references to Jews. Marcion's desire was to sever Christianity from its Jewish roots and allow it, even force it, to deny its own ancestry. He might be called the culmination of the first great wave of Christian anti-Semitism.

The church, to its credit, refused to go along with Marcion, eventually condemning him as a heretic, but Marcion's anti-Semitism was destined to continue to exert its ugly influence in the life of the church. Marcion ultimately forced the early church to draw up its own canon of scripture, which quite specifically included the Old Testament. It could hardly have done otherwise, since the canonical gospels included thousands of references and allusions to the Hebrew scriptures. Those Jewish texts had long been the primary way through which Christians had portrayed Jesus as the fulfillment of the law and the prophets. Christians even began to appropriate Jewish concepts to themselves, calling themselves "God's chosen people," or "God's elect," and identifying themselves as the "new Israel." Later the title selected for the Christian scriptures would be the New Testament. "Testament" was a poor Latin translation of the word for "covenant." God's first covenant had been made with the Jews; the second—the new and presumably the final—covenant was made with the Christians. These consciously adopted terms implied that the Jews no longer had a right even to their former claims as God's chosen or covenanted ones. They were now defined by the Christians as God's rejected, the ones who did not live up to their calling. "He came to his own and his own people received him not" is the way the Fourth Gospel described it (John 1:11).

The next step backward in this journey takes us into the New Testament itself. We Christians do not like to face the fact that anti-Semitism is present in our scriptures—especially in the gospels themselves—but it is. The book we call the "Word of God" actually teaches us to hate, so to the anti-Semitism in the New Testament portion of the Bible I now turn.

22

ANTI-SEMITISM IN THE GOSPELS

The New Testament is a repository of hostility to Jews and Judaism. Many, if perhaps even most, Christians are completely free of anti-Semitism, yet the Christian Scripture is permeated with it.

Samuel Sandmel[6]

When I was a child attending an Evangelical Episcopal (Anglican) Sunday school in North Carolina, I was taught that it was okay to hate Jews. If I doubted that, the Bible was quoted to validate that negativity. I never met a good Jew in all of my prepared Sunday school material. Jews were those evil people who were always out to get Jesus—and get him they did, I was told. I grew up never doubting that it was the Jews who were responsible for Jesus' death. Like many in the early church and for centuries afterward, I exonerated the Roman officials of any guilt in the death of Jesus. I accepted the propaganda that was so deep in our faith tradition that it even found expression in the creeds. It was simply "under" Pontius Pilate, not "because of" Pontius Pilate, that Jesus suffered, died and was buried, those sacred documents proclaim. The Roman procurator was portrayed as little more than an innocent bystander. The Jews were the real villains. There is only a vague, understated note in the scriptures reminding readers that the Jews did not have the power to execute; all executions, other than those resulting from mob violence, had to be carried out by the Romans.

In the leaflets handed out weekly as part of my church's Sunday school curriculum, it was easy to identify the Jews. They had names like Pharisees, Sadducees, scribes, Caiaphas, Annas and Judas Iscariot. Those names dripped with hostility as these stories were told. The Jews were sinister, evil people who were constantly plotting and scheming. When these Jews were portrayed pictorially, they were always painted in dark, negative colors, complete with scowls on their faces. Jews, I was taught, were people who had no principles.

In this same Sunday school no one told me that Jesus was a Jew. That seemed to have escaped their notice. When I saw pictures of Jesus, he certainly did not look like a Jew. He typically had blond hair, blue eyes and fair skin. I thought he was a Swede or at least an Englishman. It had also escaped my teachers' notice that all of the disciples, as well as Paul and Mary Magdalene and Mary and Joseph, were Jews.

The Bible stories were presented to me as episodes depicting the good guys, who were Christians, against the bad guys, who were Jews. When Paul expressed his negative feelings about the Jews, it did not occur to me that Paul, a Jew, was saying these things about another part of his own people. Paul's enemies were not the ethnic Jews, as I was taught by implication. They were rather the Jewish members of the orthodox party of Paul's own religious tradition. That was, however, too subtle a distinction for my Sunday School material to grasp. To say it in a way that contemporary church people might understand, Paul's enemies were simply the traditionalists, people that we today might call the "fundamentalist Jews." Clergy might call them the "old guard." Paul represented a challenging liberal party within Judaism that was composed of those Jews who believed that they had received a new vision of God in Jesus and that this new vision needed to be incorporated into their ongoing, ever-evolving faith story.

The heroes of the Jewish past, who were recognized as the mountaintop experiences in the Jewish tradition, had also been people who had a new vision that was destined to reform and reshape the Jewish story. There was Abraham, who left Ur of the Chaldeans to form a new people around a new idea; or Moses, who led the Jews out of slavery and stamped upon them a radical monotheism; or Elijah, who brought into a developing Judaism the role of the prophets; or Ezekiel, who reformed Judaism in the trauma of the Exile; or even Ezra and Nehemiah, who led a remnant out of the Exile to pick up the threads of their broken history and to rebuild the dream. There was also that enigmatic, shadowy figure, whose ideas were developed in Second Isaiah, as well as the writer of Second Zechariah, both of whom helped bring Judaism into a major new perspective in their times.[7]

So those revisionist Jewish followers of Jesus saw him as one more, perhaps even the greatest, in the long line of people who had kept the faith of the Jews open, living and growing. They thus challenged and destabilized that most traditional part of the Jewish community, which believed that it already possessed in its orthodox formulations the final truth of God and so needed no further expansion. What looks to the contemporary reader like a rather vehement anti-Semitic polemic in the New Testament was in fact a typical ecclesiastical dispute between traditionalists and visionaries, the closed tradition facing the new challenge. What we tend to forget today is that both parties in this instance were Jews.

That kind of face-off has happened thousands of times in religious history. It was not unlike the battle in Christian circles today between the fundamentalists and the modernists, in which epithets are hurled back and forth with little sensitivity to the feelings of the other. Fundamentalists are called ignorant, closed-minded security seekers who cannot embrace reality. Modernists are called atheists, secular humanists, traitors to the faith of their fathers and mothers. Religious battles are always visceral, emotional and exaggerated. That is because they are always about our deepest identity. Religious debates involve our sense of security and well-being. As such they are not unlike political battles where each side suggests that the ultimate disaster imaginable will occur if the opposite side or a different candidate is victorious at the ballot box.

What we have in the New Testament is primarily a story written by the Jewish revisionists, who were later to be called Christians, and who would in time open their revisionist Jewish faith story to the inclusion of gentiles. In that part of the New Testament called the epistles, we have letters attributed to such Jewish leaders as Paul, Peter, John, James, Jude and probably second-generation disciples at least of Paul, writers who were perhaps even more capable than the original Christians of making the transition into a universal vision. Then we have gospels written by the Jewish Mark, Matthew and John, who tell the story of how the meaning of Jesus broke the boundaries of Judaism to incorporate a radically new universal idea that relativized all of their previous conclusions and thus all of their religious security systems.

The one piece of this growing body of revisionist literature that did not follow this exact pattern is the narrative we call Luke-Acts. These two books, presumably authored by a man named Luke, but certainly authored by the same person, constitute the only parts of the Bible that were written by one who was not Jewish by birth. Luke appears to have been born a gentile. He seems to have been attracted to Judaism, as many first-century gentiles were, becoming one of those people who were called "gentile proselytes." He appears ultimately to have converted to Judaism. Then, probably through the influence of Paul, he entered a new kind of religious community, shaped, its adherents claimed, by one called the Messiah (translated "Christos" in Greek and "Christ" in English), who was said to have called both Jews and gentiles beyond their original tribal identities into a new humanity. The battle that was thus waged inside first-century Judaism was between the traditionalists and the revisionists. It was a battle over how the future of Judaism would be defined. The new vision could not succeed unless the old vision died. This meant that the stakes were very high and the emotions were very real.

Over a period of time, probably less than a century, the revisionist Jews formed common cause with the influx of gentiles into Christianity and, as a consequence, loosened their own ties with Judaism. The barriers that proclaimed that Jews must stay separate and therefore could not eat or intermarry with gentiles faded under pressure from the revisionists, while among the orthodox Jews those very same lines were hardening. The division was inevitable and during the last years of the ninth decade of the first century of this Common Era an actual split occurred. Traditional Judaism could not and would not change. Anything that becomes so rigid it cannot adapt to a new reality will finally die. That is how Christianity, a new religion, but born in the womb of Judaism, came into being. In the sacred scriptures of that new religion there would linger eternally the echoes of those fierce battles fought between the revisionist Jews and the orthodox Jews. The New Testament was largely the product of the revisionist tradition. The animosity between the two groups was visceral and real. Echoes of their hostility are certainly heard in those words the revisionists hurled at the orthodox party that form much of the content of the New Testament. That hostility came to reside in the books that we call epistles and gospels. When those scriptures themselves came to be viewed as inspired and holy, their hostile words achieved a new status.

Anti-Semitism as found in a book now called the "Word of God" conferred on this destructuve prejudice not only legitimacy but also holiness.

Of course, the words of the orthodox party were equally as hate-filled, but because no one was adding books to the Jewish scriptures, that brand of hostility did not enter their sacred text and so was not read over and over again through the centuries. Orthodoxy was not open to change. The traditionalists' sacred scriptures were closed. The negativity of the revisionists, however, received enormous power from its inclusion in the Christian scriptures. If God had rejected the Jews, as the Christian scriptures implied, then the Christians' continued rejection of Jews was validated. Throughout history these New Testament references would be read as if they reflected conflicts between Christians and Jews, not conflicts between liberalizing Jews and traditionalist Jews. The very Jewishness of Jesus would be forgotten. The legends of his miraculous birth, in which he was supposed to have been fathered by the Holy Spirit, would serve to make him appear to be less Jewish. His mother was just the sacred womb that nurtured the divine seed into life.

As the number of Jews in the Christian church began to shrink—a reality caused first by the influx of gentiles that reduced Jewish percentages of the whole and then by the fact that Jewish Christians more and more shed their Jewish practices and began to intermarry into the gentile world—the Christian church began to deemphasize its Jewishness. This can be seen in Luke's gospel, for example, where Jewish celebration of Pentecost or Shavuot is given an entirely new Christian thrust. Shavuot celebrated the giving of the law, God's greatest gift to the Jews. Christian Pentecost celebrated the gift of the Holy Spirit, which was said to be God's greatest gift to the Christians. In the words of Paul, "Now we are discharged from the law, dead to that which held us captive, so that we are slaves not under the old written code but in the new life of the Spirit" (Rom. 7:6, NRSV). John's gospel offered a similar contrast when it said, "The law indeed was given through Moses; grace and truth came through Jesus Christ" (John 1:17, NRSV). In time the Jewishness of the early Christians would simply fade away. By the first quarter of the second century of the Common Era, Christianity had become overwhelmingly a gentile movement.

From that day to this, the primary readers and interpreters of the New Testament have been gentiles who have had no great sense of Jewish history, of

Jewish writing styles or of the original Jewish setting of the Christian story. They identified the Jesus movement, about which the scriptures spoke, not as a movement made up of revisionist Jews but as one made up of Christians with no reference at all to their Jewish background. They identified the orthodox party in the New Testament with all Jews and thought of them as the enemies of Jesus. When they read the narratives of the Jesus movement in the Bible, they interpreted those texts not as negative comments that revisionist Jews had said to the orthodox Jews but as things that Christians, including Jesus, had said about all Jews. As these "sacred scriptures" were read through the ages in the churches of the Western world, the hostility of Christians toward Jews was reinforced anew in every century. The role of the Jews in the death of Jesus was recounted again and again as each Good Friday was observed. The presumed acceptance of the blame for this dark act of "deicide" was articulated in those scriptures by the Jews themselves. So the children of Abraham, the people who produced Jesus of Nazareth, suffered throughout Christian history, generation after generation, as the words of the Bible continued to wreak havoc against the Jews down through the ages. The face of anti-Semitism is now unmasked. It was and is a gift of the Christians to the world. It is the dark underside of the gospel of love. It is part and parcel of the Christian story. It is not a pretty, a noble or an inspiring picture.

There is one more strand of anti-Semitism, however, that must be traced before the story is complete. When the Christian gospel climaxed with the crucifixion, the antihero was pictured as a quintessential Jew. His name was Judas. He was called "Iscariot," which means political traitor or assassin. In a real sense, anti-Semitism would focus through the ages on this character. He would be the linchpin, perhaps even the ultimate source of Christianity's darkest chapter. To his story and his part in this dreadful bigotry we turn next.

23

THE ROLE OF JUDAS ISCARIOT IN THE RISE OF ANTI-SEMITISM

If the Jews were alone in this world, they would stifle in filth and offal. They would try to get ahead of one another in hate-filled struggle and exterminate one another.

Adolf Hitler[8]

I am suspicious of the historicity of Judas Iscariot and of his role in the Christian story as the traitor. That suspicion has been created by five easily identifiable, documentable facts.

First, a careful reading of the New Testament reveals the not-fully-suppressed memory of a man named Judas, in the inner circle of Jesus' disciples, who was *not* evil and who was *not* a traitor. In the Fourth Gospel John refers to a disciple named Judas, who is not Iscariot (14:22). Luke in his list of the twelve disciples names, in addition to Iscariot, another disciple named Judas, identified only as the brother of James (6:16). This Judas replaces Thaddaeus in the list recounted by Mark (3:14–19) and Matthew (10:2–4). In addition to this, there is an epistle that bears Judas' name that was included by the Christians in the New Testament. The author of this book is identified as Jude, which is simply another variation of the name Judas, and he is called in that epistle "a servant of Jesus Christ and brother of James" (Jude 1:1). There is clearly an early Christian memory of a faithful Judas in the inner circle of the Christian movement.

The second source of my suspicion comes from the fact that the act of betrayal by a member of the twelve disciples is not found in the earliest Christian writings. Judas is first placed into the Christian story by Mark (3:19), who wrote in the early years of the eighth decade of the Common Era. Prior to that time, we have the entire Pauline corpus, which was written between the years 50 and 64 CE. We may also have what scholars call the Q (or *Quelle*— i.e., "source") document, which many believe to be a lost "sayings gospel" that both Matthew and Luke are said to have incorporated into their narratives as a supplement to their use of Mark. Because we still have Mark, we can easily show that Matthew and Luke copied some of the content of Mark almost verbatim into their gospels. But when all of this Marcan material is removed from Matthew and Luke, these two gospel writers still have material so identical that it has to have had a common source. That shared material has led many to the assumption that both Matthew and Luke had a second written source other than Mark, a source that is now lost. When these identical or nearly identical passages are lifted out of Matthew and Luke and studied separately, they appear to be largely a collection of the sayings of Jesus. Hence Q is assumed to be an early collection of Jesus' sayings. Some scholars date this Q material as early as the 50s. If that is accurate, then this is a second major pregospel source that must be examined.[9]

Turning first to Paul, we discover that the concept of betrayal prior to the crucifixion enters Paul's writings merely as a dating device, with no content whatsoever. Addressing a letter to the Corinthians in the mid-50s Paul says, "For I have received from the Lord, what I also delivered to you; that the Lord Jesus Christ on the night when he was 'betrayed'; took bread and when he had given thanks, he broke it and said, 'This is my body which is broken for you.'" (1 Cor. 11:23–24). Paul's intention here was simply to tell the story of the inauguration of the Last Supper. However, in doing that he used a word that the English translators in the seventeenth century said means "betrayed." In the Pauline quote above, I placed 'betrayed' into a single quote because this word literally means "handed over," which does not project the same meaning that comes to mind when we hear the word betrayed. It is worth noting that in his entire written corpus Paul gives no evidence that he was aware of a betrayal that took place at the hand of one of the twelve disciples, but the English translators knew the later gospel stories, and so they placed that meaning into their rendition of this word. It was one more of many examples in which later Christians were guilty of reading Paul through the eyes of the gospel narratives. We need to keep in mind that Paul had died before the first gospel was written. While in this particular text Paul does not rule out the betrayal possibility, he does appear to do so just four chapters later.

In 1 Corinthians 15:1–6, Paul once again declares that he is passing on to his readers the sacred traditions that he has received. Then he gives the barest outline to the details of the final events in Jesus' life. He says that "Christ died for our sins in accordance with the scriptures, and that he was buried, and that he was raised on the third day in accordance with the scriptures, and that he appeared to Cephas [Peter], then to the twelve."

"He appeared to . . . the twelve." Judas was still among them when Easter dawned: that is Paul's testimony! When Matthew related the first biblical story of the risen Christ appearing to the disciples on a mountaintop in Galilee (Matt. 28:16–20), he asserted that it was only to "the eleven" that Christ appeared. Sometime between when Paul wrote 1 Corinthians (ca. mid-50s CE) and when Matthew wrote this account of a resurrection appearance (ca. 82–85 CE), the story of Judas as a traitor appears to have entered the Christian story. Paul did not know about this tradition. His writings in 1 Corinthians make that perfectly clear.

When we turn to the Q source, we discover that it is in this common, and presumably earlier, tradition that both Matthew and Luke quote Jesus as saying to the disciples, with Judas present, "At the renewal of all things, when the Son of Man is seated on the throne of his glory, you who have followed me will also sit on twelve thrones, judging the twelve tribes of Israel" (Matt. 19:28). Luke has this text read, "You are those who have stood by me in my trials; and I confer on you, just as my father has conferred on me, a kingdom, so that you may eat and drink at my table in my kingdom, and you will sit on thrones judging the twelve tribes of Israel" (Luke 22:28–30). The assumption here is that among the twelve disciples who will judge the twelve tribes of Israel, Judas is included. The editors appear to forget that one of the twelve will be judged unworthy. The Q material, if it was indeed a separate and earlier source, seems to have been collected before the story of Judas the traitor came into the tradition, and both Matthew and Luke failed to make their source fully conform to the changing tradition that now included the story of a traitor among the twelve. That is additional evidence that the story of the betrayal of Jesus by one of the twelve, named Judas, was not an original part of the Christian narrative. It was added later, which of course begs the question as to when and why it was added. I shall return to that question later.

The third reason I am suspicious about the historicity of the betrayal story is the way the Judas account so obviously grows once it has been introduced by Mark, somewhere between 70 and 75 CE. Mark has Judas go to the chief priests to betray Jesus. They "promise to give him money," but no amount is stated, and "he sought how he might conveniently betray him" (Mark 14:10–11, KJV). In Mark's version of the Last Supper, Jesus identifies the traitor as "one of the twelve, one who is dipping bread into the bowl with me" (14:20, NRSV). Mark then has the act of betrayal take place at midnight in the Garden of Gethsemane with a kiss (14:44–45). That is the last time we see Judas in Mark's gospel.

Matthew, writing about a decade after Mark, builds on Mark's meager details. In his growing story Matthew adds the price paid for the betrayal. It was, he says, thirty pieces of silver (26:15). Matthew also introduces dialogue between Judas and Jesus at the moment of betrayal that Mark does not mention (26:25). The disciples, Matthew tells us, resisted those who would take Jesus after this betrayal, but Jesus rebuked them (26:51–54). Matthew then tells the story of Judas repenting and trying to return the blood money. The temple leaders refused to receive the money back, so Judas cast it into the temple and, according to Matthew proceeded to hang himself. Matthew then tells us that the chief priests used the money to buy a potter's field in which strangers could be buried (27:3–10). That is the end of Judas for Matthew.

Luke, writing some five to ten years after Matthew, portrays the chief priests and scribes as aggressively seeking to lay hands on Jesus but being restrained by their fear of his popularity with the people. So they sent spies pretending to be righteous messengers trying to entrap him (Luke 20:19–20). Judas, as the traitor, is introduced against this background. Luke explains Judas' treachery by saying that "Satan entered [him]" (22:3) and caused him to strike a deal with the chief priests and officers. Finally, what it was that Judas actually betrayed is introduced in Luke for the first time: Judas was to lead them to Jesus apart from the crowd (22:6). This is a rather weak explanation. Surely the authorities could have followed Jesus at night and discovered where he slept apart from the crowd. He was easily identified, after all. When he was arrested, he reminded his accusers that he had been daily in the temple teaching (22:53). It is worth noting that what Judas actually did for them could have been accomplished without his assistance. It thus has the feel of a manufactured story. There Judas exits Luke's gospel.

However, in the book of Acts Luke adds, in a speech delivered by Peter to the disciples, that it was Judas rather than the Jewish authorities who used the reward of iniquity to purchase a field. When inspecting that field Judas fell "headlong," Luke says; "he burst open in the middle and all his bowels gushed out" (Acts 1:16–18). It was a rather more gross way to die than simply by hanging and it quite specifically contradicts the hanging account. Both situations might bring death, but one's bowels do not gush out when one is hanged by the neck. The story obviously was still growing.

John paints Judas with an even more sinister brush. Judas was really a thief, he says (12:6). He was filled by a satanic spirit (13:27). There is no Last Supper in John, but after the foot-washing ceremony that is substituted for it, John describes a discussion that took place in which Jesus identified the traitor as "he who ate my bread" (13:18). The disciples wondered and looked around at one another. The beloved disciple then asked Jesus quite specifically the "who" question, and Jesus responded, "The one to whom I give this piece of bread when I have dipped it in the dish" (John 13:26, NRSV). Then dipping the bread into the common food supply, he handed it to Judas and said, "Do quickly what you are going to do" (John 13:27, NRSV). Judas then went out of the upper room, and as he did, John comments, "It was night" (13:30). After the Last Supper was concluded, Judas arrived in the Garden of Gethsemane at the place where Jesus was praying, accompanied by a band of soldiers from the chief priests, and the traitorous act was accomplished (18:2–9). Peter fought back with a sword, John says, cutting off the ear of the servant of the high priest (John 18:10–11). That was Judas' last appearance in the gospel tradition.

The distinctions are fascinating! Clearly the story was evolving, the details supplied as each phase of the narrative entered the tradition. The whole story of Judas has the feeling of being contrived. My suspicions are not alleviated by the details.

The fourth reason for my suspicion is that the story of the act of betrayal is set very dramatically at midnight. It is just too neat a detail to have what the gospel writers believed was the darkest deed in human history occur at the darkest moment of the night. That looks more like a liturgical drama than it does a fact of history.

My fifth and final source of suspicion is the name of the traitor itself. Judas is nothing but the Greek spelling of Judah. The name of the traitor is the very name of the Jewish nation. The leaders of the orthodox party of that nation, who defined the worship of the Jews, were by the time the gospels were written increasingly the enemy of the Christian movement. It is simply too convenient to place the blame for Jesus' death on the whole of orthodox Judaism by linking the traitor by name with the entire nation of the Jews. When that fact is combined with a specific attempt to exonerate the Romans by portraying Pilate as washing his hands and saying, "I am innocent of this [just] man's blood," then we see the shifting of blame. It simply looks made up. The Romans killed Jesus, but by the eighth decade of the Christian era, when the story of Jesus was being written, something compelled the gospel writers to exonerate the Roman procurator, Pilate, and to blame the Jews. That was when Judas the traitor, identified as one of the twelve, entered the tradition. That identification sealed the fate of the Jews as the perennial object of a violent and persecuting Christian anti-Semitism.

What were the circumstances in the eighth decade of the first Christian century that made that shift seem to be both desirable and necessary and how was it accomplished? That is the story to which I turn next.

24

THE CIRCUMSTANCES THAT BROUGHT JUDAS INTO THE JESUS STORY

I regard the Jewish race as the born enemy of pure humanity and everything that is noble in it.

Richard Wagner[10]

I ask you, my readers, to suspend your critical faculties for a moment and to assume with me that the story of Judas Iscariot was a late-developing, contrived story and not a remembered bit of objective history. If this speculation is correct, as I believe it is, then I must deal with two additional questions. The first: Since the story of Judas is not remembered history, where did the gospel writers get the content that they wove into the Judas narrative? The second: What was going on at that time in history that may have been the catalyst that led to the creation of the Judas story?

I mentioned in the previous chapter that the words "handed over," which have also been translated as "betrayed," enter the Christian story in the writings of Paul (1 Cor. 11), when he relates the inauguration of the liturgy of the Lord's Supper. He dates this inauguration by writing, "On the night in which [Jesus] was betrayed [handed over], he took bread."

The Greek word that we translate as "handed over" or "betrayed" was used on one other occasion with a similar understanding in the biblical story. It was the word chosen by the Greek translators of the Hebrew scriptures to describe the decision of the brothers of Joseph to hand him over by selling him to the Midianites or the Ishmaelites and thus into a life of slavery, as that story was told in the book of Genesis (37:28). It is difficult to see the connection in the English text because the translators rendered the words as "sell," i.e., they handed him over for money. Of particular interest to me in this context is to show that all of the content of the story of Judas Iscariot comes out of other stories of betrayal in the Hebrew sacred scriptures. So I note that in this other biblical narrative, where "handed over" carries with it the sense of betrayal, is when Joseph's brother Judah suggests that they get money for their dastardly deed. Let me repeat the obvious: when the name Judah is spelled in Greek, it is Judas.[11]

There is also a story in the book of the prophet Zechariah in which the shepherd king of Israel was betrayed for thirty shekels of silver. This money, says Zechariah, was hurled back into the temple treasury, which is exactly what Matthew, who is the only gospel writer to mention thirty pieces of silver, says Judas did with his money when he repented (compare Zech. 11:12–13 with Matt. 27:5). To whom was this shepherd king betrayed in Zechariah? It was to those who bought and sold animals in the temple (11:7–17 and 14:21).

Similarly, there is a narrative in the David saga of stories where one who ate at the table of the Lord's anointed, which is what the king was called, raised his traitorous hand against King David. His treachery backfired and so he went and hanged himself. This traitor's name was Ahithophel and it is a reference to him from the book of Psalms that is quoted in the Judas story to show that his act was simply the fulfillment of the prophets ("as it is written of him," Mark 14:21, Matt. 26:24; "as it has been determined," Luke 22:22). That Old Testament text reads, "Even my bosom friend in whom I trusted, who ate of my bread, has lifted the heel against me" (Ps. 41:9). The entire Ahithophel narrative is located between 2 Sam. 15:7–17:23.

Next comes the narrative that introduces the kiss of the traitor. Its antecedent is also found in the David cycle of stories. In a rebellion led by his son Absalom, David is successful in retaining his throne but feels he can no longer trust all his former inner circle. Retiring his military chief Joab, David replaces him with a man named Amasa. Joab is not pleased and, under the guise of wanting to congratulate his successor, he seeks out Amasa. On finding him, Joab draws Amasa's face by the beard to his own, pretending to extend to him the kiss of friendship. In the process, however, he disembowels him with a dagger (2 Sam. 20:5ff.). Perhaps this is the story that colored

Luke's account of Peter's speech, suggesting that Judas died with all his bowels gushing out (Acts 1:15–18).

My point in this exercise is to show that every detail of the Judas story has been lifted directly out of the Hebrew scriptures, where it was originally part of narratives about other traitors in Jewish history. It is thus borrowed content that gives flesh to the gospel story of a traitor, and that in turn adds to the speculation that the story of the traitor itself was forced by some need other than to remember history. The plot thickens.

Turning to the time when the gospels were written, in Mark's case 70–75 CE, we ask if there is anything going on that might help us explain the necessity of shifting the blame for Jesus' death from the Romans to the Jews. Mark is crucial for this study, not only because his gospel was first, but because both Matthew and Luke incorporate Mark into their narratives. It is in Mark that Judas is first introduced as the traitor. The history occurring in the land of the Jews at this time was critical. Tensions had been rising between the Jews and the Romans from the time of the life of Jesus, when Jewish guerrilla fighters were already roaming the hills of Galilee doing hit-and-run attacks on the occupying Roman army. To the Jews, these guerrillas were heroic freedom fighters. To the Romans, they were terrorists and killers. These guerrillas were called Zealots. The fact that one of Jesus' disciples was known as Simon the Zealot may indicate a closer connection between these guerrillas and Jesus than Christians have yet been willing to admit (Luke 6:15).

In the year 66 CE, this guerrilla activity escalated into a full-scale war between the Romans and the Jews that did not officially end until 73 CE, when the total annihilation of the Jewish army at a place named Masada took place. The climax of the war, however, occurred when the Romans decided that the only way to defeat the guerrillas was to destroy Jerusalem and the entire Jewish state. Led first by a general named Vespasian, and later by his son Titus, the Romans moved into siege positions around the holy city and pounded it until the walls of the city fell in 70 CE. The Romans then moved in, smashing everything in sight, razing the buildings and demolishing the Temple. The Jewish state disappeared from the maps of history, not to appear again until 1948, when the United Nations brought into being the state of Israel under the authority of the Balfour Declaration, made near the conclusion of World War I.[12]

The Jews lost everything in the Roman devastation of the first century: their nation, their holy city, their temple, their priesthood. With their traditional sacred symbols gone, the Jews attached their identity to their scriptures, which alone gave them a sense of their past. They invested these scriptures with both absolute authority and literal truth. The whole truth of God and the divine will is in the Torah, they asserted. Nothing more is essential; nothing more is necessary. The Jews thus became increasingly rigid, fundamentalist and doctrinaire about their sacred writings. That always occurs where survival is at stake.

At the time of this tragedy, the followers of Jesus, who were still predominantly Jews, blamed the orthodox party in Judaism for bringing this disaster upon their nation. At the same time Roman hostility toward and persecution against those Jews whom they believed to be responsible for the hostilities was rampant. To separate themselves from being identified with the orthodox party, the Jewish followers of Jesus decided to tell the Jesus story by saying that they too had been victimized by these rigid temple Jews. The same people who brought this war on our nation had earlier been responsible for the death of our leader, Jesus of Nazareth, said these Jewish revisionists soon to be called Christians, to the Romans; we have a common enemy. If the agenda was to blame the orthodox party for the death of Jesus, and thus to separate themselves in the minds of the Romans from those responsible for the war, how better could they accomplish that purpose than by telling the Christ story with the chief person responsible for the death of Jesus bearing the name of the entire Jewish nation? How better could they seek Roman favor than by whitewashing the Roman procurator, Pontius Pilate, in their narrative of Jesus' final days, exonerating him of any blame in the death of Jesus? So Pilate, in the developing gospel story, was portrayed as washing his hands, proclaiming himself "innocent of this man's blood" (Matt. 27:24). The Jewish crowd was portrayed as accepting the blame: "His blood be on us and on our children" (Matt. 27:25). The shift in blame was complete. The Jews did it. *They* are the enemy. Judah/Judas did it. *He* is the enemy. Pilate was and the Romans are our friends.

With the destruction of the temple in 70 CE, the Jews could no longer observe the Festival of Dedication, later to be called Hanukkah, by celebrating the return of the light of God to the temple. So when Mark wrote his narrative, and Matthew and Luke followed him in this, he created a story in which the figure of Jesus replaced the destroyed temple. We call this story the trans-figuration, and in it the light of God, which was once said to have descended on the temple, was now said to have descended upon Jesus, making him translucent. Jesus, the Christians were claiming, had replaced the destroyed temple as the new meeting place between God and human life. It is a fasci-nating and revelatory claim. Later, in John's gospel, that identity was en-hanced when Jesus was quoted as saying, "Destroy this temple, and in three days I will raise it up" (John 2:19). The listeners did not understand, says the gospel writer, because he was referring to the temple of his own body.

So the deed was done. To survive in a hostile environment, the Christians courted the favor of the gentile Roman government, painting Pilate sensi-tively and positively while they helped shift the blame for Jerusalem's de-struction onto the laps of the orthodox authorities. So Judas, the antihero, was born and the fate of the Jews in history was sealed. The Christians could hate the Jews with impunity; they could persecute them with a clear con-science; they could make their self-centered quest for survival appear to be an act of morality and virtue. That is how anti-Semitism was born. That is how it was destined to grow: it was fed year after year when the story of Jesus' passion and death was read anew to justify again and again Christian violence against Jews.

That is the ultimate seed out of which this Christian prejudice has grown. That is the source out of which all the hostility toward the Jews has flowed. That is what allowed Christians to tolerate and even to celebrate a violent, killing anti-Jewish undercurrent that would emerge in chilling horror in the writings of the church fathers, in the Crusades, in the Inquisition, in the re-sponse to the bubonic plague, in the writings of reformers like Martin Luther and in the Holocaust. Judas is our clue. Christians took the life of one disciple who had the name of the entire nation and made him the Antichrist, thereby avoiding their own persecution as Jews by the conquering Romans, and that act brought the annual infusion of bigotry and a killing anti-Semitism into the essence of Christianity. The sin of anti-Semitism was thus transformed into a virtue in Christian history.

The only purpose in raising the sources of our prejudice into conscious-ness is to enable us to expel them from our souls. The biblical texts that we Christians have used for centuries to justify our hostility toward the Jews need to be banished forever from the sacred writings of the Christian church.

The way to begin this process is, I believe, to return to the Christ consciousness that caused the early Christians to assert, as Luke does in the Pentecost story, that to be filled with the Spirit is to transcend all tribal boundaries and to speak the universal language of love (Acts 2). It is to recover the power in Paul's words to the Galatians, that "in Christ . . . there is neither Jew nor Greek" (Gal. 3:28). Later, to emphasize this point, Paul writes, "If any one is in Christ, he [and she] is a new creation" (2 Cor. 5:17).

To enter that new creation may be what will be required for the human race to survive. At the very least, perhaps in this new creation the killing prejudice of the past that seems to affect all religions will be brought to an end. It is a vision worth pursuing.

THE BIBLE AND CERTAINTY

THE TERRIBLE TEXTS

Beloved, being very eager to write to you of our common salvation, I found it necessary to write appealing to you to contend for the faith which was once for all delivered to the saints.

Jude 1:3

No one comes to the Father, but by me.

John 14:6

He who is not with me is against me.

Matthew 12:30

25

THE SYMPTOMS

CONVERSION, MISSIONARY EXPANSION AND RELIGIOUS BIGOTRY

A spirituality revolution is taking place in Western and Eastern societies as politics fails as a vessel of hope and meaning. This revolution is not to be confused with the rising tide of religious fundamentalism, although the two are caught up in the same phenomenon: the emergence of the sacred as a leading force in contemporary society. Spirituality and fundamentalism are at opposite ends of the cultural spectrum. Spirituality seeks a sensitive, contemplative, transformative relationship with the sacred and is able to sustain levels of uncertainty in its quest because respect for mystery is paramount. Fundamentalism seeks certainty, fixed answers and absolutism, as a fearful response to the complexity of the world and to our vulnerability as creatures in a mysterious universe. Spirituality arises from love of and intimacy with the sacred and fundamentalism arises from fear of and possession of the sacred. The choice between spirituality and fundamentalism is a choice between conscious intimacy and unconscious possession.

David Tacey[1]

There is an Episcopal congregation named St. Francis in the Fields, located in a fashionable suburb of Louisville, Kentucky, called Harrod's Creek, that seems to have a hard time with the concepts of diversity and even freedom of speech. Some members of this congregation discovered, I gather to their horror, that a study group in their congregation was actually reading books that appeared to challenge what some of them called the "true faith of the church." The clergy leadership of this congregation dispatched one of its own to meet with the members of that study group. This meeting confirmed their worst suspicions. This group had actually been reading books by Marcus Borg, Elaine Pagels, Rowan Williams and Karen Armstrong.

That was an interesting list. Marcus Borg is a well-published Jesus scholar who teaches at Oregon State University. He is married to an Episcopal priest and is himself an active Episcopal layperson. Elaine Pagels is a professor of religion at Princeton University whose books are regularly on the New York Times best-seller list. She is much involved in her Episcopal congregation as a regular worshiper. Rowan Williams, the Archbishop of Canterbury, is liberal on social issues but conservative on theological issues. Karen Armstrong, a former Roman Catholic nun, is probably the best-known religious writer in the world today.

Undeterred by these credentials the priest issued an ultimatum to this group, saying, in effect, "From now on, you must read only the books which we, the clergy of this church, assign and approve." He then suggested a list of acceptable authors, all well-known traditional and, I might add, rather boring writers who would be thought of primarily as Christian propagandists rather than as Christian scholars. The list included names of those with encyclopedic, but not necessarily original, minds. Furthermore, this priest stated that if the members of this group wanted to continue meeting in that particular church, they must be monitored regularly and perhaps even led by one of the church's clergy. If they were not willing to follow this directive, said this "holy man from the office of the heavenly sheriff," they would have to leave the church. The creeds of the church, he asserted, cannot be debated since they represent the faith that has been once and for all delivered to the saints.

Perhaps this priest was not aware that the historic creeds of the church were developed in the third and fourth centuries of the Christian era and that far from falling from heaven in three neatly organized trinitarian paragraphs, complete with punctuation, they were adopted amid raucous debate, with all of the wheeling and dealing, the compromises and power plays that accompany every decision-making convention, whether it is primarily political or ecclesiastical.

I still have a difficult time believing that this scenario actually happened in my denomination and as recently as the first decade of the twenty-first century! Was not the Episcopal Church part of the Anglican Communion that bounded into existence as the result of Henry VIII's sex life and multiple wives? Do they not still define themselves as the great via media, standing between the Catholic tradition and Protestant principle? But happen it did. I have actually read the correspondence between this priest, the members of the study group and the congregation. What amazed me most was the implication conveyed by the clergy of this church, who appear to define themselves primarily as the "defenders of the faith," that the Christian faith can be and has been reduced to a set of propositional statements delivered to human beings by divine revelation. Perhaps it was even more incredible to me that they assumed that their finite human minds could define the reality of God and that their definition was ever afterward not to be subject to debate or change. That assumption was breathtaking in its naïveté. To bring this episode to its actual conclusion, the offending study group, I understand, accepted the invitation, not to be monitored or led, but to leave that church: they moved their meeting place, and perhaps their membership, to nearby St. Matthew's Episcopal Church. Perhaps there they will be able to continue their journey into the mystery of God, unimpeded by "benefit of clergy."

I wish I could assume that this rather bizarre tale was only an isolated event, triggered by an insecurity so deep as to be pitiable in the mind of one, or at least a very few, of the church's clergy; but that would be to turn a blind eye to Christian history. This behavior might seem rare and warped in our "enlightened" day, but the attitude behind it has dotted the landscape of the Christian tradition during the majority of its two thousand–plus years of life. Religious closed-minded ignorance wrapped in bigotry has even been justified by appeals to the sacred scriptures, which have again and again been quoted to demonstrate that if one disagrees with the "stated faith of the church," one is actually disagreeing with God and God's truth. When one adds to this the claim that the scriptures are themselves the very "Word of God," the circular argument becomes apparent and seemingly defensible.

The particular verse in the Bible that these Louisville clergy appear to have had in mind, and certainly the verse that has been frequently quoted to justify religious intolerance, is located in an obscure and seldom-read book in the New Testament called the epistle of Jude. In that very brief, one-chapter-long book, a reference is made in the third verse to something the author calls "the faith which was once for all delivered to the saints."

Most people would not be able to locate this epistle in the Bible if their lives depended on it. Consisting of only twenty-five verses, it nestles between the third epistle of John and the book of Revelation, which makes it the next to the last book in the New Testament. It is part of a group of writings that scholars designate as "general epistles." I have never heard any verse of this epistle quoted in any context save for this one. The implication present in this isolated text, and certainly the conclusion intended by those who quote it, is that Christianity can be and has been captured in a series of creeds, doctrines and dogmas, the truth of which is both self-evident and unchanging. Anyone who dares to question this conclusion or these core beliefs is questioning nothing less than God. Once those implications are accepted, it certainly becomes the duty of the church and its hierarchy to protect all the other people of the world from such heresy.

Whenever truth becomes set, it is inevitable that every new idea and even every new perspective becomes threatening and disturbing to the stated truth and thus it becomes an enemy to be suppressed. That clearly was the mentality underlying the behavior of the ordained persons in this Kentucky congregation, as they sought to justify both their ignorance and their arrogance in the claim that their actions possessed biblical authority and biblical respectability. When threatened religious people have a compelling need to command conformity for their own faith assertions, or to put down any challenge to the traditions of their religious past, the idea that there is such a thing as "the faith which was once for all delivered to the saints" is a godsend. It is used like a rapier's thrust in defense of "orthodoxy." It suppresses all lack of certainty. It leads the charge against any deviation. This produces the religious mentality that causes a variety of religious bodies to claim that they and they alone are "the true church." This is the source out of which the assertions come that "our pope is infallible" or "our Bible is inerrant."

When certainty combines with zeal in religious matters, horror always results. Jude's suggestion that we must "contend for the faith which was once for all delivered to the saints" has thus been the source of enormous pain and horror, as any quick look at history will reveal. The fact that this attitude is still alive and well in Kentucky in the twenty-first century is a cause for great alarm.

This text from Jude supports the claim so frequently made by Christians that there is only one way to believe and that, of course, it is the way of the one who quotes this text. This pious claim thus gives to religious arrogance the mask of respectability. To the grand inquisitor, it gives the face of a holy man. This is the mentality that provides the rationale by which destructive conversion tactics and aggressive, imperialistic missionary activities have been countenanced. For is it not obvious that once God has been captured in some kind of creedal box, once the Christian faith has been reduced to a set of propositional statements, doctrines and dogmas, then an idolatry of killing proportions becomes operative in religious life? This is why, even in the twenty-first century, religion remains one of the most divisive and hostile forces in the world. Embarrassing as it may be to those of us who call ourselves Christians, the fact is that more people have been killed in the history of the world in conflicts over and about religion than over any other single factor. Religion has so often been the source of the cruelest evil. Its darkest and most brutal side becomes visible at the moment when the adherents of any religious system identify their *understanding* of God with *God*. The two are never the same. This misguided conviction then gives rise to the idea that it is a religious duty to preserve "God's truth" from any challenge, from any source. Only with this kind of assumption would an Episcopal priest in Louisville, Kentucky, in the twenty-first century think it appropriate and even essential to tell a group of church members what books they may and may not read, or to insist that anyone who might stray outside some clearly defined box must be monitored by the clergy.

People who see themselves as "defenders of the faith" argue that without certainty, Christianity will not survive. They point to the fact that churches with fuzzy, "liberal" messages are dying and that churches with firm and unbending beliefs are growing. There is a germ of anecdotal truth in those claims. But holding fast to "firm truth" can be managed only if truth is narrowed to include just the data with which that believer is comfortable.

My contention, which I will seek to defend in this section of the book, is that the moment any religious tradition claims certainty, it turns demonic. It also gives up at that moment the very reason for which it was originally created. Whether such a tradition lives or dies, therefore, becomes of little significance. Above all, I contend that something called "the faith of the church" has never existed; truth, whether it be religious truth or any other kind, is always evolving and changing, and the moment truth is codified, it begins to die. That makes it very difficult to be triumphal and certain. We Christians are pilgrims walking into the mystery of God, not soldiers marching off to war. There is a great difference.

26

CREEDAL DEVELOPMENT IN THE CHRISTIAN CHURCH

Modern Non-Religious Man [and Woman] forms himself [or herself] by a series of denials and refusals, but he [or she] continues to be haunted by the realities he [or she] has refused and denied.

Mircea Eliade²

How did Christianity, which began in the powerful God intensity found in the man Jesus of Nazareth, change into an ecclesiastical, institutionalized religious system that has clearly defined creeds, doctrines and dogmas that have been imposed on the Western world with coercive and sometimes abusive force? To say the very least, that is quite a transition. This faith system is not intrinsically evil. That is not just my assertion. Christianity has in fact contributed things to our world of tremendous value. It preserved civilization through the dark ages. It produced exquisite music, architecture and art. It began the system of higher education that we today take for granted. It built the first hospitals and sought to establish a person's right to health care. It gave birth to the idea that life is sacred, an idea that still underlies our entire culture. Those are enormous, not trivial, accomplishments and they are not to be discounted or treated lightly.

However, Christianity has also given us religious persecution, religious wars and the Inquisition. It has produced a biblical fundamentalism that has endorsed slavery, oppressed women, justified wars, opposed scientific knowledge and persecuted homosexual persons. It has developed a history in which religious imperialism has sapped the meaning out of the very God that Christians claim to worship. It has helped to create a world where adherents of one religion feel compelled to kill adherents of another. So the question arises as to what there is inside religion in general and Christianity in particular that could compel us in these destructive directions.

Christianity was born in an experience. It moved, as all forming experiences do, into the apparently human necessity to explain that experience. Next it codified its own explanations so that they became creeds. Then it claimed for those creeds the authority of absolute truth. In time, it began to persecute and even to kill those who would not acknowledge the authority that was attributed to those creeds. In the process, it revealed ever so clearly what believers are loath to admit—namely, that religion is not primarily a search for truth; it is overwhelmingly a search for security.

Religion cannot really become organized unless it can be defined, nor can it be a source of security until it is defined. So religion needs to answer specific questions: For what do you stand? What do you believe? What makes you distinctive? But once those things are defined, religion always manifests its darkest, most destructive side. That is when we begin to hear the incredible claims of the frightfully fearful who require the possession of unchallenged authority. We have the Truth. Reject it at your own risk. We are God's messengers. To obey us is to obey God. There is no salvation outside the church. We control the doorway to God. All of these claims should sound familiar to the Christian world, for in varying levels of sophistication, those have been offered as the underlying messages of the Christian faith.

Most members of the church's hierarchy regard the creeds as the source of the church's unity. However, the fact is that the exact opposite is the case. The creeds actually guarantee the disunity of the church and were consciously intended and designed to do just that. That is a strong statement, resisted by many on first hearing, but history reveals that the primary purpose of any creed is to determine who it is that does not qualify for membership. Creeds are designed to separate the true believers from the false believers. Because creeds set boundaries, they inevitably divide.

Christianity began when people had a life-changing experience that was associated with one named Jesus of Nazareth. That experience, which called them beyond their boundaries into new dimensions of humanity, was accompanied by feelings of wonder, awe and wholeness. Yet that experience as yet had no shape or form. The best they could do at the beginning to put their experience into words was to utter an ecstatic cry. That is what Paul did when he exclaimed, "All this is from God, who through Christ reconciled us to himself. . . . That is, in Christ God was reconciling the world to himself" (2 Cor. 5:18–19). There is in this text no explanation of how God got into Christ, no discussion of when, no debate about if. Just an exclamation that somehow, in some way, through some means in the life of this Jesus, God had been encountered. That was our faith story's moment of truth. Shortly thereafter, a creed was formed to articulate that experience. Originally, it had only three words, all of which were rather vague: Jesus is *Maschiach!*

Maschiach was, as noted earlier, a Jewish word that literally meant "the anointed one." Those three words constituted the first attempt to develop a creed. Many people will assert that this was the best creed the church was destined ever to produce, primarily because it made no attempt to pin down the power of this God experience. It understood the fact that human minds might experience a sense of the holy but they will never be able to explain that dimension of their lives, to say nothing of being able to explain the fullness of God. So it was that this three-word creed left vast amounts of what might be called "wiggle room." At the very least this creed understood that God cannot be bound in human concepts. As history moved and Christianity became more institutionalized, however, the human need for the security of certainty overwhelmed the sense of awe and wonder in the experience of the divine and the creedal explanations of the church grew increasingly more complex and restrictive.

Most of the wiggle room in this original creed was found in the word *maschiach*. It entered the vocabulary of the Jews as a title for the king: Samuel anointed Saul to be king to rule over the children of Israel (1 Sam. 9:15–10:13). Later, disappointed with Saul, Samuel in an act of treasonous civil disobedience anointed the youthful David to be his successor (1 Sam. 16:1–13). As the power of the king grew in Jewish history, titles claimed by the king also grew, and so they were incorporated into the evolving word *maschiach*. The king is called "the son of God" in the Psalms: "You are my son; today I have begotten you" (2:7). This royal son of God was said to reign at God's right hand and was sometimes called the "son of man" (Ps. 80:17). Like all human words, *maschiach* took on new meanings as it journeyed through history.

When the royal family of the House of David was destroyed in the conquest of Judah by the Babylonians in the sixth century BCE, *maschiach* was set free to enter the fantasies, the hopes and the dreams of the Jews. It was then transformed into standing as a symbol for the ideal king who would on some future day come to restore the fortunes of Israel. That is how the concept of "messiah" entered the Jewish faith story.

As soon as *maschiach* was transformed into "messiah," a proliferation of messianic images came forth. For some *maschiach* was simply a white knight who would conquer the enemies of the Jews and restore the grandeur of the throne of David. For others *maschiach* was a divine being who would come at the end of the world to establish the reign of God. For still others he was a mythical servant who would absorb the pain and suffering of the world, creating in the process a new human wholeness. Even these images did not exhaust the possibilities. The heroes of the Jewish past began to be magnified in order to expand the range of messianic ideas—a new and greater Moses, a new and greater Elijah, one who fulfilled the scriptures, one who was understood against the symbols of ongoing Jewish worship. There was a veritable explosion of images so that when the earliest Christians affirmed that Jesus was *maschiach*, people heard many things according to how they understood *maschiach*. So it was that this first creed came to be translated: Jesus is Messiah! Jesus is the Christ! Jesus is Lord!

As Christianity moved out of the Jewish womb in which it was born and into the Greek-speaking Mediterranean world, words that had particular and peculiar meaning to these gentiles began to transform and replace the Jewish words. "Messiah" was deemphasized and the Greek equivalent, Christos, which was transliterated into the word "Christ," replaced it. In English, the title "Christ" has become almost the last name of Jesus. From the time of Paul Jesus was increasingly called simply Christ and not the original "*the* Christ," which is still a title. This meant that the followers of Jesus, who were originally the "followers of the way," became "followers of Christ" and ultimately Christians.

The more popular word, however, among the gentiles, and one that they understood in a variety of ways, was "Lord." As Christianity entered more and more into a gentile milieu, the word "Lord" moved their affirmations about Jesus increasingly beyond human concepts and into divine definitions. One can see this happening even in the gospel tradition. The story of Jesus' supernatural birth enters the Christian story in the writings of Matthew in the ninth decade of the Common Era. The understanding of the Easter event as a physiological resuscitation of a three-days-deceased body is the contribution primarily of Luke and John in the late ninth and tenth decades of the Common Era. The story of his cosmic ascension is a contribution Luke makes to the developing story, very briefly in his gospel (24:50–53) and then much more fully in the first chapter of the book of Acts (vv. 1–11), also written in the tenth decade.

Armed with these increasingly supernatural definitions of who Jesus was, believers began the creedal debate for real. How could Jesus be both human and divine? People knew he was human. He was "born of a woman, born under the law," said Paul (Gal. 4:4). He suffered under Pontius Pilate. He died and was buried. These events attested by every gospel writer stamped him with an uncomplicated humanity. It was inconceivable that a deity could suffer, die and be buried. Jesus was depicted as praying in Gethsemane and on the cross. The agony of those prayers was real. We are told that he prayed to a God he called "Abba," or Father. Jesus was not talking to himself. The witness of history was that Jesus was human.

Yet in that humanity, people believed that God had been encountered, met, received and experienced. So how was it that God came to dwell in a human life? This question engaged the Christian community for the first centuries of the Christian era. This was also the time when people found it more and more important to define the limits of faith, to remove the wiggle room in the earliest three-word affirmation. They were destined to move far beyond the limited debate as to whether *maschiach* should be rendered Messiah, Christ or Lord.

The church thus found itself in a deep and frequently bitter Christological debate that was destined to last for centuries. In the Greek world, the realm of the divine, which included God and heaven, was separated from the realm occupied by human beings on earth. The Greeks were dualistic, dividing bodies from souls, flesh from spirit, earth from heaven and God from the world. "Jesus is Lord" did not adequately convey to these gentile worshipers who

Jesus was. People, who claimed to be Christians, were defining what that meant in radically different ways. The chaos of uncertainty became intolerable. That is what set the stage for the expansion of the three-word creed. The faith into which people were being baptized needed clearer definition. A statement of faith was required to make the boundaries of Christian belief clear. Clear beliefs created the security of knowing that "we and only those who agree with us hold the truth." Unity in faith was to be achieved by drawing lines that would separate out those who did not believe adequately. The Christian church thus began to walk the long road that would lead to the persecution of heretics, the imposition of faith through warfare and era after era of religious intolerance.

That first expanded statement of faith was called "the Apostles' Creed." This title was a clever bit of propaganda, for it carried with it the suggestion that this was what the first apostles actually believed about Jesus. This statement of faith was thereby assumed to be rooted in antiquity, grounded in the experience of those who were closest to Jesus. It was, in fact, nothing more than an attempt to capture what Jude was speaking of in his epistle when he made reference to "the faith . . . delivered to the saints." By and large, all of the disciples, save for poor Judas, were acknowledged as saints by the time the Apostles' Creed evolved into its final form. That creed was thought to be necessary for catechetical teaching in preparation for baptism and confirmation. It cleaned up the lines of authority and it enhanced the power claims of the leaders of the church, who defined themselves as the successors of the apostles. All of these things were well served by claiming that what was in fact a third-century creedal statement of Christian beliefs was the actual faith of the apostles. There was only one liability implicit in that claim, but it was a major one: the assertion that this was the faith of the apostles was simply not true.

When this creed achieved its final form, it affirmed a trinitarian formula that the apostles had never even imagined. It followed a neat scheme, with one paragraph assigned to the Father, one to the Son and one to the Holy Spirit. It reflected the patriarchal era in human consciousness and referred to God as the masculine "Father." It identified this God as the creator of heaven and earth, which was a direct reference to the seven-day creation story of Genesis (1:1–2:3), in which God created the heavens by separating the waters under the firmament from the waters above the firmament and calling the firmament "Heaven" (vv. 6–8), and then God created the earth by gathering the waters below into a single place so that dry land would appear and calling the dry land "Earth" (vv. 9–10).

The Apostles' Creed affirms as literal history the story of the virgin birth, of which I am confident the original twelve had never heard since this tradition entered the Christian self-understanding after all of them had died. Certainly neither Paul nor Mark had ever heard of it. Paul never even mentions the name of Jesus' mother, but he does say that Jesus was born of a woman and was descended from the House of David. The word Paul uses for "woman" has no connotation of "virgin" in it. Mark portrays the mother of Jesus rather pejoratively: she thought Jesus was out of his mind and wanted to put him away. The last gospel, that of John, seems to contradict the birth narrative. Not only does he omit the birth tradition, about which he surely must by then have been aware, but also on two occasions he refers to Jesus as the son of Joseph (1:45, 6:42).

The Apostles' Creed clearly deflected the guilt that had accrued to the Romans for the death of Jesus by suggesting that it was only "under," and not at the hands of, Pontius Pilate that Jesus had been crucified and had died.

The framers of this creed opted for the phrase "on the third day," which indicates that another early dispute on the timing of the resurrection had been resolved. The earlier tradition, found in Mark, suggested that resurrection occurred "after" three days (8:31, 9:31, 10:34). Echoes of this earlier tradition are also found in Matthew's gospel, suggesting that this was the original understanding of that gospel writer (12:40, 27:63), before the pressure of making the dawn after the third day coincide with the first day of the week forced an accommodation into the timeline of the narratives. The assumption made in the Apostles' Creed was that three days was a literal measure of time and not the liturgical interpretive symbol that it surely seems to have been when the stories of the resurrection were first told. The affirmation that Jesus ascended into heaven derives from Acts 1:1–11 and clearly reflects a three-tiered universe. Yet the ascension as an event separate from the resurrection did not come into the Christian consciousness until the ninth or tenth decade. None of these concepts dates back to apostolic days; all were developed long after the apostles had departed this world.

Despite its name, the Apostles' Creed appears to have first circulated locally in the late second and third centuries as a kind of baptismal formula. In all probability it began with a variety of forms from church to church until by the end of the third century the rough edges had been smoothed over, its various emphases had been brought into harmony and it had achieved more or less its final form. The fact that neither its actual point of origin nor its author had ever been identified led to the convenient conclusion that it dated from the witness of the original twelve. With its general acceptance by common usage, it represented an enormous step away from the three-word creed that was the original summation of the church's faith and into the formulation of theological complexity, complete with doctrine, dogmas and the power to force conformity on the Christian community.

When a literal link back to the apostles became impossible to defend, the line of defense was that the Apostles' Creed was simply the working out "under the power of the Holy Spirit" of the original intention in the tradition that dates all the way back to the disciples of Jesus. Then it was said without embarrassment that the creed was exactly what the earliest Christians "had meant" when they called Jesus *maschiach*—Messiah, Christ and Lord. However, it is clear that the explanation of who Jesus was and is had become much more complex and to accommodate that complexity, the three-word original creed of the church had now expanded to a creed of ninety-three words. It would not end there.

The elusive unity that people hoped would develop around this creed also did not happen. Even with the creed expanded to its new length, the wiggle room was not removed. Many people said this creed, but they understood what it was saying and what they meant by it quite differently. No matter how hard they tried, they could not close out this perennial debate. They could not establish a consensus and they could not agree on the meaning of that faith which had been once "delivered to the saints." It did not occur to these people that the task they were trying to accomplish was not a human possibility, that the mystery of God, including the God they believed they had met in Jesus, could not be reduced to human words and human concepts or captured inside human creeds. Nor did they understand that the tighter and more specific their words became, the less they would achieve the task of unifying the church. All creeds have ever done is to define those who are outside, who are not true believers; and thus their primary achievement has been to set up an eternal conflict between the "ins" and the "outs," a conflict that has repeatedly degenerated into the darkest sort of Christian behavior, including imperialism, torture, persecution, death and war.

When Constantine won the battle at Milvian Bridge in 312 CE, he moved quickly to proclaim the Edict of Milan in 313 CE, which made the Christian religion, for the first time in its brief life, a legal religion within the Roman Empire. That edict changed the nature of Christianity dramatically and for all time. Christianity was no longer a persecuted sect. The same civil and political authorities that once had tried to stamp this movement out now relinquished their hostility and began to move first toward reconciliation and second toward submission. More important than that, the empire began to co-opt this religious tradition in the service of its own agenda, to unite the empire under a common religion and then to claim the power to put the empire's stamp of approval on particular ecclesiastical patterns. The Council at Nicaea was called by the emperor Constantine in the year 325 CE for the purpose of clarifying, presumably for all time, what the exact faith of the church was. The intention of the men who gathered for that council was to be able to state exactly what one must believe to be a Christian. The journey from three words to ninety-three words was about to be expanded mightily in that elusive quest for unity inside a clearly defined truth.

Can you imagine the task of forging an external Christian creed being the goal of a political convention? Conventions are places where deals are made, compromises are offered and secret backroom negotiations occur. How was "the faith which was once for all delivered to the saints" going to fare in this setting?

The real issue at the council that Constantine convened revolved around that perennial concern about the nature of the Christ figure. It was fought between the followers of Arius, who asserted that Jesus was "of like substance with the Father," and those who were followers of Athanasius, who asserted that Jesus was "of the same identical substance of the Father." Both camps were miles away from the Jesus of history. In the gospel of John (95–100 CE) Jesus had been identified with the eternal "logos" or "word" of God present in creation. The deification of Jesus that had been developing as the years went by was about to take an enormous leap forward. The Athanasians, who were the ultimate winners at this council, wanted to make sure that the divine nature of their Jesus was no longer subject to debate, that all the wiggle room had been removed from the Apostles' Creed.

When the smoke of battle cleared, the Christian church had a new creed that now contained two hundred and six words. From three to ninety-three to two hundred and six words represented a rather stunning chart of creedal growth and the expansion was related mostly to the task of erecting layers of defense around Jesus' divinity. He was declared to be "begotten of the Father before all worlds, God of God, Light of Light, very God of very God, begotten not made, of one substance with the Father by whom all things were made; who for us men [and women] and for our salvation came down from heaven and was incarnate by the Holy Ghost of the Virgin Mary and [only then] was made man." This creed was intended to close every loophole, to describe in a straightforward way the exact nature of the faith once delivered and to end the debate about the person of Jesus for all time. Anyone who did not subscribe to this creedal statement was separated from the church. As noted earlier, creeds never unite; they always divide. Creeds are boundary-makers.

As was inevitable, the Nicene Creed also failed in its unifying task. Wiggle room was not removed. The debate raged anew. A century or so later, another creed was adopted, called the Athanasian Creed after the winner at Nicaea, Athanasius. Unbelievably long and convoluted, it never became part of Christian liturgy. However, even with its six hundred and thirty-seven words, the debate was still not over. Finally the Council of Chalcedon in 451 CE sought to bring this debate to a conclusion, recognizing strangely enough that the task of clarifying what the church intended to teach about the nature of Christ could not be stated positively. Chalcedon succeeded only in saying what Jesus was *not*.

Anxious because God could not be reduced to a human formula, the leaders of the church contented themselves with the task of enforcing the faith they could not define. If one disagreed with these ever-more-differing explanations, one was simply evil. The problem was not in the words; it was in the hardened hearts of the heretics whose obstinacy and sinfulness prevented them from believing. The stage was thus set not for unity but for a purge. Whenever deviant beliefs were discovered, they had to be rooted out and those who espoused them killed in the service of conformity to the catholic faith. So Christianity turned demonic. Infidels like the Jews were constantly persecuted and Muslims as well as Jews were killed in the Crusades. Heretics were burned at the stake. Religious wars were waged to defeat anyone who did not worship properly. Efforts to force people to conform were accomplished by way of torture first and if that failed by execution.

The human need for certainty confronted the majesty and wonder of God and when it could not force the divine mystery into human concepts, expressed itself in violence and persecution. That was when Christians appealed to the authority of scripture and particularly to the text in Jude, seeking justification for their evil. Such an appeal, however, never works. There is no such thing as a set of propositions that constitute "the faith . . . delivered to the saints." That is nothing but idolatry. Why are uncertainty and humility before the Ultimate Mystery vices rather than virtues? Or is it the very nature of religion to demand conformity and when it is not received to turn violent and destructive? If that is so, should we not be done with it? Dietrich Bonhoeffer once proposed that we develop a "religionless Christianity." Perhaps the time has come to do just that!

If Christianity could separate itself from Judaism at the end of the first century in order to become the religion of the emerging empire, is it possible that Christianity in our generation might separate itself from religion in order to enter into a universal human consciousness? I think that is exactly the challenge of our time in history: a religionless Christianity must be born; a humanistic Christianity must come into being. That is the vision of a reformation that I see beginning to dawn. I will return to this idea in the closing section, and ultimately in a subsequent book.

27

SINCE I HAVE THE TRUTH, "NO ONE COMES TO THE FATHER BUT BY ME"

The only redeemer of God's elect is the Lord Jesus Christ.

Others, not elected, although they may be called by the ministry of the Word, and may have some common operations of the Spirit, yet they never truly come unto Christ, and therefore cannot be saved: Much less can men, not professing the Christian religion, be saved in any other way whatsoever, be they ever so diligent to frame their lives according to the light of nature [general revelation], and the laws of that religion they do profess. And, to assert and maintain that they may, is very pernicious, and is to be detested.

from the Westminster Confession, framed after the Reformation by Presbyterians in 1646

I f a particular religious system possesses the truth—something "once delivered," in an unchangeable form, to its founders, as the epistle of Jude seems to claim—then it quickly follows that this system clearly has a monopoly on salvation or on the pathway to the holy. So it should not be surprising to see that claim registered vigorously and most often offensively. If salvation is found only in our faith tradition, then those who are outside our system are lost, benighted or invincibly ignorant. If they are lost, any conversion tactic or missionary strategy is appropriate, for it is our duty and our burden "under God" to reach out to save them whether they want to be saved or not. If they are benighted, we can relate to them and their religious understandings as pitiable, uninformed and primitive without ever bothering to understand the role those religious values play in their corporate life. Finally, if they are invincibly ignorant, then any tactic that might be used to open them to truth can be justified. That makes cruelty, torture and warfare in the pursuit of the purity of religion quite legitimate. This kind of religious imperialism requires that its adherents be convinced that they, and they alone, possess absolute truth. The ever-present effect of this religious mentality is to diminish both the practices and the being of anyone who might stand outside the system for which these claims are being made. That diminishment in turn makes the outsiders fit objects for both conversion and missionary activity. All this flows from the claim that the ultimate truth of God has been or can be captured by any religious system.

Most of the missionary hymns of the Christian church were written in the service of these definitions during the eighteenth and nineteenth centuries. The nineteenth century, which church historian Kenneth Scott Latourette has described as the greatest period of Christian expansion,[3] just happens also to have been the greatest century of colonial conquest as well. That is not coincidental. However, the leaders of the Christian church never seemed to link the two in their minds or in their rhetoric. Perhaps they never heard the lament of native people that when the missionaries came, the missionaries had the Bible and the native people had the land. After the arrival of the missionaries, they and their descendants had the land and the native people had the Bible.

Missionaries in the nineteenth century were highly romantic figures who sacrificed the comforts of their advanced civilizations and sometimes even the well-being of their own children to answer the call of God to rescue the lost of the world from the fires of hell reserved for the unbelievers. Let it be said that some of these people were truly dedicated and brought many gifts of great value to areas of the world where standards of living were very low; nonetheless, the missionary effort itself was baseborn, deeply compromised, and quite imperialistic.

The old missionary hymns make that abundantly clear. Reginald Heber's hymn "From Greenland's icy mountains" winds up its last stanza with the assertion, "They call us to deliver their land from error's chain." Earlier this hymn had asked, "Can we whose souls are lighted with wisdom from on high, can we to men benighted, the lamp of life deny?"[4] Some of the images employed in these missionary hymns are quite military. I think of the hymn that proclaims, "Fling out the banner, . . ." as if an army were on the march, and concludes with words that make that concept absolutely clear: "We conquer only in that sign."[5] Still other hymns of that day refer to those "who yet have never heard the truth that comes from Jesus, the glory of his word." Among the people described in that hymn are those who inhabit the great forests of Africa where, the hymn suggests, "apes swing to and fro."[6]

As always, these offending attitudes were related to the words of scripture. The favorite text used by the missionaries in general and imperialistic Christians in particular was a verse in John's gospel in which Jesus is quoted as having said, "No one comes to the Father, but by me" (14:6). That became the basis for the ultimate assertion that Christians alone control the doorway into God. If you do not come to God through Christ, you cannot get there. It was a powerful claim wrapped inside a text that has been the source of enormous pain to many people. It is still quoted in Christian circles to justify religious bigotry and even religious persecution. It is a text, therefore, that demands inclusion in this series on the "sins of scripture."

"No one comes to the Father, but by me" is also a text that invariably comes up when I am lecturing on the vision of an interfaith future. It seems to be a hurdle that people must get over to break the spell of their romantic imperialism. So the question becomes: Does this text actually support this claim? The answer to that question is simple. It does so only if one is profoundly ignorant of the New Testament scholarship of the last two hundred years, only if one literalizes the Bible and finally only if one knows nothing about the Fourth Gospel in which alone this text occurs. I begin this analysis by putting these Johannine words under a microscope.

"No one comes to the Father, but by me" is only the last half of this Johannine verse. The first half constitutes the sixth in a list of sayings that the author of this book attributes to Jesus. All of them include the words "I am." This text reads in full, "I am the way, and the truth, and the life. No one comes to the Father, but by me." These "I am" sayings are all familiar: "I am the bread of life" (6:35), "I am the light of the world" (8:12), "I am the door of the sheep" (10:7), "I am the Good Shepherd" (10:11), "I am the Resurrection and the Life" (11:25), "I am the way, the truth and the life" (14:6) and "I am the vine, ye are the branches" (15:5). Several of these are repeated more than once. The words "I am" are used in other sayings attributed to Jesus by this gospel writer: one thinks immediately of such Johannine verses as "Before Abraham was, I am" (8:58) and "When you see the Son of Man lifted up, then you shall know I am" (8:28, my translation). The RSV translators, failing to understand this last saying, have added the words "that" and "he" to the text. They thus make it read, "Then you shall know *that* I am *he*," but there is no "that" or "he" in the original Greek. John has a purpose in the use of this "I am" symbol that these translators simply have not grasped.

Of course, Jesus never literally said any of these things. For someone to wander around the Jewish state in the first century, announcing himself to be the bread of life, the resurrection or the light of the world would have brought out people in white coats with butterfly nets to take him away. None of the earlier gospel writers give us any indication that any of them had ever heard it suggested before that Jesus taught this way. The "I am" sayings are clearly the contribution to the tradition of the Fourth Gospel. What then do they mean? Why did John add these sayings to the ongoing Christian tradition? The answer is found in the period of history in which the Fourth Gospel was written.

Allow me to go back and repeat the major events in the turbulent 70s that afflicted the Jews. In 70 CE the city of Jerusalem fell to the Roman army in the climactic battle of the Galilean War, which had begun in 66 CE. The nation of Judah after that battle disappeared from the maps of human history. The Jewish capital of Jerusalem was reduced to rubble. The temple and the priesthood were no more. I referenced this bit of history earlier in my effort to describe how the figure of Judas arose. Now I need to carry it further to clarify why the separation of the Christians from the Jews was so bitter.

The disciples of Jesus were destined not to separate from the synagogue's worshiping community before about 88 CE. Until that moment, they continued to think of themselves as Jews who found in Jesus a new way to approach the God of Israel. They were aware that throughout the empire, gentiles were coming into the Jesus movement, but these gentiles had agreed to be respectful of Jewish traditions even if they did not adopt them (see Acts 15).

The compelling task of the first Jewish disciples of Jesus was to relate the story of Jesus to the traditions of their Jewish faith. That is why the gospels are filled with references to Jesus as the fulfillment of the prophets. That is why Moses stories are retold about Jesus. For example, the story of a wicked king who sought to destroy the promised deliverer by killing Jewish boy babies was told about both Moses and Jesus (compare Exod. 1:22 with Matt. 2:16–18), and there are obvious parallels between Moses' Red Sea experience and Jesus' baptism and between Moses wandering for forty years in the wilderness and Jesus wandering for forty days in the wilderness. That same attempt to connect Jesus to the traditions of the Jewish faith explains why Elijah stories were wrapped around Jesus. For example, both Jesus and Elijah ascended into heaven (compare 2 Kings 2:1–12 with Acts 1:1–11), and both poured spirit out on their disciples.

As the orthodox party after the defeat of the Jewish nation grew more and more fundamentalist, however, their ability to tolerate these revisionist Jews who kept reinterpreting the Jewish scriptures lessened. The very existence of these "revisionists" seemed to proclaim that the Torah was not perfect, that something more had to be added. Thus these Jesus people appeared to relativize the orthodox claims about the completeness of the Torah, which meant they tampered with the ultimate source of the security of the orthodox Jews. The tensions grew more and more strained until finally the rupture occurred and the followers of Jesus were excommunicated from the synagogue by the orthodox Jews. The hostility that flowed between the two groups was fierce and bitter. "You are no longer part of the faith of your mothers and fathers," the orthodox party would shout. "You no longer can claim Abraham, Isaac, Jacob and Joseph as your fathers in faith. You are no longer part of the traditions of Moses and the Torah."

The excommunicated revisionists fought back with counterclaims. Playing on the Torah's opening chapter, John wrote, "In the beginning was [not just God, as the Torah claims, but] the Word" (1:1). What we have met in Jesus, the revisionists said, is that Word enfleshed. They used the Greek word *Logos* to communicate Jesus' relationship with God. Jesus was identified with the Word of God that came forth in the dawn of creation and thus he was more deeply related to the Jewish God than either Abraham or Moses. In other words, the revisionists were claiming to be more orthodox than the orthodox! They possessed in Jesus the earliest revelation of God in creation. To make this identity even more specific and concrete, the Christians began to say that the God who revealed the divine name as "I am who I am" to Moses at the burning bush (see Exod. 3:14) was the same God they had met in Jesus of Nazareth.

So the battle raged on, as all battles do when religious feelings are at stake. The gospel of John was the product of these excommunicated revisionists. That is why references appear in this gospel to the followers of Jesus being put out of the synagogue (see 9:22 and 12:42). That is why this gospel reinterprets the opening chapter of the Torah (compare John 1 with Gen. 1). That is also why this gospel, over and over again, claims the divine name "I am" for Jesus of Nazareth. The Christians (formerly the revisionist Jews) were saying, "We have met the holy God who was once revealed to Moses and who has now been revealed anew, and perhaps more fully, in Jesus. We are not separated from the God of our fathers and mothers as the orthodox party was asserting. Jesus is the very way through which we walk into the same divine mystery that our ancestors in faith also knew. We know of no other way that we can come to the God of our fathers and mothers except through this Jesus." That was a testimony to their experience. It was not a prescription claiming that they possessed the only doorway into the only God. It is amazing to me that this attempt on the part of the early disciples of Jesus to validate their experience journeying through Jesus into the mystery of the God they had known in Israel would someday be used to judge all other religious traditions as unworthy, wrong or even evil. Yet that is the path this text has followed as Christianity moved from minority status into majority power.

There is a difference between my experience of God and who God is. There is a difference between affirming that I walk into the mystery of God through the doorway called Jesus and that in my experience this is the only doorway that works in my journey, and asserting that there is no doorway through which anyone can walk except mine. Imagine the idolatry present in the suggestion that God must be bound by my knowledge and my experience! Yet that claim has been made and is still being made by imperialistic Christians today. The text written by persecuted minority members of the early Christian community to justify their claim to be part of the larger people of God becomes a text that is interpreted in such a way as to become a claim that issues in religious imperialism. Is it not interesting how little attention is paid to another text that proclaims an open and inclusive faith? It is found in the words attributed to Peter in Acts 10:34ff.: "Truly I perceive that God shows no partiality, but in every nation any one who fears him and does what is right is acceptable to him."[7]

We live in a religiously pluralistic world, but there is only one God. This God is not a Christian, nor is this God an adherent of *any* religious system. All religious systems are human creations by which people in different times and different places seek to journey into that which is ultimately holy and wholly other. Until that simple lesson is heard, human beings will continue to destroy each other in the name of the "one true God."

28

MY VISION OF AN INTERFAITH FUTURE

All positive religion rests on an enormous simplification of the manifold and wildly engulfing forces that invade us: it is the subduing of the fullness of existence. All myth, in contrast, is the expression of the fullness of existence, its images, its signs; it drinks incessantly from the gushing fountains of life. Hence religion fights myth where it cannot absorb and incorporate it.

Martin Buber [8]

There is a specific antidote in the gospels that challenges the exclusiveness that is claimed by the words "No one comes to the Father, but by me." It is found in three sayings attributed to Jesus in the synoptic tradition that at first glance appear to be quite similar. Closer examination, however, reveals them to be not only radically different, but diametrically opposed. Each illustrates how a saying can get twisted when the context in which it is spoken is different. I am certain that behind their textual confusion there was an original, consistent and inclusive saying of Jesus. The present confusion reveals much about how the religious needs of people drive us to accentuate the negative when we are in conflict with another faith tradition.

These three sayings are found in Mark 9:40, Matthew 12:30 and Luke 9:50. Because this difference is so important, I want my readers to see them exactly as they are printed in the gospels themselves. I quote from the translation we call the Revised Standard Version:

Mark 9:40: "*He that is not against us is for us.*"

Matt. 12:30: "*He who is not with me is against me.*"

Luke 9:50: "*He that is not against you is for you.*"

The wording is so similar that we almost have to read these verses twice to catch the difference, even if the difference is profound.

Mark is the earliest writer, so one might suggest that his version is the original one. In his rendition of this saying of Jesus is the suggestion that Christian allies are the ones who are not overtly negative to those people or concepts in the Jesus movement. That removes the claim that there is only one true pathway to God, and it opens the door to countless ancillary relationships.

Both Matthew and Luke have Mark in front of them when they write. However, Matthew changes this text into the exact reverse of what Mark has suggested that Jesus said. He has Jesus declare that if you are not in complete agreement with him, then you are against him. His suggestion is that people are either in or out of the Christian movement. There are no gray areas. That attitude supports the "only my way" mentality and closes the door to everyone who is not single-minded in devotion to that primary way of acting and believing. Luke, who writes after Matthew, reverts to the Marcan original and once again poses Jesus as suggesting that even in a religious world, agreement to walk arm in arm does not require unanimity of belief or identity in practice. In other words, two out of three renditions of this saying of Jesus are open to a variety of approaches to the wonder of God, while one out of three says there is only one way: agree with me or you are against me. To our great discredit, institutional Christianity has always acted on the basis of the minority report of Matthew.

This did not constitute a critical issue for anyone but the Jews through most of the centuries of Christianity simply because the world was so large and communications were so slow that generally we lived in great ignorance of other people and other religions. Even as recently as the nineteenth century, during the War of 1812, which was in some sense round two of the American Revolution, the final battle of New Orleans was fought well after the treaty of peace had been signed. The word of peace did not get through to Andrew Jackson, the American general, for some three months. Communications are so rapid and the world is so small today that such an occurrence would now be inconceivable.

Because the Jews lived primarily as minority voices in a predominantly Christian world, however, they bore the brunt of the fact that they were different. They stood outside the majority system. No one stopped to ask what were the things Jews and Christians had in common, the areas in which they walked together. Yet those binding shared realities included such significant things as a single unbroken religious heritage, one God, a commitment to ethical behavior as the way to serve that God, the requirement to love that God with our hearts, souls, minds and strength and to love our neighbors as ourselves and finally a willingness to care for and show mercy to all who are in need. Surely in these great commitments, Jews and Christians could never have been against each other. But that is not how the relationship was acted out. Imperial Christianity simply asserted, "Christians have the truth; the Jews are not Christians and do not accept Christ as Messiah, so they are not with us," which was interpreted to mean, "They are against us." So Jews were treated as enemies of Christianity, to our great shame and to their great persecution.

The rest of the religions of the world were simply not on our radar screen for most of Christian history. Of course, there were moments when we touched each other. The journeys of Marco Polo made us vaguely aware of the religions of Asia. The rapid growth of Islam after the death of the prophet Muhammad caused the Christian world and the Islamic world to bump into each other on the edges of the Mediterranean Sea, in Turkey, in Croatia and in North Africa. The Battle of Tours in 732 CE stopped the encroachment of Islam into Christian Europe and divided the world into religious spheres of influence. The Crusades represented a hostile invasion of Christian power into Islamic strongholds. Each of these, however, was minor in the scheme of things, and none of the great religious systems of the world ever really interacted with each other except on the most superficial of levels. So all of our grand religious claims to be the true faith, to have a corner on the market of salvation, never really got tested. They remained as the pious mantras of an unchallenged religious system. We assumed the truth of our claims without fear of being contradicted by reality. That luxury lasted until airplanes, radio, television, the Internet and the World Wide Web came along and changed the world.

In the twentieth century, however, the Western world, by engaging during World War II with the empire of Japan, discovered a non-Christian religion that was so vibrant that Japanese pilots would dive their planes into American and British ships in suicide missions because "to die for the emperor is to live forever." It was startling both to the Western psyche and to our religious consciousness to realize that a "pagan" religion could elicit such levels of devotion. In the Korean War, we watched the Chinese army accept losses that would have been intolerable in the Western world because the religions of China did not affirm the value of individual life in the same way that the Christian West had always done. We found it difficult to defend ourselves against an army that would run wave after wave of troops over a field of land mines, allowing the later waves to go safely once the first waves had cleared the mines with their now deceased bodies. It was another witness to the power of what we thought of pejoratively as a "pagan" religion. In the Vietnam War, we watched Buddhist monks immolate themselves in acts of religiously inspired protest. Buddhism, we discovered, still possessed great power. In the 1970s and '80s, we confronted Islamic power tied to oil—power that had the ability to topple Jimmy Carter, a sitting president, and to require the *Wall Street Journal* to hire its first religion writer, Gustav Niebuhr, since religion, even a "pagan" religion, now had economic consequences. Today we face the specter of Muslim militants who do not hesitate to offer themselves in suicide missions if it furthers their religious aims. The *New York Times* quoted a young Islamic fanatic speaking in a mosque in West Virginia as saying, "To love the Prophet Muhammad is to hate those who hate him."[9]

A veritable renaissance of religious terror now confronts us and is making against us the claims we have long made against religious traditions different from our own. It feels very different when we confront the religious claims of being the true faith, of controlling access to God, of being committed to the task of converting the world to our religious thinking and discover that we are the object of that religious invective rather than being the ones who are making the claims. The time has surely come to abandon what was a minority idea in the gospels, created when Matthew changed Mark's original wording—the idea that for one not to be identical in faith with us is to be our enemy. The probability is that the literal word of Jesus was the original text as Mark recorded it,[10] and that earlier wording suggested that if other religious traditions are not against us, they are in fact for us. Jews, Buddhists, Muslims and Hindus are not against our religion, so we can embrace them as sisters and brothers, honor the pathway that each walks in their quest for God and begin a new era of religious cooperation. We can lay down the misinterpreted claim that we possess the only doorway to God.

Does the interfaith future mean that all the religious traditions of the world must seek to come together in an attempt to find our lowest common denominator? I do not think so. That would only reduce each tradition to something bare and bleak. It would be nothing more than a manifestation of our least divisive and therefore least characteristic affirmations. No richness, no uniqueness would be found there.

Is our only alternative then to seek to honor positive traditions in all religious systems, creating in the process a pantheon large enough to hold us all together, a religion of consensus where the edges are blurred and the divisions are papered over? Some traditions, like B'hai, seek to do that, and they do it with great integrity, but that pathway, while positive for many, does not seem to me to offer the best hope for either religious toleration or a religious future.

I propose, rather, a different route into what I think is our inevitable interfaith future. Each of us as participants in our own particular faith must journey into the very heart of the tradition that claims our loyalty. I, as a Christian, must plumb the depths and scale the heights of my own faith system. I must learn to separate the essence of Christianity from the compromises this religious system has made through history. It is tribal boundaries, not creedal affirmations, that most deeply shape the various Christian denominations. In the New World, Lutherans come from northern Germany and Scandinavia, Anglicans from England, Presbyterians from Scotland, Roman Catholics from Ireland and southern Europe and so on. We Christians must journey beyond these forced political divisions to the core of our faith and there allow ourselves to discover its essence, to enter its meaning and finally to transcend its limits. We do that, however, while still clinging to what we call our ultimate Truth and what we regard as our "pearl of great price." That must also be the pathway that every Jew, Muslim, Buddhist, Hindu and any other participant in any other religion of the world must walk.

Then—when we have all walked into our own depths, found the deepest essence of what our faith is all about and separated out that essence from the compromises of history—we can each lift up what is our most precious gift. I envision the adherents of these various faith traditions of the world all sitting in a circle of equals addressing one another. I, as a Christian, would say to the others, "This is the essence of Christianity that I have discovered on my journey; this is my 'pearl of great price,' and I want to offer it to you." Then the Jew would say, "This is the essence of Judaism, my 'pearl of great price,' and I want to offer it to you." In turn, the Muslim, the Buddhist, the Hindu and any other would do the same. No one sacrifices his or her own tradition. Every person is enriched by the gifts of others. Competition fades into complementarity. Each of us becomes richer and more full. Our humanity is enhanced; the threat, the fear and the need to conquer disappear. The opportunity to share replaces them. The world moves out of the quest for tribal or religious survival and into an interfaith future in which the pathway each of us walks into holiness is honored and we recognize that the essential truth about all religion is its goal, not its highway. No system captures God. All systems finally empty into God.

No one holds a corner on the market of salvation. There is no one way into God that all must follow if they hope to arrive. There is, however, an Ultimate Reality beyond all human religious traditions. We call that Reality God, and into that Reality all religious systems must journey. We follow our own path with integrity. We spit on no alternative path that might shake our confidence. We join hands in our common humanity and rejoice in the journey that each of us has taken. A new day dawns and it maybe begins to look vaguely like the Realm of God.

READING SCRIPTURE AS EPIC HISTORY

29

THE HEBREW SCRIPTURES COME INTO BEING

Blessed Lord, who caused all Holy Scriptures to be written for
our learning: Grant us so to hear them, read, mark and inwardly
digest them.

Book of Common Prayer[1]

Part 1: The Dawn of Human History

In the ancient Greek world there were two epic poems that citizens of that day
treasured. They were called the *Iliad* and the *Odyssey*. Under the guise of describing the ancient history of the Greek people, which included their mighty
military exploits, these epic poems accomplished an even more important
function in human development. The *Iliad* and the *Odyssey* told their people
who they were, what their life was all about, why they held the values they did
and how their human fears and anxieties could be managed or conquered.
The *Iliad* and the *Odyssey* thus provided the people with a mirror into which
they could gaze at themselves. That is what an epic is, and so the rise of the
epic poems represented a new stage in human development.

These narratives were the means by which human beings, who were at
that time only beginning to understand the idea of history, could embrace
the meaning of time. The *Iliad* and the *Odyssey* enabled people to relive vicariously the exploits of their ancestors, so they served to stretch the human

consciousness until men and women could begin to see themselves as people who had a past that could be remembered and a future that could be anticipated. In this manner, time-bound creatures began to contemplate timelessness. Finite men and women began to enter infinity and earth-bound people began to engage the experience of transcendence. The poet Homer, whoever he was—and it matters not if he was one person or many persons—captured in this poetry something of the essence of what it meant to be human and of what humanity looked like to people perhaps five thousand years before the Common Era.

The *Iliad* and the *Odyssey* surely began as oral stories passed on by word of mouth. That was essential, because no written language existed in the early days of human consciousness.

Most people are not aware of how recent the development of written language is. It came as a surprise to the European explorers who first touched the shores of the New World to discover that among the native American people they found here, there was no such thing as a written language. Anthropologists now believe that the native Americans migrated from Asia across the Bering Strait sometime between fifteen thousand and twenty-five thousand years ago, when Asia and North America were still connected by a land bridge.

Spoken language appears to be no older than fifty thousand years, having begun, anthropologists now believe, in the Upper Paleolithic Period, while written language appears to be no older than five to ten thousand years. These two steps, however—learning first how to speak and then how to write—were dramatic steps in our human evolutionary development, and together they ushered us into self-consciousness, which was the experience that finally separated human beings from the natural world that had produced them. If one defines human life as marked by language and self-consciousness, we are a very late development in the history of the world.

Words are by definition abstractions, which serve to unify the common experience of those who develop them. The use of words implies the ability to remember. That is why students of language believe that nouns were the first thing to enter human vocabulary. Our ancestors used nouns to name things that looked alike, both inanimate things and animate things. It is of interest to note that in the oldest biblical story of creation, Adam named all the animals as God created them (Gen. 2:19–20). Nouns were born when the same sound was applied by common consensus to various manifestations of the same thing. That is how a rabbit, a bird, a fish, a bush, a flower, a tree, a fruit, a tiger, water or a dwelling place, just to name a few, came to be known. A new noun would have to be developed whenever a new thing entered the human consciousness with consistency.

Adjectives to modify these nouns came next, pushing language beyond the specific to the abstract. Since all tigers, rabbits, trees and fruits were not the same, descriptive words developed to distinguish them from one another. I suspect that words for size, taste and color came first. These developed adjectives pushed language deeper into abstraction. For example, color emerged when these speaking creatures observed the same color on more than one thing: a red flower, a red leaf and a red bird; or a black dog, a black lynx and black coal; a white cloud, a white duck and a white bear. Things that had a color in common gave rise to the much more abstract ideas of redness, blackness and whiteness.

Verbs appear to have developed next. A mind that remembers, that lives in the flow of time, was essential for this development to take place. People needed to describe what it is that creatures or plants do: rabbits run, birds fly, fish swim, plants grow, flowers bloom, trees bear fruit. In this way action, which requires a sense of the passing of time, remembering what things were and anticipating what things will become, entered the human vocabulary.

Pronouns probably came next and since pronouns are abstract nouns, they served to increase the flexibility of language. They not only enabled our speech to expand, but once again forced our consciousness to stretch. Adverbs were born when actions needed modifiers. Some birds flew higher; some animals ran faster; some humans grew older. But once again this process took centuries.

Putting sounds, now turned into words, into recognizable written signs was an incredible advance, but one that was absolutely essential to human development. Written language probably began when trade required some mechanism for counting, but of that almost no certainty is guaranteed. What is certain is that this new skill of writing, the process of making words into symbols, enabled a cohesive sense of community to develop within the tribe. It was also through writing that people began to pass on to their successive generations the most basic questions of self-awareness: Who am I? Where did I come from? Who are my ancestors? What is my purpose? Why am I here?

What is my meaning, my destiny? Why was I born? It was in the experience of answering these questions that every people walking through history developed an epic of self-understanding. An epic was first oral, but as it found expression in the growth of written language it began to enter into timelessness, transcending generations.

Some ancient tribes did not remain an identifiable people long enough for their epic history to achieve written form and so it perished without a trace. Other tribes lost their epic after they were defeated or enslaved and their history was incorporated into the epic of a more dominant and successful tribe of people. The epics that endured, like the *Iliad* and the *Odyssey*, were powerful devices in human development and therefore epics that must be valued as a great reservoir of human wisdom. Each epic sought to explain the existence of the earth and the centrality of the people whose story it was. As such it began to explain how their values emerged, what was the significance of their achievements and why it was that a particular people basked in the favor of the gods or God.

Exorbitant claims were in time always made for these epic tales. At the very least the gods or God had directed the affairs about which the epics were written. Then the values espoused in the epics were said to be values of that which was called divine. Next it was said that these gods had inspired the human authors to write as they did. Finally, for some people, the writings themselves came to be held in such high esteem as the source of all wisdom that they were said to be the very words of God, holy, true, unchanging and inerrant. That is a familiar pathway that has been traveled by many an epic. Every epic is the sacred history of the people who created it.

So I invite you to journey with me into the biblical origins, a journey that must begin by setting aside the idea that a supernatural being either wrote or inspired the narratives. Only then will we ever be able to see why these epics are still worthy of being honored in a special way.

Part 2: The Hebrew *Iliad*—the Yahwist Document (ca. 950 BCE)

Like other ancient tribes, the Hebrew people had an *Iliad* and an *Odyssey*. The Hebrew *Iliad* is called by scholars today the "Yahwist Document." It is the oldest continuous narrative that we can identify in the Bible. It seems to have achieved written form during the middle years of the tenth century before the birth of Jesus. The Hebrew *Odyssey* is called the "Elohist Document." It is the second oldest continuous narrative that we can identify in the Bible. It dates from the middle years of the ninth century before the birth of Jesus. Both epics give evidence of having been orally transmitted for centuries before achieving written form. These epics had an interesting relationship, beginning separately, merging and undergoing massive revisions in the light of a changing history.

Like all epics, these ancient Jewish sacred traditions were designed to explain some of the observed mysteries of their very human experience. Why do people become ill if they eat certain foods? What is the source of evil? Why do human beings feel alienated from the world of nature? Why are there differences in language? Why is this land our land? Why is God our God? How did we become God's chosen people? Epics always address the questions of existence. The Jewish epics were no different. These questions, found in every national epic, are all but universal. They are human questions designed to help human beings make sense out of their existence.

When the Yahwist writer wrote the original strand of the Jewish faith history, the author did so from within a very specific historical context. The Jewish nation was settled victoriously in what they called their "Promised Land." A monarchy of some power had been established. A city named Jerusalem had been conquered and transformed into the capital city of the Jews. That city had originally been erected on a hill, making it easily defensible. Jerusalem also possessed an internal water supply, which was the basis of its life. Inside that city a temple, in which the God of the Jews might live, was promised and indeed might well have been actually under construction. That temple would solidify the claims that God had chosen the Jews for a special purpose. This writer had access to the rich oral history of his people. Part of that history purported to tell the story of how the world was made. It was primitive and quite patriarchal. God created the first human being, who was fashioned in a "hands on" way, which suggested that God had molded the dust of the earth into a human form and then had breathed life into this form through the creature's nostrils.

A sense of alienation that was deep in the human psyche, however, could not be ignored. So the story was told of the human family's expulsion from the Garden of Eden and the separation from the Creator that resulted from that expulsion. The human quest was a quest for a restoration of unity with

God and/or nature. This would be a dominant theme of the Jewish epic. These people who saw themselves as the direct descendants of the original man and woman would, according to their sacred story, seek to build a tower so tall it could reach the heavens in an attempt to be one with God. That project would fail. It did, however, help them account for the fact that each tribe spoke a different language. One of the descendants of Adam was then said to have been chosen by God to help overcome this alienation. That is why God called Abraham to leave Ur of the Chaldeans in order to form a new people. The struggles of this people to survive and to keep the dream of restoration alive is chronicled in wondrous detail. In the pursuit of their destiny, this chosen people did not always follow the traditional laws by which the people of the world seemed to operate. For example, it was Isaac, the second son of Abraham, not Ishmael, the firstborn, who was to be the heir of the promise. It was Jacob, the second son of Isaac, not Esau, the firstborn, who was to be the line through which the life of this nation was to flow.

The enemies who lived in the world around these special people defeated them, enslaved them, corrupted them and exiled them, but God's promise was never lost and that meant that God's faithfulness required that the promise be redeemed. Their destiny was to be the nation through whom all the nations of the earth would be blessed. It was a high purpose, a noble vocation.

As the Yahwist writer put this oral history into writing, it was the monarch, the city of Jerusalem and the temple that seemed to this author to guarantee the promise. God had anointed David to begin the monarchy. God had led David to conquer Jerusalem and to transform it into the holy city of God. God had instructed David's son and heir, King Solomon, to build the temple. So the Yahwist writer's view of all the world and all of human history was seen through the lens of these three institutions. God, to the Yahwist writer, seemed to work from the top down. God made the divine covenant with the king. Through the king the people were incorporated into the covenant. God began the ordered tradition of divine worship that marked these people's lives with Aaron, the brother of Moses and the first high priest. Through obedience to the high priest and the temple, the people were incorporated into this worship. To rebel against the king, the temple or the priest was to rebel against God. As long as these institutions existed, the promises of God were in effect. That was the operative thesis of the author.

The writer of this first Jewish epic called God by the name of Yahweh, or at least that is our best guess as to how the Jewish letters JHWH or YHVH were pronounced. In one sense the name for God was never to be uttered, for to speak the holy name implied some control over the one whose name it was. That constituted, of course, the definition of blasphemy.

The Yahwist Document was the Hebrew *Iliad*. It described the origins of the Jews. It articulated their destiny. It told the people by whom that epic was created who they were, why they mattered, where they had come from, who God was and why the Jews were special people. It was their defining story. In this epic the earliest strand of the Hebrew Bible is located. It was not, however, destined to remain a single story.

But this was the first step through which the Bible came into being. To grasp this origin is to take the first step in the process of reclaiming the Bible as a worthy guide to our life today. This is neither to denigrate the Bible nor to demote it. It is, however, to be honest about the Bible and to sweep away the excessive claims that have been laid upon it. Perhaps as the story unfolds we will grow more comfortable with this first conclusion.

Part 3: The Hebrew *Odyssey*—the Elohist Document (ca. 850 BCE)

The Yahwist Document, the Hebrew *Iliad*, hardly looked like the "Word of God" in its earliest form. Neither did the "Elohist Document," which I think of as the Hebrew *Odyssey*. It too rose out of a very human situation that marked the Jewish nation about a century after the Yahwist document was written. It grew not only out of a time but also out of a situation that rendered the Yahwist document no longer able to be the defining story for part of the Jewish people. That is why a new epic was required, or perhaps at the very least a new chapter in the ongoing epic of the Jewish people. We look now briefly at step two in the very human development of what we would later call the Bible.

The Jewish nation, as we noted earlier, was never really a unified people. Perhaps that was because they were the union of two different tribes with two different histories. In a real sense it was a merger that never quite merged, leaving a cleavage as big as a fault line deep in the middle of Jewish history. That division was always acknowledged in their sacred literature.

Scholars, historians and anthropologists go back to the moment of the Exodus to locate the original separateness that would always plague the Hebrew people. To understand this division requires that we challenge one of the basic assumptions we have all made about biblical history.

The overwhelming probability is that not all of the Jews were numbered among the escaping slaves from Egypt. Enslaved people in Egypt appear to have been only a segment, albeit a significant segment, of the people who would someday create the story of the national history of the Jews. The other constituent part of the Jewish nation appears to have been nomadic Semites who roamed the wilderness and never were the slaves of Egypt. The escaping slave people recognized an ethnic kinship with these fellow Semites and so formed an alliance with them during their wilderness years. This merger may have occurred in a place called Kadesh in the wilderness of Zin, for there are numerous references in the Hebrew scriptures to the fact that the children of Israel resided there for some period of time.

The name Kadesh appears first in Genesis 14:17. It was identified with Ishmael in Genesis 16:14. Abraham dwells there in Genesis 20:1. The children of Israel abide there in the book of Numbers, and Moses even brings water out of the rock at Meribah in Kadesh, which was said to have been a great sin since it put God to the test. The story says that Moses was punished for this action by not being allowed to go into the Promised Land (Num. 10:11–13:26, 20:1–122, 27:14, 33:36–37). Deuteronomy reports that the Israelites remained in Kadesh many days (1:46). The book of Judges attests that Kadesh was a place of sojourning (11:16–17). Kadesh receives further references in 2 Samuel 24:6 and in Psalm 29:8.

The theory has been advanced that at Kadesh the escaping slave people and the nomadic wilderness Semites came together, formed an alliance and began to share their oral histories, so that their separated lives began to blend into a single story. The difference, however, was never lost. Perhaps this was the time when the patriarchs that we know as Abraham, Isaac and Jacob were added to the epic. Originally they may have been only the names of Canaanite holy men associated with sacred shrines in that land located at Hebron, Beersheba and Bethel, historical figures who were later woven together by suggesting that Abraham was the father of Isaac, Isaac was the father of Jacob and Jacob was the father of the twelve sons who would make up the nation of the Jews. In their common ancestry of Abraham, Isaac and Jacob, to whom they said God had promised the land they were prepared to conquer, these two groups of people found a sense of oneness and a moral blessing on their violence. In the different wives of Jacob, however, they found the sources of their divisions.

Jacob had two wives, the story said, Leah and Rachel, who were sisters and so their sons were both half brothers and first cousins. There were other sons of Jacob—not children of these two sisters, but of their servants. They were thus the children of concubines, racially mixed, and their descendants were destined to live on the fringes of the Jewish nation. The ultimate division and rivalry would, however, be between the two legitimate lines, a rivalry that would always threaten the unity of the Jewish nation. It is interesting to watch how the Elohist writer portrays the separation and makes the claim for the superiority of those who were the people for whom the Elohist wrote.

The Elohist narrative does not just include, but lingers over, an account of their ancestor Jacob wrestling with an angel and having his name changed to Israel (Gen. 32). As the Jacob story is developed, we are told that Jacob agreed to work for seven years for a man named Laban in order to secure as his wife Laban's beautiful younger daughter, Rachel (Gen. 29:1–20). However, Jacob was tricked by Laban, for the veiled daughter to whom Jacob was eventually married turned out to be not his beloved Rachel at all, but her older sister, Leah, who was described in less than flattering terms. Her eyes were weak, said the text (Gen. 29:17), or perhaps cowlike, seeming to pop out of her face. When Jacob in the cool light of dawn discovered this deception, he was irate. Laban justified this chicanery by saying it was inappropriate for the younger daughter to be married before the older daughter. In a world where multiple wives were not a problem, the situation was rectified by giving Rachel to Jacob to be wife number two and Jacob agreed to work for Laban seven additional years. As this story developed the unattractive and unloved wife Leah became the mother of Judah, who was to be the dominant patriarch of the Southern Kingdom. King David was a descendant of Judah. The holy city of Jerusalem with its temple was in the land of Judah. But Rachel became the mother of Joseph, who was destined to be the dominant patriarch of the Northern Kingdom. Since Rachel, according to this story, was the favorite wife of Jacob/Israel, it followed that Joseph would be portrayed as his favorite son, the one upon whom Jacob/Israel lavished his affection (Gen. 37–50).

It was for this favored son that the coat of many colors was made. Because Joseph basked in this status, it was said that he excited jealousy among his brothers (who were the sons of Leah and of the concubines) by dreaming of the day when all his brothers would bow down before him and serve him. Finally this family tension reached the place where the brothers decided to kill Joseph. They captured him, threw him into a pit and planned to leave him there to die. Their plan was to kill an animal and sprinkle the blood of that animal on Joseph's ostentatious coat of many colors, so that their father would think that his son had been destroyed by a wild beast. At that moment, however, according to this story, some traders in a caravan headed for Egypt came by and Leah's son, Judah, suggested that they not kill Joseph but instead sell him into slavery, which they did, gaining for him the price of twenty pieces of silver. That evil deed was to set in motion the drama that represented this nation's first understanding of what it meant to be the saved people.

Through a series of exciting adventures that served to extol the virtues of Joseph, this young man went on to rise to great prominence in Egypt, until he was second in command to the pharaoh. In that power position Joseph was actually able to save his brothers from death in a great famine. He did not leave them to starve in the land of Canaan, though they had intended starvation to be *his* fate when they threw him in the pit, but rather he moved them with their entire extended families into Egypt, where they settled in the land of Goshen. Over a period of some four hundred years, the story says, these Hebrews who began their life in Egypt as the privileged family of the pharaoh's closest advisor gradually declined into being an underclass, then sank into being a slave people—which is what finally set the stage for the Exodus.

Joseph, the son of Rachel, was clearly the hero of this story. When the slave people came out of Egypt under Moses, they carried with them the bones of Joseph (Exod. 13:19). When under Joshua they set up their new nation in the land of Canaan, the northern part of the territory was assigned to Joseph's heirs (Josh. 17:7–18). His importance was such that the descendants of his two sons, Ephraim and Manasseh, were given the status of full tribes and were assigned land in the Northern Kingdom. This kept the number of tribes at twelve, since the tribe of Levi was reserved for priestly duty (Josh. 13:14). So the division between the two groups of the Jews was written into Jewish history. The descendants of Joseph, the son of Rachel, were to dominate the north; the descendants of Judah, the son of Leah, were to dominate the south. I suspect that the Joseph tribes were the escaping slaves from Egypt and the Judah tribes came from the nomadic Semites of the wilderness.

When we come later to the time when a monarchy was set up in Israel, Saul, who was from the tribe of Benjamin, became the first king (1 Sam. 9). It was an interesting choice since Benjamin was said to be Rachel's second son after Joseph, but the tribe of Benjamin was located in the south as a satellite of the tribe of Judah. Thus in some sense he minimized the split among the Jews—indeed, the tensions between the two groups may have been factors in the choice of their king. Saul, however, could not establish his monarchy and so was not able to hand the throne on to his son. The kingship then passed to David, who was Saul's popular general and a member of the tribe of Judah (2 Sam. 1ff.). After a forty-year reign in which David expanded his kingdom and pacified the immediate area with military conquests, he abdicated his throne while on his deathbed, so that his son Solomon might be placed on the throne and the nation spared conflict over succession (1 Kings 1). It worked and Solomon reigned for another forty years. During this reign, however, the tensions between the north and the south reached a fever pitch. Upon Solomon's death his son and heir apparent, Rehoboam, assumed the throne but was immediately challenged by a northern general named Jeroboam, who demanded a redress of northern grievances. Rehoboam refused and civil war broke out. The south was unable to quell the uprising and so the kingdom of the Jews was split into two provinces: one was called the Southern Kingdom or Judah and the other was called the Northern Kingdom or Israel (1 Kings 12ff.). The Jewish nation was never to be reunited. The date of this split was about 920 BCE.

The north always had the harder task of nation building. They had no holy city like Jerusalem that could serve as a symbol of unity, and so in time they set about building their capital at Samaria (1 Kings 16:21ff.). This new capital would never rival Jerusalem in grandeur. Samaria possessed no temple in which God was supposed to dwell. To minimize this sense of loss, the Jews of the north built shrines in their land, but these shrines never compared favorably with the temple. There was no royal family in the north, just a series of military dictators who were regularly overthrown. Last but not least, the northerners had no separate and justifying epic history that was their own. So the Northern Kingdom was never as stable as the Southern Kingdom. Northern Jews tended to be looked down upon by the Jews of the south, who acted as if nothing good could come out of Galilee (which was the first-century CE name for what was left of the Northern Kingdom).

What the people of the north did, however, somewhere around the midpoint of the ninth century, was to write their own epic, to give themselves a vision of who they were. The Yahwist version of Jewish history would not do. That older epic extolled the institutions of the south. It suggested that rebellion against either the king or the high priest was rebellion against God. Since the citizens of the north had rebelled against both, they needed an epic justification. So it was that representatives of the Northern Kingdom began to put into writing their own version of what had heretofore been an oral history. That was how the Hebrew *Odyssey* came into being.

This work is called the "Elohist Document" because it used the name Elohim, rather than Yahweh, for God. It suggested that God made the covenant not with Moses but with the people, who then chose Moses as their leader. God's covenant was not with the king, but with the people, who allowed the king to rule by their consent. The implication was clear that if the king misruled, the people had the right to overthrow him. Kings served in the Northern Kingdom not by divine right but by the will of the people. In many ways the Elohist Document shared much of the same history as the Yahwist Document, but it reflected the values of the revolutionary north. The northerners glorified their own origins by suggesting that they were the heirs of Jacob's favorite son and, thus, the descendants of Jacob's favorite wife. They wrote their negativity against their neighbors in the south into their history by suggesting that the citizens of Judah were descended from the rejected and weak-eyed Leah, who was so unattractive her father had to scheme to marry her off. They further suggested that it was their noble ancestor Joseph who had actually saved the ancestors of the tribe of Judah from starvation by taking them down into Egypt to live. He did this despite their earlier attempts to kill him by starvation in the pit. They also shamed their southern neighbors by suggesting it was Judah, the chief patriarch of the south, who had suggested that their ancestor Joseph be sold into slavery for money that he pocketed. They challenged the sacredness of Jerusalem and its temple, and they defined God much more democratically. The Jewish epic of the Northern Kingdom nonetheless did what all epics are designed to do. It rooted the people in history. It provided a common past. It anticipated a common future and it located God in their midst. It was, as all epics are ultimately, an intensely biased tribal story. It was hardly the "Word of God."

When the Northern Kingdom fell to the Assyrians in 721 BCE the citizens of this part of the Jewish nation were deported and resettled in other parts of the empire. Because they had no deep sense of cohesion, they literally disappeared into the gene pool of the Middle East, becoming the ten lost tribes of Israel. Some unknown person or persons, however, from the Northern Kingdom escaped the conquering Assyrians and, taking their northern epic story, the Elohist Document, with them, fled to Jerusalem. There the common history was recognized and the two stories, the Hebrew *Iliad* and the Hebrew *Odyssey*, were woven together, not in a seamless way, but woven together nonetheless. So it was that the epic of the Jews grew to contain the combined story made up of the dominant Yahwist Document and the recessive Elohist Document. From this point on the Jewish epic was known as the Yahwist/Elohist account of the history of the Jews. Clearly it was revered as their sacred tribal story. Just as clear, however, was the fact that this was a human-created national history, not God's dictated or God's inspired holy writing. This merger of the two epics occurred at about the time that the eighth century turned into the seventh century BCE. Though the epic was not yet finished, as we shall see, what we now call the Bible was coming into view.

Part 4: The Deuteronomic Writer (ca. 625 BCE)

In the latter years of the seventh century BCE, another massive revision of the Jewish epic was undertaken. It came about as a result of a frantic search for the means to win God's favor and therefore God's protection in a radically insecure Middle Eastern world. In that day if a tribe was defeated in battle it meant one of two things: either the god of the defeated tribe had been defeated by the superior god of the victorious people, or the defeated people had somehow offended the powerful deity they were supposed to serve and were therefore being punished. The first of these possibilities was not likely to be part of Judaism, since the Jewish people had begun to catch a glimpse of a dawning universalism: there was but one God who ruled the world. They still believed that this God had a special relationship to and a special vocation for the Jews, however, so overwhelmingly defeats and disasters for the Jews were interpreted to mean that the holy God was punishing the disobedient nation. This idea was particularly emphasized in the difficult years of the seventh century BCE, when the nation of Judah roiled in the insecurities of world history, caught as they were between the Egyptians to their south and west and the mighty nations bent on world domination that were emerging in the east. The Assyrians had conquered and laid waste to Israel, the Northern Kingdom, in the eighth century BCE. Now, however, these Assyrians were absorbed with fending off first the Babylonians and later the Persians. Judah was too weak militarily and politically to do much more than seek to win divine protection by holy living. They were pawns on the stage of history.

When the Assyrians had come down against the Northern Kingdom of Israel in the 720s, Judah had refused to come to Israel's aid. Instead, Judah's king had negotiated with the Assyrians to be given vassal status in exchange for not resisting. That maintained a modicum of independence but little more. The Jews paid tribute to their masters. Stripped of all wealth they remained free, but only in their poverty (2 Kings 19:14–28). It was better at least than deportation. In the minds of the prophets, who were their religious leaders at that time, all that could save them was faithfulness in worship and righteousness in living. The prophets despaired and wrote scathingly about what they regarded as the evil of their King Manasseh, who ascended the throne in Jerusalem at age twelve and reigned for fifty-five years as the seventh century rolled into history. According to the sacred story of the Jews (2 Kings 21:1ff.), King Manasseh "did what was evil in the sight of the Lord." He built "altars for Baal" in the land and "made an Asherah," a symbol of a fertility goddess. He "worshiped all the host of heaven, and served them," and he even sacrificed his own son as an offering. He allowed wizards, soothsayers and mediums in the land. To these abominations the prophets promised the wrath of God: "Behold, I am bringing upon Jerusalem and Judah such evil that the ears of everyone who hears of it will tingle. . . . And I will wipe Jerusalem as one wipes a dish . . . turning it upside down" (1 Kings 21:12–13). The prophetic word continued: "I will cast off the remnant of my heritage, and give them into the hand of their enemies, and they shall become a prey and a spoil to all their enemies, because they have done evil in my sight and have provoked me to anger" (2 Kings 21:14–15). It was a fearful word to hear. People wondered when the wrath of God would fall.

Yet Manasseh died in peace at the age of seventy-seven and was succeeded by his twenty-two-year-old son Amon (2 Kings 21:18). In the eyes of the prophets Amon continued in his father's evil. Perhaps because of that Amon was subsequently murdered by his servants, and the heir, an eight-year-old son named Josiah, came to the throne (2 Kings 21:23–24). Josiah appears to have had a godly mother and to have been tutored by the prophets, who invested great hope in him. His faithfulness to the traditions espoused by the prophets, it was hoped, might temper the prophetic words of doom.

When King Josiah was twenty-six years old, his religious zeal led him to undertake renovations on the temple. During those renovations a book of the law, purporting to have been written by Moses himself, was discovered in the walls of the temple by Hilkiah, the high priest, who brought it to the attention of the king. When the king heard the words of this book, he "rent his clothes" and inquired of the Lord about what he should do, "because our fathers have not obeyed the words of this book" (2 Kings 22:3–13).

On the basis of that discovery, which is believed by scholars to be substantially the book of Deuteronomy (which literally means "the second law"), Josiah initiated the greatest transformation in the way people worshiped in Judah in all of that nation's history (2 Kings 23:15–27).

Was the book a plant? I suspect so. I also suspect that it reflected the work of, or at the very least the involvement of, the prophet Jeremiah. However, under the purging zeal of the Deuteronomists, as this reforming group came to be called, the epic story of the Jews was modified in two dramatic ways. First, the book of Deuteronomy was added to the Yahwist/Elohist Document, turning it into the Yahwist/Elohist/Deuteronomic Document. Second, this entire text was now edited in the light of the Deuteronomists' values, and thus a mighty reformation of Jewish worship practices was carried out. That book became the next building block in the development of Jewish scriptures. Once again it was events of very human origin that added a new layer to the epic of the Jews. As this development shows, the Bible is not the "Word of God." It was never intended to be the "Word of God." It has its roots in the tribal sacred story of the Jewish people. It was simply the chronicle of their walk with who they believed God was through their own national history. It rooted them in time and it gave them a past to remember.

Josiah reinstituted the Passover as a liturgical means whereby the Jewish past might be captured and even entered. The Passover had not been observed by the Jews since the time of the judges, the scriptures stated (2 Kings 23:21–23). In addition to connecting with the past these reformers gave the Jewish people a future to anticipate. The reinstated Passover related them to a transcendent sense of God, who stood always beyond their grasp, calling them into those patterns of worship that forced them to think beyond the limits of their human capacities.

The great reform movement under Josiah, as dramatic as it was, did not, however, bring about divine favor. Shortly thereafter Pharaoh Neco of Egypt went up to battle the Assyrians. King Josiah intercepted him on the plains of Megiddo and was killed. It was such a traumatic moment in Jewish history that Megiddo gave rise to the mythological battle of Armageddon, which would take place at the end of time. Now the nation of Judah began to cascade toward what would be the most traumatic moment in its national life until the Holocaust in the twentieth century. In that tragedy, however, the final editing of the Hebrew epic would be accomplished.

Part 5: The Priestly Writers (ca. 580–520 BCE)

It was within twenty-five years of the time of Deuteronomic reforms and the traumatizing death of King Josiah that the little nation of Judah faced an ultimate challenge. To their north and east the Babylonians had conquered the Assyrians and were now the dominant military power in that part of the world. Under the command of their general, Nebuchadnezzar, the Babylonians swept down on the nation of the Jews in 598 BCE, and after a bitter two-year siege they conquered Jerusalem in 596 (2 Kings 24–25). A puppet ruler, but still part of the royal House of David, named Zedekiah, was set on the Jewish throne and a state of vassalage began. Ten years later an unwise rebellion led to a Babylonian reconquest of Jerusalem. This last Davidic king of the Jews was forced to watch the execution of all of his sons. Then his eyes were put out. He died a blind man in captivity. Almost all the Jewish people were carried into a Babylonian captivity that was destined to last for two or three generations. The prophet Jeremiah, closely allied with the Deuteronomic reforms, escaped to Egypt and died there. What history has called the Babylonian Exile of the Jewish people had begun. Among the people carried into exile was a priest-prophet named Ezekiel, who along with his priestly cohorts would radically rewrite the sacred epic of the Jewish people in the light of the needs of their particular time.

It would be hard to overestimate the trauma of this period of Jewish life. The chosen people lost every symbol of their Jewish identity. They could no longer even observe their defining calendar of feasts and fasts. Most of them thought of God as one bound to their land in Judah, so they believed they had lost their God also. They wondered how they could ever "sing the Lord's song in a foreign land" (Ps. 137:3, 4). The Davidic monarchy was gone forever as an institution in history, but it was destined to reemerge in their fantasies about an ideal king, one that they called Messiah, who would someday come to restore the fortunes of the Jews. Messiah gave the Jews a future hope that probably nothing else could have given them.

The one thing the Jews had and to which they clung with a tenacious ferocity was their sacred story, their defining epic, now represented by the merger of the Yahwist Document and the Elohist Document together with the new inclusion and editing of the Deuteronomic writers. Their new circumstances were of such painful significance that it was felt with an overwhelming intensity that their defining epic had to be revised anew. So it was that Ezekiel and a group of fellow priests undertook that responsibility. When they finished this work the Jews finally had what we today call the Torah. In the process the Yahwist/Elohist/Deuteronomic Document was massively edited and expanded by the priestly addition, almost doubling the size of their sacred story. The survival of the Jews' identity as a people was the first priority of these priestly writers. In order to survive as a separate people, these Jewish leaders believed, the Jewish people had to be distinct and different. Three traditions were therefore either inaugurated or revived to create this distinctiveness. All three are still today major identifying aspects of what it means to be Jewish.

The first was the observance of the Sabbath. The Jewish people were to be set apart from the other peoples of the world by their refusal to work on the Sabbath day. To give that tradition the force of divine command, the story of the seven-day creation was written. Its intention was not to tell people how or in what timespan the world was created. To use this story as Christians did in the nineteenth century to counter Charles Darwin's writings about evolution is the height of biblical ignorance. Its whole purpose was to enjoin on the

Jewish people in exile the mark of the Sabbath. God had blessed and hallowed the seventh day by resting on it. The worshipers of this God were bound to do likewise.

The second tradition inaugurated in the Exile was the collection of the ritualistic laws that bound the Jews into proper worship. These laws are spelled out in detail by the priestly writers in the latter part of the book of Exodus and in the entirety of the book of Leviticus, which were both the products of the Exile. The holiness code of the book of Leviticus, which includes the prohibitions we have already discussed about sexuality, were designed to make the Jews morally different from their pagan captors. Here are located the prohibitions against touching menstruating women and engaging in same-sex unions, as well as hundreds of other prohibitions. Needless to say, the Jews knew little about either menstruation or homosexuality, but they treated both as somehow unclean. It was their way of maintaining a separate kind of ethical puritanism. The kosher dietary laws are part of these religious regulations in the book of Leviticus. Their purpose was to prohibit the Jews from eating with anyone who was not Jewish. Not only did the Jews have to refrain from both the meat of swine and shellfish, among many other prohibitions, but the kitchens in which Jewish food was prepared had to be kosher. If one does not eat with another outside his or her clan, one can hardly develop a relationship that might grow into a friendship or a marriage. That was, of course, the point. The Jews were to remain isolated from all other people. Otherwise there could be no survival.

The third tradition that was revived and made mandatory for Jewish males was the rite of circumcision. This habit, which appears to have had much earlier Middle Eastern roots, had fallen into general disuse, but now it served the primary need of Jewish survival. The scriptures were thus revised so that circumcision was said to have been the requirement of God at the time of the covenant with Abraham (Gen. 17:10), a sign of being part of the chosen people from the time of Moses (Exod. 12:48), and a mark of what it meant to be Jewish from the time of birth (Lev. 12:3). Every Jewish male had to wear on his body the mark of his Judaism so that marrying or conceiving outside their tribe would be difficult. Jewish identity was not to be hidden.

The synagogue replaced the temple during the Exile. The scriptures were made central to Jewish identity and to Jewish worship. The Torah, now in its newly revised Yahwist/Elohist/Deuteronomic/Priestly version, had to be read in its entirety in the synagogue on the Sabbaths of every single year. The holy days that are interspersed in the Jewish calendar were designed to recall the Jewish heritage. Passover was a liturgical remembrance of the Exodus. In the Josiah reforms it could be celebrated only in Jerusalem. In the Exile it became a family rite with the hope that someday—perhaps next year—it could be celebrated in Jerusalem (Lev. 23:5–8). Shavuot or Pentecost, which means fifty days after Passover, celebrated and recalled the giving of the law to Moses at Mount Sinai (Lev. 23:15–21). It was a twenty-four-hour vigil for which the long Psalm 119, a hymn to the beauty and wonder of the law, was written. Rosh Hashanah or Jewish New Year was, according to the priestly writers, set for the first day of the seventh month of the Jewish year (Lev. 23:23–25). Its purpose was to provide a liturgical time to pray for the kingdom of God to come, and with it the restoration of the Jews to their ancestral lands. Yom Kippur, the Day of Atonement, was to be observed on the tenth day of the seventh month, when the sacrificial lamb was slain and its innocent blood sprinkled on the people so that they could, in a phrase that Christians would later borrow, be made clean by the blood of the Lamb, speaking yet again to that human need to be at one with God (Lev. 23:26–32). Then the eight-day celebration of the harvest called Sukkoth or Tabernacles would begin on the fifteenth day of the seventh month. There were other, minor holy days, but these were the major ones that the priestly writers incorporated into the Torah in their massive revision of the epic story of the Jews.

The priestly writers also edited the text of their epic to make certain that the *ancestors* of the Jews had observed the rules which the priestly writers were developing as the marks of Judaism. This means that the Noah story had to be edited to make sure that Noah could carry out ritualistic sacrifices without ending the existence of an entire species of animals who were supposedly on board in a single pair consisting of one male and one female. So for the purposes of sacrifices, seven pairs of some animals were put on board (Gen. 7:2). The story of manna falling in the wilderness was edited to assure us that God did not work on the Sabbath. God sent two days' supply of manna on the day before the Sabbath so that the Jews in the wilderness did not have to violate the Sabbath by gathering the manna on the day of rest (Exod. 16:4–5).

So the Torah, the Jewish epic, achieved its present form. It is surely a human epic filled with human passion, human ignorance and human insight. It defined the people who created it. It gave to them a past that enabled them to claim their history. It projected them into a future that enabled them to live in hope. It did what epics are designed to do—namely, it interpreted life. That is not an insignificant accomplishment.

The Torah was the anchor of the scriptures and for the Jews the holiest part of the sacred story. The story was, however, still not complete. We must now chronicle the rest of its development, which was destined to include an expansion of the narrative from simply a tribal story of the Jews to a universal story of the human race. This transformation is an exciting chapter in human religious history.

30

ESCAPING THE
LIMITS OF THE EPIC

THE PROPHETS, THE WRITINGS,
THE DREAM

They [the prophets] summoned Israel to remember the living
sources of its life and to live in expectation of the fulfillment
and resolution of the divine. . . . They were messengers sent
with a message from the Invisible One. . . . They were sent to
speak for the Speaking One whose word could accomplish
its purpose.

James Muilenburg[2]

While the epic of the Jewish past was being shaped into the Torah's
guiding force, the life of the Jewish people continued to move in
history. This meant that the sacred story expanded not only with the revisions
we have chronicled, but with new adventures that had to be absorbed. Present history, however, never achieved the status of the past. So to make something have great value for the Jews one still had to locate it in the Torah. That
foundational story, though reflecting the editorial changes of a much later
period, nonetheless began with creation, moved through the patriarchs, and
closed with Moses. According to the Torah, however, Moses never entered

the Promised Land (Deut. 34). He died after only having seen from the mountaintop the vision of that land flowing with milk and honey. The Torah was, however, destined to remain the most sacred part of the defining epic of the Jewish people.

· However, to keep their developing post-Moses past inside the corporate memory of the Jews, the works of a group of people called the "former prophets" were next added to their sacred story. The writings of the former prophets—Joshua, Judges, 1 and 2 Samuel and 1 and 2 Kings—were designed to give to the epic some sense of Jewish history between the death of Moses and the defining moment of the Exile.

This work was further supplemented by the fact that beginning in the eighth century before the Common Era yet another movement arose inside Judaism that was destined to change the character of the Jewish people and to stretch dramatically their sacred story. It was led by reformers called by the Jews the "latter prophets," but outside Judaism this movement, which came to be called simply the prophetic movement, was regarded as so distinctively different from anything that developed in Judaism before that the word "prophet" tends to be reserved for these figures without any reference to their earlier antecedents. How was it that Judaism alone produced this string of incredible figures who would make a contribution to the world unparalleled among any ancient people? That is a question that we need to address. The prophets provided the bridge whereby the God of the Jews could emerge into being the universal God that the people of the Western world began to see. So it is essential to spend a brief time looking at how those reformers shaped the sacred epic.

I tend to identify a man named Nathan as the founder of this movement. His story is told in 2 Samuel. Nathan is introduced in chapter 7 of that book as a prophet who encourages David to be about the task of planning for the building of the temple. Nathan delivers the word that this project, however, is to be David's dream, not his fulfillment. The temple is to be built by David's son. But then in chapter 12 of 2 Samuel Nathan establishes the role of the prophet as one who speaks for God in the citadels of power.

It was Nathan who confronted David, the king, when David entered into his adulterous relationship with Bathsheba and subsequently arranged for the murder of her husband, Uriah. Kings in that time were normally thought to be able to have anything they wanted. Nathan would give birth to the idea in Judaism that even the king was bound by the moral law of God. Armed with nothing more than his moral courage and a sense of divine righteousness, he stood down the most powerful king in Jewish history and bore witness to the fact that the Jewish way of life did not exempt kings from the judgment of God. It is one of the most dramatic stories in the Bible.

Nathan approached the king seeking permission to tell him a story of a grave injustice. A rich man who owned many flocks lived near a poor man who had only a single ewe lamb. This single little lamb was a family pet, eating and sleeping with the owners almost as a member of the family.

One day the rich man had a guest for whom it was required that he prepare a banquet. Instead of going to his own flocks for a lamb to slaughter, he went to the home of the poor man and took his pet lamb, which he killed, dressed, roasted and set before his guest.

When David heard the story he was filled with wrath and said, "As the Lord lives, the man who has done this deserves to die!" (2 Sam. 12:5).

Nathan, then staring straight into the king's eyes, said, "Thou art the man" (v. 7, KJV).

David, in a precedent-setting act that established the power of the prophets, publicly repented and accepted the judgment and the punishment pronounced on him by Nathan. The Jewish nation would never be the same.

Elijah in the eighth century institutionalized that prophetic role when he took on King Ahab and his wife Jezebel (1 Kings 17ff.). In time the prophetic movement produced a group of people known as the "writing prophets," who are unique in the history of the world. It was these prophets whose works were ultimately grafted into the biblical story, bringing a whole new dimension to that still growing epic. The tribal history of the Jews was now joined by penetrating prophetic insights into the meaning of life itself.

A man named Isaiah was the most dominant figure in the movement. He served as the advisor to several kings in Jerusalem in the generations before the fall of that city to the Babylonians. Jeremiah came next and was the prophet who lived at the time of Judah's defeat by the Babylonians. As we mentioned earlier, he was probably a force behind the Deuteronomic revision of the Jewish epic. He portrayed himself as a weeping, depressed, somewhat tragic figure who watched his nation collapse. Ezekiel the priest/prophet then took up the torch. He went into captivity in Babylon and was, as we have noted, the major player behind the priestly revision of the Jewish

epic that was instrumental in guiding the Jews through the Exile without losing their identity.

Other voices, whose writings were shorter in length but not necessarily in
power, began to walk in this pathway of writing giants, adding their penetrating voices to the expanding text of the Jewish epic story. A man named Hosea
led this tier of prophets. He was the prophet who saw in his own domestic crisis a new insight into God. He was also the prophetic figure who made love
the central meaning of God. His work served to draw his nation beyond the
level of survival and into the life of serving and caring. It was an enormous
step in spiritual development.

Then came Amos, who drove the values of the Jewish epic into the social
arena. Amos suggested that human justice was nothing but the worship of
God being lived out among the people and that divine worship was nothing
but human justice being offered to God. He too added a new dimension to
the Jewish epic: the poor were never allowed after Amos to be invisible.

Next came Micah, who pretended that he was something like a "country
lawyer" called to put Israel on trial for unfaithfulness. The case was tried before a jury of the mountains and hills, so that God, the Judge, could utter the
ultimate command for Jewish worshipers: "What does the Lord require of
you but to do justice, and to love kindness [mercy], and to walk humbly with
your God?" (Mic. 6:8). The Jewish epic was becoming something more than
just a collection of national self-serving heroic tales.

Two other prophetic voices deep in the Hebrew tradition would exercise
enormous influence upon these people and would in the process elevate the
epic of the Jews to new dimensions. Both were unnamed prophets whose
writings got attached to the scrolls of earlier prophets, and so they are called
respectively Second Isaiah and Second Zechariah. Both planted the seeds
that were to become dramatically influential later in Jewish history.

Second Isaiah, whose writings are believed to constitute chapters 40–55 of
the present-day book of Isaiah, developed a mythological figure that he
called the "Servant" of the Lord or sometimes the "Suffering Servant." This
figure, most scholars believe, was designed to be a theological symbol for the
whole Jewish nation—the embodiment, if you will, of a new and dramatically different vocation for the Jewish people. This prophet saw no hope for
the restoration of the popular Jewish dream of power and earthly grandeur.

The Jewish epic was destined to be bent by this writer in a remarkably different direction. The role of the "Servant" was to bring wholeness to human life by absorbing life's pain, accepting life's abuse and entering life's evil. He would drain the anger from people's souls with all of its destructive power and restore the world to health. No ancient epic had ever conceived of such a role for any tribal people. The Jewish epic was developing a pathway in uncharted waters. The creation of this image of a national hero inside the Jewish epic would lay the groundwork for people hundreds of years later to interpret the memory of Jesus as living within a legitimate expectation of the Jewish people, for Jesus and this "Servant" figure were destined to be deeply intertwined.

Second Zechariah, whose writings are believed to constitute chapters 9–14 of the book of Zechariah, also wrote about a mythical figure, who once again was a symbol for the whole Jewish nation. Second Zechariah's hero was called the "Shepherd King of Israel." He was set upon by those whose greed for increased wealth led them into the business of buying and selling animals in the temple. When the traders were opposed by this "Shepherd King," they rid the land of him for the sum of thirty pieces of silver, which, as guilt money, was hurled back into the temple (Zech. 11:4–14). This picture of Zechariah's "Shepherd King" would be influential in shaping the Jewish epic, which in turn defined the Jewish worldview and the Jewish expectations. The work of both of these unknown figures would in time be understood quite differently from what the writers intended by simple believers, who did not recognize that epics were not created in a superstitious way. Instead of understanding that the memory of Jesus was simply interpreted through the lens of Second Isaiah's "Servant" and Second Zechariah's "Shepherd King," these people began to suggest that the theistic God had inspired these unnamed voices to prophesy events that would take place in the future, events that Jesus would miraculously fulfill. The epic of the Jews was beginning to turn into magic, and what had come into being as tribal history was turning into the "Word of God."

Is that view of an epic story even a possibility that we should entertain? Hardly! Epics are never literally true. They contain tales of supernatural power but are always designed to show divine favor being displayed toward the tribe that created them. What these unique Jewish prophets did, however, was to reveal that inside the people who created this original epic a new dimension of thought was emerging that was accompanied by a different value system unique in human history.

It was the destiny of this minority within the Jewish community to see the world from a universal perspective, to escape their tribal limits, to entertain global understandings, to seek transcendence and to transform national history into a vision of service for others instead of power over others. They were even able to allow their epic to reflect these minority positions. In time Jewish liturgies incorporated the Jewish epic into the worship life of the people, and they invested it with an aura of sacredness. But the important thing was, they incorporated it *all*. Yes, it included tales of Jewish grandeur, of great nations like Egypt being pulverized by the power of Israel's God, of deliverance for the favored people accomplished by the mighty hand of their tribal protector, who could split great bodies of water to allow the favored ones to walk through the seas on dry land and then rain upon them heavenly bread to prevent starvation in the wilderness. It incorporated the national ambition to conquer the land of others, to make it their home, calling it the Promised Land. They even suggested in their epic that God had committed this land to them as the descendants of those ancestors who, they claimed, lived on that land hundreds of years earlier.

The sacred story of the Jews, however, also included the prophetic voices that saw love as the primary nature of God, saw social justice as the goal of God and saw the necessity of having the covenant marked not with power images exclusively but with their responsibility to do justice, to love mercy and to walk humbly with their God. They also included in this far-reaching sacred story the divine calling to live for others, to absorb pain, to bear abuse, in order to drain the hostility out of life and thus to create wholeness. In these incredible portraits they heard the call of their God and knew that the word of their God had been heard in the midst of their sacred story. It never occurred to them to mask the warts or to diminish the evil that their epic included. Their genius was not that they were somehow pure or morally superior, but that they allowed minority voices to shape their national epic and to enable a different word to be heard in their epic than in any other epic in human history. They purged neither the evil nor the wonder from their history. That is why our Bible today still sends out such mixed messages.

To complete this brief but sweeping analysis of the forces that conspired to expand the Hebrew epic in such different directions, let me add that contrary to religious propaganda, some parts of this sacred story we call the Bible are not even inspiring. It includes some works written by petty people, who are by and large unknown because what they had to say did not transcend their day. I think of names like Nahum, Obadiah and Haggai, for example. Few people, even among the educated clergy, can cite one detail out of these biblical works.

There are also in this remarkable epic what might be called protest stories—that is, Jewish books written once more by minority voices, designed to counter the prevailing religious ideas. One of them sought to answer such questions as: Why do the righteous suffer? Why is the world not fair? The purpose of this writer was to counter the answers of popular religion, which asserted that God blesses the good and punishes the evil. If a good man suffers, is it proof that he has hidden sins? That was the common explanation. Not so said the unknown poet who told the ancient tale of a very good man named Job, who suffered calamity after calamity and who was urged by his "comforters" to confess his secret evildoing and to ask God to withdraw the divine wrath. Job refused, and his voice of protest brought into being a new understanding of both God and suffering.

A second voice of protest was one raised against that religious idea so dear to our tribal mentality that the love of God stops at the boundary of "my people." God's love hardly embraces gentiles like the people of Nineveh, said the common wisdom, but God's prophet Jonah was called to preach to the Ninevites at the very time that the Jewish reform movement under Ezra was purging the land of mixed marriages and half-breed children. In Jonah the protest against limits being placed on God's love was heard.

A similar theme is registered in the protest book of Ruth. The background to this story is that the super patriots of the post-exilic period were holding up King David as the quintessential Jew and expressing the national yearning to restore that throne so that Israel could once again dominate her enemies. There was also a not-so-well-hidden note of the racism present in Jewish life at that time, with David being cited as "exhibit A" of that Jewish racial superiority. The author of the little book of Ruth wrote in response a charming protest in which the purpose of the book is not exposed until the last verse. In this narrative, an exemplary young Moabite woman named Ruth was widowed when her Jewish husband died. Rather than return to her Moabite family, which would have been the social norm of that day, she chose to stay with Naomi, her Jewish mother-in-law, and to care for her with an incredible devotion that lived out the highest expectations of the Jewish law. She was rewarded for her faithfulness in this story by a marriage to Boaz. A child of this union between the Jewish Boaz and the Moabite Ruth was named Obed. He became the father of Jesse, who was the father of the revered King David. This meant that the greatest king of the Jews was one-eighth Moabite! Racial superiority was exposed for what it is: bigoted nonsense. This remarkable story was also incorporated into the epic of the Jews. The religious tradition of the Jews was capable of challenging the voices of the religious establishment of their day. Perhaps that was where the claim that these words were the "Word of God" began. The establishment resisted, but it did not, perhaps it *could* not, purge from its epic the challenge that was deep in the text.

The epic of the Jews also had places within its sacred tales where the invitation was heard that kept the boundaries of both their tribe and their religion flexible. People would find in its words the voice of God that would tell them that God welcomes all people—all races, ethnic backgrounds, genders and sexual orientations—to find their place at the table of the Lord. It was a voice of God that proclaimed that there are no restrictions on the love of God. This remarkable Bible evolved into being not a weapon to enforce prejudice, but an invitation to come as you are in order to become all that you can be.

Next in the biblical text of this thoroughly human but mysteriously expansive saga we call the Old Testament there are two minor liturgical books that were designed for special moments in Jewish history. The book of Esther was written to help the Jews celebrate the fourteenth day of Adar, the Feast of Purim, when the Jews recalled their deliverance from the Persians; and the book of Lamentations was written to be read on the ninth of Ab to recall the destruction of the temple by the army of Nebuchadnezzar in 596 BCE.

Then there are the so-called wisdom books of the Jews, the best known of which are the book of Proverbs, which dispenses practical, if culturally compromised, advice; and a philosophical book called Ecclesiastes, in which Qoheleth the preacher meditates on the apparent meaninglessness of life: "Vanity of vanities! All is vanity" (Eccles. 1:2).

Next there is the Jewish hymnal, called the book of Psalms, which includes songs of praise for both God and the king that range from the bloodthirsty to the profound.

Finally, there are books added to the epic of Jewish life very late in Jewish history. These include 1 and 2 Chronicles, basically a rewrite in a later age of the books of 1 and 2 Kings to make them fit the needs of a new time in history, and the document of the last prophet, called Daniel, written in the second century BCE but projected back into the Exile of the sixth century, in which various familiar images entered our vocabulary—images like the fiery furnace that did not consume Shadrach, Meshach and Abednego (Dan. 3), the lions' den into which Daniel was thrown (Dan. 6) and the "clay feet" that rendered all of the protective armament worthless (Dan. 2:34). The book of Daniel also transformed a mythical figure described as "like a son of man" (Dan. 7:13), which first appeared in Ezekiel as a synonym for probably Ezekiel himself, into a supernatural figure who would someday come riding on the clouds at the end of history to inaugurate the kingdom of God. It was yet another lens through which the memory of a man named Jesus would someday be interpreted.

When this epic, with its various layers, its grandeur and its pathos, its triumphalism and its minority voices, is put together, it represents a rich treasure trove, a national story like none other in human history. It was born in a dialogue between ongoing human experience and that pervading sense of the holy that calls us beyond human limits into the wonder of transcendence, the mystery of God. We read this epic. We mark it, learn it and inwardly digest it, not because God wrote it, dictated it or even inspired it, but because it is an intensely human book describing a human journey where neither the vision of tribal glory with all of its triumphant pain nor the yearning of those who see beyond the range of the sight of most people is left out. That is how our Bible came into being.

Today, religious people read this part of the sacred story that is shared by both Jews and Christians, but more often than not we read it all wrong. The inspiration of the Bible is not found in its tales of supernatural occurrences and transforming miracles, narratives that speak of divine intervention or fulfilled prophecy. Its inspiration lies rather in those parts of this epic that probe the inner recesses of the human heart and tell us something about who we are, what our values are and what it means to touch the holy. In its pages we listen to the wisdom of the ages even in its dated forms, in search of meaning, transcendence, and ultimately God. This book, which in time came to be called the Holy Bible, is not the ultimate court of appeal on all human questions, nor does it contain the final answer in the attempt to discern God's will. It is rather a call to walk in the faith tradition it reflects, to be part of this ongoing story and even to write the next chapter in this ever-expanding epic so that you and I can also see ourselves as the people of God, always in an exodus from that which binds us, always in exile from the faith of yesterday, always listening for the voice of the holy both in the life of the world and in the depths of our own being. That is what the Bible is, the epic of our life. To try to make it more than that, the source of religious authority or the ultimate definer of truth, is to turn it into being demonic. It is from those who have claimed too much for this literalized Bible that the sins of scripture embedded in its "terrible texts" have emerged. They are texts wrenched out of this epic tale and used to enhance violence, to destroy the holiness of God's world, and to hurt, maim or kill certain of the children of God. The day of using the Bible to claim for your prejudice that it has "the authority of the Word of God" is quite frankly over, and we should give thanks for that fact. The churches of the world must learn that truth or they will die. There is no alternative.

We turn next to see how the story of Jesus was grafted onto this epic, and with it the call to a new universal consciousness.

31

JESUS AND THE JEWISH EPIC

I will change your names. You will no longer be called wounded,
outcast, lonely or afraid. I will change your names. Your new
name will be confidence, joyfulness, overcoming one,
faithfulness, friend of God, One who seeks my face.

D. Butler [3]

To our knowledge Jesus left no written records. There is only one occasion in the entire gospel tradition where we are told of Jesus writing anything, anywhere, at any time. That single note is found in a disputed
narrative about Jesus and the woman who was taken in the act of adultery
(John 8:1–11). In that account the text says that Jesus, facing the woman's accusers, "bent down and wrote with his finger on the ground." No attempt was
made in this text to say what it was that he wrote, leaving it to screenplay writers and preachers to translate that writing for each generation. Whatever else
the gospels are, they are certainly not the writings of Jesus.

It is equally clear that the gospels are not the result of Jesus' dictation
found in the written notes from his disciples. They are not like the table-talk
collections that were to be gathered by the fervent sycophants of later Christian heroes like Thomas Aquinas and Martin Luther, for fear that a single
gem might fall from the lips of the hero and not be recorded.

Some years ago while on a book tour, I was the primary guest on a nation-
wide late-night talk show that originated in Burbank, California. The host

was Tom Snyder, a radio and television figure well known in the 1990s. The book that we were to discuss, first between the two of us and then with listeners who would call in with questions and comments, was *Rescuing the Bible from Fundamentalism*. As the dialogue progressed, I went into some of the dating consensus around the books of the New Testament. There was for Tom Snyder no problem with my dating of the Pauline corpus between 50 and 64 CE. When we turned to the gospels, however, and I began to suggest dates between the early 70s CE for Mark, the first gospel to be written, and 100 CE for John, the last, my host became apprehensive.

"Wait a minute, Bishop," Tom Snyder said. "I've just gotten out my short pencil, and those dates suggest to me that the gospels were not written by eyewitnesses since they would have been too old."

"That is correct, Tom," I replied. "Only the gospel of John actually claims to be an eyewitness account, and I know of no reputable New Testament scholar who believes that John, the son of Zebedee, was actually the author of the Fourth Gospel. He would have been approaching one hundred years of age, and almost no one lived to that age in the first century. Even if they had, writing a book is not what they would do at that age. The other gospel writers do not even suggest such a claim. Luke goes so far as to outline the sources of his research in Luke 1:1–4."

"But Bishop," Tom continued, "when I was in parochial school as a kid, the nuns told me that the disciples followed Jesus around and wrote down everything he said, and that was the source from which the gospels have emerged. It never occurred to me before to question that!"

"Tom," I responded, "did the nuns tell you that they wrote Jesus' words down in spiral notebooks using ballpoint pens?"

It was a consciousness-raising "aha" kind of moment for my genial host. In the first century very few people possessed the skill of writing. That is why we discover a group of people in the New Testament who are called "scribes." So few people could write that a trained professional subgroup was required to handle the writing needs of the whole community. Writing parchment was incredibly expensive, ink and quills were quite difficult to come by and books were transcribed on scrolls, making it all but impossible to do anything except read a book from beginning to ending. Scrolls do not lend themselves to skipping around.

So in the gospels we do not have the eyewitness recorded recollections of the disciples. The question therefore arises, what do we have? That is the story we need to unravel.

The gospels were written forty to seventy years after the earthly life of Jesus had come to an end. They were written in Greek, a language Jesus did not speak except in a most casual way. Internally at least, Mark and the two gospels that copied Mark, Matthew and Luke, reveal evidence of having been shaped by the liturgical life of the synagogue.[4] They are interpretive portraits, not eyewitness accounts. All of that must be embraced before we can begin to see just what the Jesus story adds to the Jewish epic, for that is exactly what happened when the Christian faith was born. That was no small accomplishment, for the addition of the Jesus story to the epic of the Jews transformed the Jewish story into the *human* story, with the potential that is still present to make that story the *universal* human story.

That powerful truth is not always easy to see, because most of the readers and interpreters of the gospels throughout Christian history did not know they were reading a human epic. They interpreted the gospels wrongly as either biography or history. In the process they assumed that the entire Jewish epic had to be either *true* biography or *accurate* history. But no epic is ever that.

There is no doubt that the gospels are in touch with a powerful God experience that their writers believed that they and the faith communities for whom they wrote had had with the man Jesus. One cannot *write* an experience, however. All one can write is an attempt at explaining that experience. That is what the gospels are: first-century, primarily Jewish explanations of the Jesus experience. About experiences one can only offer ecstatic utterances: "In Christ God was reconciling" (2 Cor. 5:19), or "God was in Christ" (Gal. 2:20). Those are unexplained attempts to articulate an experience. Ecstatic utterances cannot be passed on to another, so explanations that can be passed on become inevitable. How did the early Christians explain their primal experience that somehow, in some way, through some means God had been met in the life of this Jesus? Basically the New Testament is the story of those explanations.

How did God get into Jesus so that we could have that experience? That was the question the New Testament writers sought to answer. Their answers are both fascinating and contradictory, but later Christians hammered these contradictions into precise doctrines. God simply declared Jesus to be the Son of God at the time of the resurrection by the action of the Spirit, said

Paul, when he wrote his epistle to the Romans (1:1–4). We miss the power of this verse because the later gospels have confused us so deeply about what the resurrection actually was. For Paul the resurrection had nothing to do with the physical resuscitation of a deceased body; it had to do with raising Jesus into the eternal life of God.[5] There was no split between resurrection and ascension in Paul. That would be introduced primarily by Luke, who more than anyone else transformed Easter into a physical emergence from a tomb and was required thereby to develop the ascension story in order to remove the resurrected physical body from this world to the realm of God.

When Mark, writing in the early 70s, faced the question of how it was that God could be experienced in the life of this Jesus, he explained it with his baptism story. God declared Jesus to be the Son of God by the action of the Spirit, said Mark, in perfect agreement with Paul (Mark 1:1–11). The difference was in the timing and in the graphic illustration. It happened, said Mark, not at the time of the resurrection, as Paul had suggested, but at the time of the baptism. Then Mark proceeded to tell the story of the heavens opening, the Spirit descending on Jesus, and the heavenly voice off-stage saying: "Thou art my beloved son!"

Matthew, writing in the early to mid-80s, also faced this same question, but he too changed the timing and his description of the experience in which God declared Jesus to be the Son of God. This declaration for Matthew came from an unnamed angel in a dream to Joseph. It was still mediated by the action of the Holy Spirit, but it now took place at the moment of conception. Jesus for Matthew was Emmanuel, God with us, and he was "conceived . . . of the Holy Spirit." "Joseph, son of David," the angel said, "do not fear to take Mary your wife, for that which is conceived in her is of the Holy Spirit" (Matt. 1:20). That is when the story of the virgin birth was born (Matt. 1:18–25).

Luke, writing in the late 80s or even the early 90s, repeated the miraculous birth story, but he both made it more specific and changed the details. In Luke, the announcing angel is not nameless but is Gabriel, who communicates not to Joseph in a dream as the unnamed angel did in Matthew, but to Mary in real time. The child you will bear, says Gabriel, when "the power of the Most High will overshadow you[,] . . . will be holy; he will be called Son of God" (Luke 1:35, NRSV).

When John wrote the Fourth Gospel in the late 90s he decided that there never was a time when God was not in Christ, so he told the story of Jesus as the enfleshment of the Word of God that had been spoken at the dawn of creation. This became the place where the preexistence of Jesus, so essential to later doctrines of the incarnation, the atonement and the Trinity, first entered the Christian story.

From Paul suggesting that God entered Jesus in the resurrection when God raised him into God's life, to John suggesting that Jesus was the enfleshed Word of God and part of who God is (since God spoke in creation and said, "Let there be light"), is quite a range of human explanations. Paul and John and all the other New Testament writers were attempting, each in his own way, to make sense out of an experience that proclaimed, in ecstatic language, "We have met God in this life of Jesus."

I am not interested in debating the details of these competing biblical explanations. I am interested rather in what it was that created the experience that God had been met in Jesus. I regard all explanations as time-bound and time-warped. When they become supernatural tales that purport to hear the voice of God speaking from the sky or see the Holy Spirit descending on a particular life, or suggest a miraculous birth that occurred without benefit of human father, I recognize that I am reading mythology. I do not dismiss mythology as untrue. I ask, What was there about this life that required this elaborate mythology to develop? Of course God speaking in a voice that human ears can hear and presumably record, the Holy Spirit descending from the sky and virgins giving birth do not actually happen except in great epic stories, but something occurs to make these mythologies seem appropriate.[6]

How was it that people became convinced that death could not contain Jesus? What was the experience that lay behind the various biblical explanations of resurrection? Of course the resurrection narratives are mythological. Dead bodies do not walk out of tombs three days after execution. Angels do not descend out of the sky, earthquakes do not announce earthly events, soldiers are not reduced to a state of stupor by angelic power, stones are not rolled away from tombs to let the dead out or to allow the gaze of witnesses to come in, bodies do not materialize on the road to Emmaus or dematerialize after the breaking of bread (Luke 24:13–27), nor do they walk through walls to enter a room where the windows are shut and the doors are locked in order to have Thomas explore the divine wounds (John 20:19–29). These are mythological details involved in human attempts to explain an experience. My interest is in raising the question about how it is that people believe they have met in this human being a power of life that the grave cannot contain and that death cannot extinguish. That is a very different question from the one Christians usually ask about the accuracy of the resurrection stories. Of course they are not accurate; they are explanations. Is the experience, however, behind them real and what was it? That is my concern.

Of course stories of cosmic ascensions are mythological. One does not get to heaven by rising off the ground and heading into the sky. One might end up in orbit instead. That would present an interesting portrait: Jesus circling the earth in eternal orbit! Failing that, one might rise into the infinity of space. It would be a long journey. If the ascension of Jesus could occur at the speed of light, approximately one hundred and eighty-six thousand miles per second, it would still take Jesus more than one hundred thousand years just to escape our single galaxy, to say nothing of the other two hundred billion or so galaxies in the visible universe. So I have no desire to debate whether or not this story is literally true. What I am interested in is seeking to determine what the experience was that caused people to say his life and the life of God must somehow be in touch with one another. Jesus must be where God is. That is not often said about human beings. Some compelling experience demands that our language be stretched beyond the human limits to capture undoubted reality. What was it? That is the question that requires our attention.

There is no doubt that stories were told about Jesus doing miraculous things like giving sight to the blind, hearing to the deaf, mobility to the crippled and speech to the mute. That was the expectation present among the Jews, that such signs would accompany the in-breaking of the kingdom of God. Isaiah had spelled that out in his thirty-fifth chapter: "Then the eyes of the blind shall be opened, and the ears of the deaf unstopped; then the lame shall leap like a deer, and the tongue of the speechless sing for joy" (vv. 5–6, NRSV).

The question I seek to answer is not whether these miracles actually happened. I do not live in a world of miracles, like the world in which the biblical stories were created. My question is a deeper one. What was it about the Jesus experience that caused people to say that in his life the signs of the in-breaking of the kingdom of God had been seen? That is a very different concern.

No, I do not believe that Jesus stilled the storm, walked on water, or took five loaves and two fish and with them fed the multitude. But I do want to understand what the experience was with Jesus that caused people to apply the God language of the Hebrew scriptures to him. It was Isaiah who said that God provides a shelter from the storm (Isa. 4:6, 25:4). What was there about Jesus that made it appropriate to apply that language to him? What caused a first-century Jew to apply to Jesus the words of Isaiah that God can make "a path in the mighty waters" (43:16) or of the Psalmist that "thy way was through the sea, thy path through the great waters; yet thy footprints were unseen" (Ps. 77:19)? What was there about Jesus that prompted people to write stories about him claiming that, like Moses (Exod. 16:31ff.), he could feed the multitude in the wilderness with heavenly bread? For that is what the feeding of the five thousand tries to say (Mark 6:30ff., Matt. 14:13ff., Luke 9:12ff., John 6:1–13).

We cannot become mired in a meaningless debate about the accuracy of first-century explanations. We do not serve our faith tradition well by literalizing the explanations of antiquity. That is to make a deity out of human words. Our concern when reading epic history is to seek the experience behind the explanations and to ask whether or not that experience was real.

Jesus was not believed to have been a God experience because of his miraculous birth, his walking out of the tomb or his cosmic ascension. Rather, the exact reverse is the fact. Stories of his miraculous birth, his walking out of his tomb and his cosmic ascension were written to try to make human language big enough, dramatic enough and supernatural enough to capture whatever it was that the early followers had experienced in Jesus. Once one believes that in a particular life the holy God, the power of the divine, has been met, then explanatory language inevitably breaks the boundaries imposed by the rational mind to try to capture the moment. The explanations are always expansive, filled with wonder and expressive of the perceptions of reality known by the writer. The explanations are therefore always rejectable whenever they are literalized. That, however, does not dismiss or even call into question the experience that made those explanations necessary. That experience is our goal. The experience is that which is transcendent, wondrous, lifting us to a new level of consciousness. What was the Jesus experience, and why does it matter? When we enter that question, then we begin to understand how the Jesus story got added to the epic of the Jewish people and how in the process it transformed that epic into one that embraces all humanity. To that story we turn next.

32

JESUS BEYOND RELIGION

THE SIGN OF THE KINGDOM OF GOD—THE EPIC UNIVERSALIZED AND HUMANIZED

They drew a circle that shut me out
Heretic, rebel, a thing to flout.
But love and I had the wit to win
We drew a circle that took them in.

Edwin Markham[7]

Those creatures that we today call Homo sapiens are a product of the same evolutionary flow that produced all the plants and all the animals. We are connected on the DNA charts to all living things. Are Homo sapiens therefore identical with human beings? I do not think so. To be fully human a creature needs to cross that anxious line between consciousness and self-consciousness. That means that we have to develop that fearful capacity to see ourselves as separate from all that is, living in a medium called time that has a past that can be remembered and a future that can be anticipated. I doubt if that experience is fully possible until we develop language, which assumes the ability to think symbolically and thus abstractly. That enormous evolutionary step, as I previously noted, is probably no more than fifty thousand years old. Language and self-consciousness seem to have evolved together. The basic verb in every language of the world is the verb *to be*. Without that verb no one can say "I am," which is the essence of self-consciousness. When language finally becomes so symbolic that it can be written, then we have the ability to capture the past, to freeze it and to celebrate it. We can even embrace the reality of a time before we were born, our first hint of eternity. Then as our consciousness grows, an awareness of our own mortality dawns, enabling us to contemplate a time when we will be no more and even begin to plan for that eventuality. Finitude is a gift of self-consciousness. Human beings are Homo sapiens who live in history.

Our ability to embrace the world was quite limited at the dawn of humanity's birth. We had no sense of how large the planet was. We did not know what lay beyond the mountains, the river or the sea that marked our own environment, to say nothing of what lay beyond the oceans. We knew only two kinds of people: those who were members of our family, clan or tribe and those who were different. We assumed that "different" was somehow evil, or at the very least, strange. We assumed also that to be different was to be dangerous, so we were always on guard.

Our ancestors lived under skies that were clear. They watched the sun rise and set. They learned the rhythm of light and darkness and adjusted to that rhythm even though darkness and night were shrouded with fear. These early humans surely wondered why the sun rose and set, why the moon turned until it disappeared, only to reappear just three days later. They had theories about everything that moved, about the purpose of streams, trees, bushes and living things. They lived in fear that enemies lurked around every corner. Defensiveness, even a certain degree of paranoia, was part of their nature and is part of ours. They wondered what it meant to die. The threat of nonbeing produced so much anxiety that they made survival their highest value. That resulted in human cooperation, which is adaptive, survival-oriented behavior. They embraced only as much reality as they could process. The human world was, in those days, a very small world.

It still is today for many people. I come from very humble stock. My mother, who died in 1999 at age ninety-two, grew up in rural North Carolina near Charlotte in a place called Griffith Station. It was on a rail line, but the train did not stop there. Once a week, she said, the train would slow down enough to kick a keg of salt fish off the boxcar for the local country store. That was the connection that Griffith Station had with the wider world.

My mother did not finish the ninth grade. She was a girl; and girls, said her father, who was a farmer become mill worker, do not need to be educated. They need to know only how to cook, how to sew, how to keep house and how to care for babies. A person did not learn that in school, he said, so school for girls was a waste of time. My mother was thus functionally illiterate. She lived her life in a very small orbit and died within twenty-five miles of the place where she was born. She could name on both hands the number of trips that took her more than a hundred miles away. Her honeymoon was one. A trip to be in attendance when I was ordained as the bishop of Newark was another. That was her first and only ride in an airplane. I met her at the gate. That was possible in those pre-terrorist days. She came off the plane on the arm of the flight attendant. When I got her in the car she said, "Son, the people on the plane were so nice, they gave me a free Coca-Cola."

Later in her life she heard on the radio about a tornado in Texas. She called my brother who lived in Texas to make sure he was safe. She had no idea how big Texas was. She read in the paper that there was a demonstration in New York. She called to make sure I was not in danger, for she knew I lived near New York.

When I became controversial in the church over matters dealing with sexuality, she became aware of this only after I had done some lectures in Charlotte on the subject of homosexuality that were well covered by the press. Those stories resulted in a spate of letters to the editor in which some not very flattering things were written about her son. She read them and worried.

When I called one Saturday morning in the midst of this controversy, she said something like, "Son, I don't understand why everyone doesn't like you; you're such a nice boy." I responded by saying that if she would just tell me what it was she did not understand, I would be happy to explain it. "Well, son," she said, "what is a heterosexual?" She perceived only a very little bit of the reality that engaged my life.

I say these things not in any way to be derogatory. I adored this special mother and owe her more than I can ever say. She was born when a horse and buggy was the primary mode of transportation. She died after space travel had become commonplace. Reality kept breaking in upon her, as it does upon all of us. Hers was an incredible life, given the circumstances with which she had to deal. She illustrates for me, however, something of the various levels of consciousness that human beings must engage, based upon their opportunities and life experiences.

In some sense the human race has always had to do just that. It is the destiny of the human being to move into new vistas, embrace new realities, grow into new awarenesses and develop new levels of consciousness. It is therefore not easy to be human. Consider how traumatic such new insights must have been for the fragile, newly self-conscious human creature when the vast size of the universe began to explode into his or her awareness. It actually took years for the insights of Nicolaus Copernicus, Johannes Kepler and Galileo Galilei to gain a hearing. When they did, however, the insecurities and fears that those insights unleashed were palpable. It is no wonder that the church, the voice of values and the source of stability in that society, was so negative to Galileo that it sought to silence him. He presented a vision that was more than the human people of that day could absorb. It loosed the demons of insecurity. What if there is no superhuman parent God above the clouds who watches over us, guards and protects us, keeping the tides inside their boundaries and the rains timely and moderate? Could we survive psychologically; could we manage the trauma of aloneness? Or would we simply fall apart, close our minds and pretend that nothing had ever changed and that the sky was not just the roof of the earth but also the floor of heaven?

When Charles Darwin challenged our special status as creatures just "a little lower than the angels" who bore God's image, suggesting that we too had emerged from the evolutionary process, we recoiled in fear and struck back with hostility. We were simply not ready to face the fact that human beings might be nothing more than one more species of living animals that inhabit this earth, perhaps of no more ultimate value or worth than a cockroach or a bird. That was a lot of reality to embrace. Unable to bear the message, we ridiculed the messenger.

Our security was further shattered when Sigmund Freud suggested that our gods were simply parental projections in the sky, and again when Albert Einstein suggested that the truth by which we lived was never objective and real, but was always subjective and relative. We have had to learn how to live with the anxiety of uncertainty, the angst of watching our security systems crumble. That is what happens when the world expands and consciousness increases. Better not to enter that world than to fall apart. That is why closed minds are still with us today. In a small world we can identify our enemies, control at least to some degree our destinies, protect our lives, sustain our values and cling to our image of a God who justifies and shapes all of these defining realities. If the world in which we live keeps expanding, however, then even our God is not able to keep up with the pace. So God totters, the "Word of God" is revealed to be much less than ultimate, the linchpins of certainty are pulled and humanity appears to float freely on an ever-changing sea. That is where we live today and inside that kind of world with that kind of consciousness we must shape our values, our beliefs and our purpose. Some human beings validate that truth and give substance to that insight when they opt to live inside religious systems by rejecting the world. Others choose to live in the world by rejecting all religious systems. Both bear witness to the fact that yesterday's religious systems cannot continue to live in today's world.

It is quite possible, maybe even probable, that the Jesus served in most of the Christian churches of the world today is simply an idol created in a primitive time that is destined to die. The story of a theistic deity who assumes human form suggests as much. When this incarnate one is said to have entered history via the miracle of the virgin birth and to have departed via the miracle of the cosmic ascension, one's suspicions should be heightened. Trinitarian language likewise does not communicate in our world; neither does the image of the vicarious savior who absorbs on the cross the punishment due to us for our sinfulness so that God's righteousness can be fully served even as we are washed in the saving blood of the sacrificial Lamb of God.

What if Jesus was not that, however, but was rather the dawning of a new consciousness in human life? What if he was a human life who saw beyond the traditional boundaries of our security system, whose mission was to lift our vision, to empower us to embrace a reality that we never before even knew existed, enabling us to walk into a new humanity? What if God is not a being who lives beyond the sky who can be manipulated by the prayers of the faithful and of the fearful? What if God is not a security-giving heavenly parent who hands out threats and favors, rewards and punishments and who wants us to remain childlike, docile and dependent? What if God is not a judge who delights in our quivering before the throne of judgment, a deity who urges us to be born again so that we will never have to grow up into mature beings? Would we welcome such a god? Or would we kill this deity because the threat we perceived at the divine hand was still intolerable to our security?

To step beyond religion is to grow into human maturity. It is to leave behind all of the security boundaries that we have erected against our fears. It is to recognize that the world is so large that differences can be embraced and honored. It is to step beyond tribal boundaries into a new and fuller sense of human identity. Perhaps another way to say it is that in Christ there is neither Jew nor Greek, Jew nor gentile. Tribal divisions come out of limited consciousness. A universal sense of what it means to be human is a gigantic step into something quite new, an expanded consciousness. Perhaps this is why a gentile soldier was placed at the foot of the cross in the earliest gospel, to point to that life on the cross that had been given away (Mark 15:39), that life that did not grasp at survival. This gentile said that that is what God is like: a life of endless giving, endless loving. Jesus' was a life so full that he did not resist hostility, a life so complete he had no need to cling to survival. His capacity to give was without limit. It was total. Nothing held in reserve. When we read Mark's story of the crucifixion we hear this centurion's words and translate them to say, "Truly this man was the son of God" (15:39), as if he was affirming the creedal orthodoxy of the third and fourth centuries.

That is not what this story means, however. It is a narrative about one who stood on the other side of the great security divide that separated Jews from unclean gentiles and who crossed it to embrace the vision of a new humanity. The experience of Jesus meant to him that human life was not bounded and that God was not external. We human beings enter God and life simultaneously the moment we step beyond our fears and become free. One cannot be human and reject those who are different. One cannot limit God to that sense of holiness we meet only inside the boundaries of tribal worship. That is why Jesus could be heard to say that the first step into God is to "love your enemies and pray for those who persecute you" (Matt. 5:44), or to "do good to those who hate you, bless those who curse you, pray for those who abuse you" (Luke 6:27–28). This Jesus was perceived as one who removed all fear.

Perhaps that is why those inside the Christ experience wrote that human life could never have produced the experience they found in him. He must have been of another realm. Perhaps his birth was said to have been announced by a star because a star does not illumine just a single nation; its rays shine over the entire world. His life drew all nations and all people beyond their limits. That is why the wise men came to present him gifts and to worship him. They were gentiles who recognized a new humanity in him. By their gift of gold they pronounced him king, the highest symbol of human achievement. By their gift of frankincense, they acknowledged that humanity at its fullest participates in the meaning of divinity from which it follows that the way into divinity is to become fully human. It was a new consciousness that overcame an old boundary. By their gift of myrrh they acknowledged that it was through the pathway of self-giving, including the giving of one's life, that the way is found into infinity. Death becomes the doorway into life. One dies every time one has the courage to give himself or herself away (Matt. 2:1–12). That is a new consciousness, the doorway into a new humanity. That is the Christ presence.

Are males superior to females, free people superior to slaves, parents superior to children, heterosexuals superior to homosexuals, white people superior to people of color? That is the wisdom of a world dedicated to survival and driving all things into power relationships. But humanity is always impaired when it builds its sense of worth by denigrating the worth of another. What the Jesus experience showed was a vision of a new humanity and in that vision no one is diminished.

Jesus crossed the boundaries separating males from females and invited women into full discipleship. His followers would say that in Christ there is neither male nor female, bond nor free, both of which were radical pronouncements in a rigidly patriarchal and slavery-practicing world. These followers of Jesus would also write that women were the first to stare into a tomb that they perceived could not contain Jesus' humanity and the first to draw the right conclusions (Mark 16, Matt. 28, Luke 24, John 20).

Jesus also embraced the outcast. He touched the rotting flesh of the leper and gave him back his own humanity (Matt. 8:2–3). You are not repulsive, Jesus conveyed; you are human. Jesus welcomed the touch of the woman with the chronic menstrual discharge, though by touching him in her uncleanness she rendered him unclean according to the Torah (Mark 5:25–34). Jesus stood between the woman taken in the act of adultery and her accusers (John 8:1–11). No sinful deed made anyone ultimately rejectable, he said, certainly not worthy of death. That is the power that people experienced in him and it was so freeing, so life-giving, that they said God was in Christ. Given hope by that power, they stepped beyond the barriers of their security and began to taste the new humanity.

Even religious rules are not ultimate, Jesus said time after time. Religious rules are seen to be invested with divine authority only because they have become part of our security systems. But, said Jesus, even the Sabbath is not to be treated as a rule into which human life has to fit. The Sabbath has value only to the degree that it enhances our humanity. The Sabbath was made for human life; human life was not made for the Sabbath (Mark 2:27). So it is with every religious doctrine, practice and rule. God is not met in the religious symbols that serve our insecurity and that enable us to pretend that we are the saved, the true believers, the holders of ultimate truth. Those attitudes are not only a reflection of the evil present in religion, but also the sources of enormous human violence and pain. God can never be identified with religion. No human tradition can ever corner the market on salvation and pretend that it controls the only doorway to God. Human folly is all that those claims are!

One who is fully human is not bound by all that seems to bind human life—tribe, prejudice, gender, sexual orientation, religion, finitude, fear. We are free of all of those things. That is the Jesus message. Or as St. Paul once observed, "Who shall separate us from the love of Christ? Shall tribulation, or distress, or persecution, or famine, or nakedness, or peril, or sword?" No! shouts Paul, answering his own question: "In all these things we are more than conquerors through him who loved us. For I am sure that neither death, nor life, nor angels, nor principalities, nor things present, nor things to come, nor powers, nor height, nor depth, nor anything else in all creation, will be able to separate us from the love of God in Christ Jesus our Lord" (Rom. 8:35–39).

That is the Christ experience. That is what the New Testament is all about. Jesus, understood as the Christ, is both a call and the empowerment needed to answer that call. The call is to embrace a new humanity, to grasp a new consciousness, to enter a new order of being, to become fully human. The empowerment comes when that new humanity is claimed. Empowerment is experienced in the recognition that humanity and divinity are two sides of the same coin. Was he divine, we ask of Jesus? Yes, but only in the sense that by living fully and freeing his new humanity he was able to enter into the realm of divinity, of God. The two cannot be separated.

The doctrines, dogmas and creeds of our tribal religious past were a stage in our development. They were part of our religious childhood. Nothing more. They are certainly not eternal. When they become lifeless, they should be allowed to die. Artificial respiration of yesterday's religious forms is a pious waste of time and energy. All creeds, doctrines and sacred forms serve only to point toward an experience they can never capture. That is why religious people spend so much time pretending that truth has been secured in these human forms. Our security demands that we be convinced of that. That is why we kill those people who threaten our religious convictions. That is why we reject those people who approach God and truth from a context different from our own. We call them infidels and pagans if they are in different religious systems; heretics if they were once part of our worldview. That is why we play religious games designed to prove our spiritual superiority.

Humanity is expanding in consciousness. In the expansion of that consciousness God is less and less the supernatural parent figure who is our divine protector and becomes instead the ultimate consciousness in which our own consciousness participates and is a part. We cease being dependent recipients and become God-bearers to one another. That is why our ancestors in faith came to experience God in the person of Jesus. This Jesus, they perceived, understood and lived out the fact that he shared in the consciousness of God. He invited us to step into that divine power by stepping into our potential and full humanity. His invitation carried with it the power to risk. By doing these things Jesus reversed the human value system that was dedicated to survival and self-preservation. He lifted up the downcast and humbled those who trusted in their own power (Luke 1:51). He valued the contributions equally of those who had labored only one hour and those who had toiled through the heat of the day (Matt. 20:1–16). He proclaimed that half-breed heretic Samaritans, when they obeyed the first law of the Torah and showed compassion on those in need, were more the children of Abraham than were the priest and the Levite who passed by without showing compassion (Luke 10:29–37). He honored the prodigal son because he came to himself, and Jesus made him equal to the elder brother who never ventured from home or duty (Luke 15:11ff.). He ordered the outcasts from the highways and byways to be compelled to come into the kingdom (Luke 14:12–24). He placed as great a value on a single lost sheep as on the entire flock (Matt. 18:12, Luke 15:4). He expanded the concept of humanity to include both our enemies and the objects of our prejudice and scorn (Luke 17:16). He called on his followers to love their enemies (Matt. 5:43) and to be willing to let their enemies love them (Luke 10:29–37). He entered humanity so deeply, possessed his own being so significantly, gave his life and his love away so freely, expanded the boundaries of his existence so totally that he became the human channel through which the reality of God was able to flow into human history. That is what people meant when they said, "God was in Christ." This was the experience that forced them to describe his entrance into life through a miraculous birth, his inability to be bound by finitude and the tomb in his resurrection and his union with God depicted in the cosmic ascension. People experienced in him the in-breaking of the kingdom of God and attributed its signs to him. They saw the fulfillment of the scriptures in him and portrayed him as living out its intimate details.

Jesus was a product of the epic story of the Jews. On the eighth day following his birth, he was circumcised and became part of the Jewish story. Their history was his history. His genealogies portrayed him as the son of Abraham (Matt. 1:1–17, Luke 3:23–38). He was shaped by the epic that produced the tribal religion of the Jews, who understood themselves to be God's favorite ones, God's chosen, who assumed that their enemies were God's enemies, who portrayed God rejoicing over the Egyptians who drowned in the Red Sea. But he was also part of the growth of that tribal God through the Exile as reflected in the demands for love and justice that the prophets added to the epic of the Jews. He was heir to the budding universalism that appeared in the latter days of the Jewish story when the Jews' God consciousness began to grow past the model of the tribal deity. Second Isaiah captured that universalism, which Jesus eventually embodied when he wrote, "For my thoughts are not your thoughts, neither are your ways my ways, says the Lord. For as the heavens are higher than the earth, so are my ways higher than your ways and my thoughts than your thoughts" (Isa. 55:8–9).

Jesus seemed to understand that no one can finally fit the holy God into his or her creeds or doctrines. That is idolatry. We cannot continue to create God in our own image and expect God to serve our needs. We cannot continue to pretend that we are the chosen and all other people the unchosen. God is not an idol of our own creation. God is not our parent, our protector, our defender. God does not do our bidding or answer our prayers. God is God. You and I are not. The tribal deity of the Jewish epic was growing with the expanded consciousness of the people. Finally, in the words of an unknown prophet who called himself the voice crying in the wilderness, a messenger who we know as Malachi,[8] we hear that the boundaries on God imposed by our security needs are being broken open and the divine shackles are falling off from who God is. Malachi heard God saying, "From the rising of the sun to its setting my name is great among the nations, and in every place incense is offered to my name, and a pure offering; for my name is great among the nations, says the Lord of hosts" (Mal. 1:11).

In the life of Jesus following the lead of the prohets, the God of Israel was becoming the God of the universe.

The Psalmist added to this universal, inescapable image of God when he or she wrote:

> Whither shall I go from thy Spirit?
> Or whither shall I flee from thy presence?
> If I ascend to heaven, thou art there!
> If I make my bed in Sheol, thou art there!
> If I take the wings of the morning and dwell in the uttermost parts of
>   the sea,
> even there thy hand shall lead me,
> and thy right hand shall hold me.
> If I say, "Let only darkness cover me,
> and the light about me be night,"
> even the darkness is not dark to thee,
> the night is bright as the day;
> For darkness is as light with thee. (Ps. 139:7–12)

The tribal deity of the Jewish epic was growing. Universalism was dawning. This deity was still a being until Jesus transformed God first into a presence and then into a life-giving, permeating spirit, revealing for everyone to see the Ground of All Being.

Jesus commissioned his disciples to go into all the world (Matt. 28:16–20). They were to go beyond the boundaries of their nation, their tribe and most specifically their religion. When they would finally escape all of these boundaries inside their expanded and open humanity, they were to proclaim the gospel—that is, the infinite love of God for all that God has made, a love that recognizes no barriers. Boundless love will even love those who have sought to crucify the Love of God. It includes every species, every plant, every planet, every tribe, every person. All become God's chosen. No one is an alien. No one is separate from God. We live in God; God lives in us. We are to be witnesses in Jerusalem, in Judea, in Samaria, and "unto the uttermost part of the earth" (Acts 1:8, KJV). The name of Jesus is now Emmanuel, which means God with us (Matt. 1:23). When he says "Lo I am with you always" (Matt. 28:20, KJV) he is claiming the Emmanuel title. When God is set free as spirit, the boundaries of the nation-states, symbolized by their different languages, are erased and every person speaks the language of a universal love (Acts 2:1–4). As that spirit rolls through history, the barriers fall. Peter hears God say in a dream: "What God has cleansed, you must not call common [or unclean]" (Acts 10:9–16). Peter rises from that vision and baptizes Cornelius the gentile. The Jewish epic breaks into universality and becomes the human epic.

The movement is furthered when Philip the deacon baptizes the Ethiopian eunuch (Acts 8:26–40). He was escaping the boundaries of the Torah, which stated quite specifically that "he whose testicles are crushed or whose male member is cut off shall not enter the assembly of the Lord" (Deut. 23:1).

Time and time again this biblical epic that began as a Jewish tribal story paused at what once was a boundary marking a human division. Ultimately the boundary was hurdled and the uninhibited love of God rolled on past the limiting tendencies of gender and race, sexual orientation and religion, until one human community came into our vision. Yes, we see still barriers of tribe, race, sex and religion in the human family. Many there are who think they serve God with murderous acts against the peace of the world. Some are Christians, some are Jews, some are Muslims, some are Hindus, some are Buddhists, but all are serving an idol, a tribal deity whose time in history is passing away. Do not mistake that passing away as something evil, even if it is marked by a rise of human fear and an increase of human hate and human killing. The vision of a new humanity is still emerging, and it will not be denied, for Luke has Jesus proclaim that the kingdom of God is near when sickness dissolves into wholeness (10:9). In Luke Jesus says that the kingdom of God is in the midst of us, that it is within each of us (17:21).

That is why Jesus is a God experience. That is why he was said to be the life that could not be contained by death or the grave; the life who made God available outside all the forms of the past, including the forms of religion. That is why the Jesus story was grafted onto the Jewish epic and served to increase the pace whereby that epic turned from a tribal history into a universal story of humankind.

Homo sapiens are evolving into Homo spiritus. A new humanity is emerging. Jesus is the first fruits of that new humanity.

This is why the scriptures that tell his story must be transformed into a universal story, true (as a time- and place-bound story could never be) to who Jesus was and what he said and did. This is why these scriptures can never again be used to denigrate, hurt, oppress, enslave or diminish the humanity of any person. This is why the church must cease its quest for power, authority and that most insidious temptation of all, internal unity, and begin to transform the world, to reconcile our differences and to make known a barrier-free humanity. We cannot pray the Jesus prayer, "Thy kingdom come, Thy will be done on earth as it is in heaven," unless we are willing to act as agents of that in-breaking kingdom by giving up our petty divisions, our excessive claims and our symbols of power and begin to devote all our energies to building a different kind of world.

In the kingdom of God for which our world yearns, every person will have a better opportunity to live fully and thus to worship the God who is the Source of Life; every person will be freed to love wastefully and thus to worship the God who is the Source of Love; and every person will have a better chance to be all that each person can be in the infinite variety of our humanity—every race, ethnic group, gender, sexual orientation—for that is what it means to worship the God who is the Ground of All Being. That is the Christ function and to serve this Christ is the only ministry that the church, which calls itself the Body of Christ, has. All else is human folly born out of human survival games.

Jesus, according to the Fourth Gospel, did not come to make us religious, to make us righteous or moral, or even to make us orthodox. All of those are demonstrably killing formulas throughout our world. John said Jesus had only one purpose and that was to call us into life more abundantly (10:10). That is the meaning of God in our post-tribal and even post-religious world.

The use of the Bible to justify our prejudices must be abandoned. We do not abandon that sacred story in which the sins of scripture are embedded in the "terrible texts," however. We rather claim it for our own. We recognize its humble tribal birthplace. We celebrate its growth, its breaking of barriers and boundaries. We watch it move from tribal deity to universal deity, and even beyond. Then we observe that in the person of Jesus this God presence drew near and entered our humanity, calling us beyond limits into a new consciousness. We place ourselves in this ever-expanding epic and write the next chapter as we embrace that new humanity. We have entered into the consciousness of God. That is what it means to discover that we are now God's dwelling place. There is no supernatural deity beyond the sky working miracles. There is only a God-infused humanity through whom the Source of Life, the Source of Love and the Ground of Being lives. We are the God-bearers of the world. We must rise to our new vocation and be God for one another. For in each of us is the promise of "Emmanuel," which means God with us. The only way that God can be with us now and through the ages is for each of us to allow God to live and love through us, through our humanity.

This why I am a Christian and why I treasure the Holy Scriptures that chronicle my journey through time to this moment of both reformation and revelation. That is why we need now to write the next chapter of our universal epic.

Shalom.

NOTES

Section 1

1. Paul Tillich, *The Protestant Era*, p. 226. See bibliography for details.

2. Among my treasured guides in this study were Gerhard Von Rad's work on Genesis entitled *Genesis: A Commentary*, Brevard Childs' and Martin Noth's works on Exodus, George B. Caird's and Hans Conzelmann's works on Luke and Michael Goulder's monumental two-volume commentary on Luke, titled *Luke: A New Paradigm*, which I discovered later in life. Ernst Haenchen led me through my study of Acts. Edwin Hoskyns, C. H. Dodd, William Temple and later Raymond Brown guided my work on the Fourth Gospel. Samuel Terrien introduced me to the book of Psalms, and James Muilenburg to the prophets and the theology of the Old Testament. My Pauline studies were guided by a series of scholars as old as Martin Luther and as modern as Rudolf Bultmann, with additional help coming from Krister Stendahl, Paul Van Buren, Samuel Sandmel and a host of others. The details for each of these authors are contained in the bibliography.

3. Dr. Bailey Smith was the gentleman's name. It was in the early 1990s.

4. Jean Holloway, "Scripture," written to be sung to the tune *Aurelia* or the tune *Munich*. Used by permission.

5. President Bill Clinton.

6. A good example might be to compare Mark 3:7–10, where the author of this gospel writes in typically garbled Marcan prose (here from the RSV):

> Jesus withdrew with his disciples to the sea, and a great multitude from Galilee followed; also from Judea and Jerusalem and Idumea and from beyond the Jordan and from about Tyre and Sidon a great multitude, hearing all that he did, came to him. And he told his disciples to have a boat ready for him because of the crowd, lest they should crush him; for he had healed many, so that all who had diseases pressed upon him to touch him.

. . . with Luke's edited version in 6:17–18:

> And he came down with them and stood on a level place, with a great crowd of his disciples and a great multitude of people from all Judea and Jerusalem and the seacoast of Tyre and Sidon, who came to hear him and to be healed of their diseases.

7. John Greenleaf Whittier put this biblical episode into a poem that later became a hymn (taken from Hymn 435 in the Episcopal hymnal, 1940, published by the Church Pension Fund, New York, 1943):

> Dear Lord and Father of Mankind,
> Forgive our foolish ways!
> Reclothe us in our rightful mind,

In purer lives thy service find,
In deeper reverence, praise.

Breathe through the heat of our desire
Thy coolness and thy balm;
Let sense be dumb, let flesh retire;
Speak through the earthquake, wind, and fire,
O still small voice of calm.

Section 2

1. Frank McCourt, *Angela's Ashes*, chap. 1. See bibliography for details.

2. The account of Agatha Yarnell is based on a true story well publicized in the press and television. I have not used her real name, however, to keep from adding one more bit of notoriety to those family members who have endured so much. I have also altered the details but not the substance of this tragedy.

3. I will explain the relationship between the oldest story of creation, which begins with Gen. 2:4 and goes through Adam and Eve, and the newest story of creation, which is in Gen. 1:1–23, as the text of this chapter unfolds.

4. Even though I will not take time to analyze this text, I think it is important to note the interesting use of pronouns found here. This is the product of a very patriarchal age, and yet this ancient story has God speak of the divine self in the plural. Let us make man in *our* own image. The text goes on to say God created man in *his* own image, in the image of God created *he* him. Male and female created *he them*. In the older version of the creation story, which begins with Gen. 2:4, only the man is created in God's image, then the animals and finally the woman out of Adam's rib. I will return to this text in a subsequent chapter. Here I simply want to note the unusual use of pronouns.

5. Pike was a former Episcopal/Anglican bishop of California who while dean at the Cathedral of St. John the Divine in New York City, prior to being elected bishop, led the fight inside the Episcopal Church to see birth control and family planning as a moral option not an immoral practice.

6. James Russell Lowell, 1845. Hymn 519 in the Episcopal hymnal, 1940. See bibliography for details.

7. Jürgen Moltmann, *God in Creation*, p. 21. See bibliography for details.

8. This is quoted from the annual report of a stockholders' meeting of this company.

9. Quoted from a statement by the United Nations Environmental Programme (UNEP), Dec. 1, 2000. Taken from *Nature's Way* by Ed McGaa, Eagle Man, chapter 9 in particular. See bibliography for details.

10. Many of the details from this paragraph and the next are taken from chapter 8 of the book *Nature's Way* by Ed McGaa, Eagle Man. See bibliography for details.

11. Andrew C. Revkin, "Glacier Loss Seen as Clear Signs of Human Role in Global Warming," Reuters, Feb. 19, 2001.

12. From an Associated Press story, Jan. 22, 2001.

13. Mr. Putin reversed himself just prior to this book's publication and signed the Kyoto Treaty on behalf of Russia.

14. Lynn White, "The Historical Roots of Our Ecological Crises," *Science* 155 (1967): 1203–1207, part of a compendium of essays.

15. Charles Birch, *Faith, Science and the Future* (Geneva: Church and Society, 1978), quoted from Moltman, p. 50.

16. Rachel Carson, *Silent Spring*. See bibliography for details.

17. Canon 4 of Rite II of the Holy Eucharist in the 1979 version of the Episcopal Church's Book of Common Prayer refers to "Our Island Home."

18. Wendell Willkie's *One World* was published in 1943.

19. Ed McGaa, Eagle Man, *Nature's Way*, p. xiii. See bibliography for details.

20. Jürgen Moltmann, *God in Creation: A New Theology of Creation and the Spirit of God*, pp. 49–50. See bibliography for details.

Section 3

1. Tertullian, *De Cultu Feminarum*, book 1, chap. 1.

2. All of the above quotations about the relationship between men and women were taken directly off the Internet from women in the religions of the world.

3. Joseph Campbell and Bill Moyers, *The Power of Myth*. See bibliography for details.

4. Television evangelist Pat Robertson in a 1992 fundraising letter.

5. "I permit no woman to teach or to have authority over a man" (1 Tim. 2:12).

6. This issue became crucial in the nineteenth century in Catholic theology because in the eighteenth century scientists had conclusively documented the existence of the egg cell in the woman, which made her cocreator of every life that has ever been born. Jesus was assumed now to have received 50 percent of his genetic makeup from his mother. Since she too was a child of Adam, she too carried the stain of original sin. So in order for Jesus to be born sinless, Mary herself had to have a special birth. The Immaculate Conception solved that problem.

7. Carl Jung, *Aion*, chap. 4. See bibliography for details.

8. St. Jerome, from his commentary on Ephesians 3:5. Quoted from Marina Warner, *Alone of All Her Sex*, p. 73. See bibliography for details.

9. St. Jerome, from his commentary on Zechariah. Quoted from Marina Warner, *Alone of All Her Sex*, p. 76. See bibliography for details.

10. U.S. Supreme Court case, *Bradford v. the State of Illinois* (1873). Chief Justice Salmon P. Chase was the sole voice of dissent.

11. Quoted from Marina Warner, *Alone of All Her Sex*, p. 76. See bibliography for details.

12. Dionysius, letter to Basilides, canon 2.

13. A ninth-century Islamic scholar, Al-Razi, made reference to this while commenting on Qur'an 4:11. The citation can be found on the Internet under "Citations: The Position of Women in Islam."

14. See Joan Morris, *The Lady Was a Bishop*, pp. 105–112. See bibliography for details.

15. Teresa Heinz Kerry, July 2004. Quoted from her speech at the Democratic National Convention in Boston, Massachusetts.

16. See Matt. 27:56, 61; 28:1; Mark 15:40, 47; 16:1; Luke 8:2, 24; 10; John 19:25; 20:18.

Section 4

1. Television evangelist Pat Robertson on the *700 Club* television program. Dec. 24, 1973.

2. Before this book went to press the Reverend Dr. Jeffrey John was appointed and installed as dean of St. Alban's Cathedral in the Church of England. It was compensation for the shameful way he was treated in this process. Oxford lost a great bishop; St. Alban's gained a great dean. The Church of England appears to be saying that an honest homosexual is prohibited from being a bishop but allowed to be a dean. The rationality of that position escapes me.

3. The Right Reverend John Howe of Central Florida to Presiding Bishop Frank Griswold. This correspondence was copied to all the bishops following the General Convention in September 2003.

4. Pat Robertson on the *700 Club* television program, Dec. 24, 1973.

5. The Right Reverend V. Gene Robinson, an acknowledged gay man whose fourteen-year partnership is a matter of public record, was elected by the clergy and people in the Episcopal Church in New Hampshire and confirmed by the General Convention of the entire Episcopal Church in 2003.

6. Taken from a speech given by Dean Moore and printed on the Internet in 2003.

7. Michael Massing, "Bishop Lee's Choice," *New York Times* magazine, Jan. 4, 2004.

Section 5

1. Billy Graham, *Just As I Am*, pp. 7 and 19. See bibliography for details.

2. A reading from Proverbs occurs only once in the three-year lectionary used by many Christian bodies. It is not on a Sunday, but on the Feast of St. Matthew, observed on September 21. That reading from the Hebrew scriptures is Proverbs 3:1–6. Otherwise Proverbs is never read in this liturgical cycle.

3. Isaiah 40–55: the work of an unknown prophet that was attached to the scroll of Isaiah.

4. James Dobson, *A New Dare to Discipline* and *Temper Your Child's Tantrums*. See bibliography for details.

5. Philip J. Greven, *Spare the Child*. See bibliography for details.

6. *The Journals of Merriwether Lewis and William Clark*, Oct. 15, 1804. Read on the Internet.

7. Charles Dickens, *Nicholas Nickleby*; Mark Twain, *The Adventures of Tom Sawyer*; and William F. Buckley, *Saving the Queen: A Blackford Oakes Mystery*. See bibliography for details.

8. *New York Times*, May 6, 2004, p. A10.

9. This was true in the Buckley novel *Saving the Queen*, which was set in an upper-class English boarding school.

10. The institution was Woodlawn School outside Charlotte, NC, a grades 1–8 school that counted among its alumni evangelist Billy Graham. Graham describes similar memories of this school in his autobiography, *Just As I Am*. See bibliography for details.

11. Alex Haley, *Roots*. See bibliography for details.

12. Suzanne Fonay Wemple, *Women in Frankish Society: Marriage and the Cloister, 500–900*. See bibliography for details.

13. Both Pat Robertson and Jerry Falwell have used this language in their attacks on the women's liberation movement. Robertson seems particularly eager to suggest that "women's lib" is lesbian-dominated and therefore antifamily.

14. Karen Armstrong, a former nun, has emerged in the last twenty years as one of the most profound commentators on religion in the world today. See bibliography for details on her books.

15. Thomas à Kempis, *Imitation of Christ*, p. 62. See bibliography for details.

16. John A. T. Robinson, *The Human Face of God*, p. 233. See bibliography for details.

17. William Boyd Carpenter, text set to the tune *St. Petersburg*. Hymn 435 in the Episcopal hymnal, 1940. See bibliography for details.

18. Johann Heerman, text set to the tune *Herzliebster Jesu*. Hymn 71 in the Episcopal hymnal, 1940. See bibliography for details.

19. Pierre Teilhard de Chardin, *Science and Christ*, p. 64. See bibliography for details.

20. Matthew Fox, *Original Blessing*. See bibliography for details.

21. My next book has as its working title *Jesus for the Nonreligious*. I will address these themes there, *Deo volente*.

22. John A. T. Robinson, *The Human Face of God*, p. 43. Robinson gets this reference from Friedrich Schleiermacher's book *The Christian Faith*. See bibliography for details.

23. The title of John A. T. Robinson's book on Christology. See bibliography for details.

Section 6

1. September 1998 press release, Westboro Baptist Church, Topeka, Kansas; Fred Phelps, pastor.

2. Jesse Jackson in his quest for the presidential nomination in 1988.

3. Patrick Buchanan in 1992 in his presidential campaign.

4. Mahathir Mohamed, Malaysia's prime minister from 1981 to 2003. This particular comment was made in late 1997.

5. John Cornwall, *Hitler's Pope*. See bibliography for details.

6. Samuel Sandmel, *Anti-Semitism in the New Testament?* p. 166. See bibliography for details.

7. As noted in the previous section, Isaiah 40–55, or Second Isaiah, is the work of an unknown prophet that was attached to the scroll of Isaiah. Zechariah 9–14 is also the work of an unknown prophet, written at least a century after Zechariah 1–8 and attached to the scroll of Zechariah.

8. Adolf Hitler, *Mein Kampf*, p. 302. See bibliography for details.

9. I have some genuine doubts about the Q hypothesis. That is why I have framed the words in this chapter with qualifiers such as "is assumed to be," "has led to the assumption," and "if this is accurate." For those who want to pursue what I believe is the most significant challenge to the Q hypothesis, I commend the preface to Michael D.

Goulder's commentary on Luke, which is entitled: *Luke: A New Paradigm*. (See bibliography for details.) However, I must say that the vast majority of American New Testament scholars are committed to the Q hypothesis and assume the historicity and the reality of this early book.

10. Quote from Karen Armstrong, *Holy Wars*, p. 510. See bibliography for details.

11. The entire Joseph story is found in chapters 37–50 of the book of Genesis.

12. There was a brief revival of the Jewish state in 135 CE, but it was only momentary.

Section 7

1. David Tacey, *The Spirituality Revolution*, p. 11. See bibliography for details.

2. Mircea Eliade, *The Sacred and the Profane*, p. 204. See bibliography for details.

3. Kenneth Scott Latourette, *The History of the Christian Faith*. See bibliography for details.

4. Reginald Heber, 1819. Hymn 254 in the Episcopal hymnal, 1940. See bibliography for details.

5. George Washington Doane, 1848. Hymn 259 in the Episcopal hymnal, 1940. See bibliography for details.

6. Percy Dearmer, 1929. Hymn 262 in the Episcopal hymnal, 1940. See bibliography for details.

7. It was a Finnish theologian named Hannu Saloranta who helped me to see these two texts as staking out radically different perspectives. The second text remains appropriate for the world in which I live.

8. Martin Buber, *The Legend of Baal-Shem*, p. xi. See bibliography for details.

9. A column by Asra Q. Nomani on the op-ed page of the *New York Times*, May 6, 2004.

10. It is of interest to me that the Jesus Seminar color-codes all three of these synoptic sayings gray, which means that "Jesus did not say this but the ideas contained in it are close to his own." I would make Mark's version pink, which means "Jesus probably said something like this," and I would make Matthew's version black, which means "Jesus did not say this."

Section 8

1. Book of Common Prayer (1979), p. 236.

2. James Muilenburg, *The Way of Israel: Biblical Faith and Ethics*, p. 75. See bibliography for details.

3. Text by D. Butler, taken from the Swedish Lutheran Hymnal published by Vanguard Press.

4. I treat this brief hint much more thoroughly in my book *Liberating the Gospels: Reading the Bible with Jewish Eyes*. See bibliography for details.

5. I treat Paul's view of resurrection in much greater detail in my book *Resurrection: Myth or Reality?* See bibliography for details.

6. I treat the full meaning of the miraculous birth traditions in my book *Born of a Woman: A Bishop Rethinks the Virgin Birth and the Place of Women in a Male-Dominated Church*. See bibliography for details.

7. Edwin Markham, the poem "Outwitted."

8. Malachi simply means "my messenger."

BIBLIOGRAPHY

Allport, Gordon. *The Nature of Prejudice*. Garden City, NY: Doubleday Anchor Books, 1958.

Armstrong, Karen. *The Battle for God*. New York: Knopf, 1993.

———. *Beginning the World*. New York: St. Martin's Press, 1983.

———. *A History of God*. New York: Ballantine Books, 1993.

———. *Holy War: The Crusades and Their Impact on Today's World*. New York: Doubleday Anchor Books, 1988.

———. *One City, Three Faiths*. New York: St. Martin's Press, 1995.

———. *The Spiral Staircase: My Climb Out of Darkness*. New York: Knopf, 2004.

———. *Through the Narrow Gate*. New York: St. Martin's Press, 1980.

Ashcroft, Mary Ellen. *The Magdalene Gospel*. Garden City, NY: Doubleday, 1995.

Batchelor, Edward J. *Homosexuality and Ethics*. New York: Pilgrim Press, 1980.

Berger, David, ed. *History and Hate: The Dimensions of Anti-Semitism*. Philadelphia, New York and Jerusalem: The Jewish Publication Society, 1986.

Berne, Eric, MD. *Sex in Human Loving*. New York: Simon and Schuster, 1973.

Blackman, Edwin Cyril. *Marcion and His Influence*. London: SPCK, 1948.

Bonhoeffer, Dietrich. *Letters and Papers from Prison*. Edited by Eberhard Bethge. London: SCM Press, 1953, 1991; New York: Macmillan, 1997.

Boswell, John. *Christianity, Social Tradition and Homosexuality*. Chicago: Univ. of Chicago Press, 1980.

Bowers, Margaretta. *Conflicts of the Clergy*. New York: Thomas Nelson, 1963.

Bowker, John. *Problems of Suffering in Religions of the World*. Cambridge: Cambridge Univ. Press, 1975.

Breasted, James Henry. *The Dawn Of Conscience*. New York: Scribner, 1933.

Bridge, Anthony. *The Crusades*. New York: Watts, 1982.

Brown, Raymond. *The Birth of the Messiah*. Garden City, NY: Doubleday, 1977.

Buber, Martin. *I and Thou*. Translated by Walter Kaufman. New York: Scribner, 1970.

———. *The Legend of Baal-Shem*. Translated by Maurice Friedman. New York: Harper and Bros., 1955.

———. *On the Bible: Eighteen Studies*. New York: Schocken Books, 1968.

Buchanan, George Wesley. *To the Hebrews*. Garden City, NY: Doubleday, Anchor Bible Series, 1972.

Buckley, William F. *Saving the Queen: A Blackford Oakes Mystery*. Garden City, NY: Doubleday, 1976.

Bultmann, Rudolf. *The Gospel of John: A Commentary*. Translated by G. R. Beasley-Murray. Oxford: Oxford Univ. Press, 1971.

———. *Jesus and the Word*. Translated by Louise Pettibone Smith. New York: Scribner, 1958.

Caird, George B. *St. Luke: A Commentary*. Baltimore, MD: Penguin Books, 1963.

Campbell, Joseph. *The Hero with a Thousand Faces.* New York: Pantheon Books, 1949.
———. *The Power of Myth* (with Bill Moyers). Garden City, NY: Doubleday, 1988.
Carson, Rachel. *Silent Spring.* Boston: Houghton-Mifflin, 1962.
Childs, Brevard. *The Book of Exodus: A Critical Theological Commentary.* Philadelphia: Westminster Press, 1974.
Chilton, Bruce. *Judaic Approaches to the Gospels.* Atlanta: Scholars Press, 1994.
———. *Rabbi Jesus.* New York: Doubleday, 2000.
Conzelmann, Hans. *The Theology of Luke.* London: Faber and Faber, 1960.
Cornwall, John. *Hitler's Pope: The Secret History of Pius XII.* New York: Viking Press, 1999.
Crossan, John Dominic. *Jesus: A Revolutionary Biography.* San Francisco: Harper-Collins, 1990.
———. *Who Killed Jesus?* San Francisco: HarperCollins, 1995.
Cupitt, Don. *After God: The Future of Religion.* London: Weidenfeld and Nicolson, 1997.
———. *Christ and the Hiddenness of God.* London: SCM Press, 1985.
———. *Mysticism and Modernity.* Oxford: Blackwell Press, 1998.
———. *Radicals and the Future of the Church.* London: SCM Press, 1989.
———. *The Religion of Being.* London: SCM Press, 1998.
———. *The Sea of Faith: Christianity in Change.* London: BBC Publishing, 1984.
———. *Solar Ethics.* London: Xpress, 1993.
———. *Taking Leave of God.* London: SCM Press, 1980.
Darwin, Charles Robert. *The Origin of Species by Natural Selection.* London: Penguin, 1989. First published 1859.
Davies, Paul. *God and the New Physics.* London: Dent, 1984; New York: Simon and Schuster, 1992.
———. *The Mind of God.* New York: Simon and Schuster, 1992.
Dawkins, Richard. *The Blind Watchmaker.* London: Hammondsworth, 1991; New York: Norton, 1996.
———. *The Selfish Gene.* London: Granada, 1978; New York: Oxford Univ. Press, 1990.
Delaney, Janice, Emily Toth, and Mary Jane Lupton. *The Curse: A Cultural History of Menstruation.* New York: Dutton, 1976.
Dickens, Charles. *Nicholas Nickleby.* Oxford: Oxford Univ. Press, 1950. First published 1838–1839.
———. *A Tale of Two Cities.* Oxford: Oxford Univ. Press, 1950. First published 1859.
Dobson, James. *A New Dare to Discipline.* Carol Stream, IL: Tyndale, 1996.
———. *Temper Your Child's Tantrums.* Carol Stream, IL: Tyndale, 1998.
Dodd, Charles H. *The Epistle of Paul to the Romans.* London: Hodder and Stoughton, 1949.
———. *The Interpretation of the Fourth Gospel.* Cambridge: Cambridge Univ. Press, 1953.
Durden-Smith, Jo, and Diane Desimore. *Sex and the Brain.* New York: Arbor House, 1983.
Eakin, Frank E., Jr. *The Religion and Culture of Israel: An Introduction to Old Testament Thought.* London: Allyn and Bacon, 1971.
Eliade, Mircea. *The Sacred and the Profane.* New York: Harcourt-Brace, 1959.
Episcopal hymnal. New York: Church Pension Fund, 1940.
Evans, Craig A., and Donald Hagner, eds. *Anti-Semitism and Early Christianity: Issues of Polemic and Faith.* Minneapolis: Fortress Press, 1993.

Fineberg, Solomon A. *Overcoming Anti-Semitism.* New York and London: Harper and Bros., 1943.

Fox, Matthew. *The Coming of the Cosmic Christ.* San Francisco: HarperCollins, 1988.

———. *One River, Many Wells: How Deepening Ecumenism Awakens Our Imaginations with Spiritual Visions.* New York: Jeremy Tarcher/Putnam, 2000.

———. *Original Blessing: A Primer in Creation Spirituality.* Santa Fe: Bear Publishing, 1983.

Freud, Sigmund. *The Future of an Illusion.* Translated by James Strachey. New York: Norton, 1975.

———. *Moses and Monotheism.* Translated by Katherine Jones. New York: Vantage Books, 1967.

———. *Totem and Taboo.* Translated by James Strachey. New York: Norton, 1956.

Funk, Robert. *Honest to Jesus: Jesus for the New Millennium.* San Francisco: HarperCollins, 1996.

Funk, Robert, Roy Hoover, and the Jesus Seminar, eds. *The Five Gospels: What Did Jesus Really Say?* New York: Macmillan, 1993.

Gade, Richard E. *A Historical Survey of Anti-Semitism.* Grand Rapids, MI: Baker Book House, 1981.

Geering, Lloyd G. *Christianity Without God.* Santa Rosa, CA: Polebridge Press, 2000.

———. *Tomorrow's God.* Wellington, New Zealand: Bridgett Williams Books, 1994.

Gomes, Peter. *The Good Book.* New York: Morrow, 1996.

Goulder, Michael Donald. *The Evangelist's Calendar.* London: SPCK, 1978.

———. *Luke: A New Paradigm.* Sheffield, UK: Sheffield Academic Press, 1989.

———. *Midrash and Lection in Matthew.* London: SPCK Press, 1974.

Goulder, Michael Donald, and John Hick. *Why Believe in God?* London: SCM Press, 1983.

Graham, Billy F. *Just As I Am: The Autobiography of Billy Graham.* San Francisco: HarperCollins/Zondervan, 1997.

Greven, Philip. *The Protestant Temperament: Patterns of Child-Rearing, Religious Experience and the Self in Early America.* New York: Knopf, 1977.

———. *Spare the Child: The Religious Roots of Punishment and the Psychological Impact of Physical Abuse.* New York: Knopf, 1991.

Habel, Norman C., and Vicky Balabanski. *The Earth Story in the New Testament.* Sheffield, UK: Sheffield Univ. Press, 2002.

Haenchen, Ernst. *The Acts of the Apostles: A Commentary.* Philadelphia: Westminster Press, 1971.

Hahn, Thich Nhat. *Living Buddha, Living Christ.* New York: Riverhead Books, 1995.

Haley, Alex. *Roots: The Saga of an American Family.* Garden City, NY: Doubleday, 1976.

Hall, Douglas John. *The End of Christendom and the Future of Christianity.* Harrisburg, PA: Trinity Press, 1995.

Hamilton, William. *The New Essence of Christianity.* London: Darton, Longman and Todd, 1966.

Hamilton, William, and Thomas J. J. Altizer. *Radical Theology and the Death of God.* Indianapolis: Bobbs-Merrill, 1966.

Hampson, Daphne. *After Christianity.* London: SCM Press, 1996. Harrisburg, PA: Trinity Press, 1997.

Harnack, Adolph. *The Expansion of Christianity in the First Three Centuries.* Translated by James Moffatt. Freeport, NY: Books for Libraries Press, 1959.

Hick, John. *God and the Universe of Faith.* London: Macmillan, 1993.

——. *The Myth of Christian Uniqueness.* London: SCM Press, 1987.

Hitler, Adolf. *Mein Kampf.* Translated by Ralph Manheim. Boston and New York: Houghton-Mifflin, 1943.

Holloway, Richard. *Godless Morality.* Edinburgh: Canongate Press, 1999.

Horney, Karen. *Feminine Psychology.* New York: Norton, 1967.

Hoskyns, Edwin. *The Fourth Gospel.* London: Faber and Faber, 1939.

James, Fleming. *Personalities of the Old Testament.* New York: Scribner, 1955.

James, William. *The Varieties of Religious Experience.* New York: Random House, 1999.

Jones, Clinton R. *Homosexuality and Counseling.* Philadelphia: Fortress Press, 1974.

Jung, Carl G. *Aion: Researches into the Phenomenology of the Self.* Princeton, NJ: Princeton Univ. Press, Bollingen Series, 1959.

——. *Answer to Job.* London: Routledge, Kegan and Paul, 1954.

——. *Memoirs, Dreams and Reflections.* New York: Vintage Press, 1965.

——. *On Evil.* Princeton, NJ: Princeton Univ. Press, 1998.

——. *Psychology and Religion, East and West.* New York: Pantheon Books, Bollingen Series, Collected Works of C. G. Jung, 1958.

——. *Psychology and Western Religion.* New Haven, CT: Yale Univ. Press, 1960.

Kempis, Thomas à. *The Imitation of Christ.* Garden City, NY: Image Books, 1955.

King, Karen. *The Gospel of Mary.* Santa Rosa, CA: Polebridge Press, 2004.

Latourette, Kenneth Scott. *Christianity in a Revolutionary Age: The 19th Century—the Great Century in the Americas, Australia and Africa, 1800–1914.* New York: Harper and Bros., 1943.

Luther, Martin. *Lectures on Romans.* Vol. 25 of Luther's Works. Edited by Hilton C. Oswald. St. Louis, MO: Concordia Publishing House, 1972.

Mann, Jacob. *The Bible as Read and Preached in the Old Synagogue.* New York: KATV Publishing House, 1971.

Marx, Karl. *Das Kapital.* Vol. 50 of *Great Books of the Western World.* Chicago and London: Encyclopedia Britannica, 1952.

McCourt, Frank. *Angela's Ashes.* New York: Scribner, 1996.

McGaa, Ed (Eagle Man). *Nature's Way: Nature's Wisdom from Living in Balance with the Earth.* San Francisco: HarperCollins, 2004.

McNeil, John J. "Homosexuality: The Challenge of the Church." *Christian Century* 104, no. 8 (Mar. 1987): 242–248.

Meier, John P. *A Marginal Jew: Rethinking the Historical Jesus.* New York: Doubleday, 1991.

Meredith, Lawrence. *Life Before Death: A Spiritual Journey of Mind and Body.* Atlanta: Atlanta Humanics, 2000.

Milgram, Abraham E. *Jewish Worship.* Philadelphia: Jewish Publication Society of America, 1991.

Moltmann, Jürgen. *God in Creation: A New Theology of Creation and the Spirit of God.* San Francisco: Harper and Row, 1985.

Morris, Joan. *The Lady Was a Bishop: The Hidden History of Women with Clerical Ordination and the Jurisdiction of Bishops.* New York: MacMillan, 1973.

Moule, Charles F. D. *The Origins of Christology.* Cambridge: Cambridge Univ. Press, 1977.

Muilenburg, James. *The Way of Israel: Biblical Faith and Ethics.* New York: Harper and Bros., 1961.

Nelson, James B. "Reuniting Sexuality and Spirituality." *Christian Century* 104, no. 8 (Feb. 1987): 187–190.

Nock, Arthur. *St. Paul.* New York: Harper and Bros., 1937.

Noth, Martin. *Exodus: A Commentary.* Philadelphia: Westminster Press, 1962.

Pagels, Elaine. *Beyond Belief.* New York: Random House, 2004.

———. *The Gnostic Gospels.* New York: Random House, 1979.

Parrinder, Geoffrey. *Sex in the World's Religions.* New York: Oxford Univ. Press, 1980.

Pelikan, Jaroslav. *The Emergence of the Catholic Tradition (100–600).* Vol. 1 of *The Christian Tradition: A History of the Development of Doctrine.* Chicago and London: Univ. of Chicago Press, 1971.

Pittenger, Norman. *Making Sexuality Human.* New York: Pilgrim Press, 1970.

Richardson, Herbert W. T. *Nun, Witch and Playmate: The Americanization of Sex.* New York: Mellen Press, 1971.

Robinson, John A. T. *Honest to God.* Philadelphia: Westminster Press, 1963.

———. *The Human Face of God.* Philadelphia: Westminster Press, 1973.

Sanders, E. P. *Jesus and Judaism.* Philadelphia: Fortress Press, 1985.

Sandmel, Samuel. *Anti-Semitism in the New Testament?* Philadelphia: Fortress Press, 1978.

———. *The Genius of Paul.* New York: Farrar, Straus and Cudahy, 1958.

———. *Judaism and Christian Beginnings.* Oxford: Oxford Univ. Press, 1979.

———. *We Jews and Jesus.* New York: Schocken Books, 1970.

Schillebeeckx, Edward. *Christ: The Experience of Jesus as Lord.* New York: Seabury Press, 1980.

———. *Jesus: An Experiment in Christology.* New York: Seabury Press, 1979.

Schleiermacher, Friedrich. *The Christian Faith.* London: T. and T. Clark, 1908. Originally published 1821.

Spong, John Shelby. *The Bishop's Voice: Selected Essays.* Compiled and edited by Christine Mary Spong. New York: Crossroads Press, 1999.

———. *Born of a Woman: A Bishop Rethinks the Virgin Birth and the Treatment of Women in a Male-Dominated Church.* San Francisco: HarperCollins, 1992.

———. *Liberating the Gospels: Reading the Bible with Jewish Eyes.* San Francisco: HarperCollins, 1996.

———. *Living in Sin? A Bishop Rethinks Human Sexuality.* San Francisco: HarperCollins, 1988.

———. *A New Christianity for a New World: Why Traditional Faith Is Dying and How a New Faith Is Being Born.* San Francisco: HarperCollins, 2001.

———. *Rescuing the Bible from Fundamentalism: A Bishop Rethinks the Meaning of Scripture.* San Francisco: HarperCollins, 1991.

———. *Resurrection: Myth or Reality? A Bishop Rethinks the Meaning of Easter.* San Francisco: HarperCollins, 1994.

———. *This Hebrew Lord: A Bishop Rethinks the Meaning of Jesus.* San Francisco: HarperCollins, 1973, 1988, and 1993.

———. *Why Christianity Must Change or Die: A Bishop Speaks to Believers in Exile.* San Francisco: HarperCollins, 1998.

Stendahl, Krister. *Paul Among the Jews and Gentiles.* Philadelphia: Fortress Press, 1996.

Swidler, Leonard, and Arlene Swidler, eds. *Women Priests: A Catholic Commentary on the Vatican Declaration.* New York: Paulist Press, 1977.

Tacey, David. *The Spirituality Revolution.* Sydney: HarperCollins, 2003.

Taylor, John V. *The Go-Between God.* Philadelphia: Fortress Press, 1973.

Teilhard de Chardin, Pierre. *Science and Christ.* London: Collins, 1968.

Terrien, Samuel. *The Psalms and Their Meaning for Today.* Indianapolis and New York: Bobbs-Merrill, 1953.

Tillich, Paul. *The Courage to Be.* New Haven, CT: Yale Univ. Press, 1952.

———. *The Eternal Now.* New York: Scribner, 1963.

———. *The New Being.* New York: Scribner, 1935.

———. *The Protestant Era.* Translated by James Luther Adams. Chicago: Univ. of Chicago Press, 1948.

———. *The Shaking of the Foundations.* New York: Scribner, 1948.

———. *Systematic Theology,* vols. 1, 2, and 3. Chicago: Univ. of Chicago Press, 1951–1963.

Toynbee, Arnold J. *Christianity Among the Religions of the World.* New York: Scribner, 1977.

Twain, Mark. *The Adventures of Tom Sawyer.* New York: Barnes & Noble Classic Books, 1999. Originally published 1876.

Van Buren, Paul. *The Secular Meaning of the Gospel.* London: SCM Press, 1963.

Von Rad, Gerhard. *Genesis.* Philadelphia: Westminster Press, 1972.

———. *Old Testament Theology.* New York: Harper and Row, 1965.

Warner, Marina. *Alone of All Her Sex.* New York: Knopf, 1976.

Wemple, Suzanne Fonay. *Women in Frankish Society: Marriage and the Cloister, 500–900.* Philadelphia: Univ. of Pennsylvania Press, 1982.

Zachner, Robert Charles. *The Comparison of Religion.* Boston: Beacon Press, 1967.

———. *The Concise Encyclopedia of Living Faiths.* Boston: Hawthorne Books, 1959.

SCRIPTURE INDEX

The Old Testament

Genesis 1:1–2:3, 224
Genesis 1:2, 64
Genesis 1:6–8, 224
Genesis 1:9–10, 225
Genesis 1:24, NRSV, 33
Genesis 1:25, 33, 43
Genesis 1:26, 27, 33
Genesis 1:27, 33
Genesis 1:28, 27
Genesis 2:18–19, KJV, 75
Genesis 2:18–23, 69
Genesis 2:19–20, 248
Genesis 2:20b–23, KJV, 75
Genesis 4:8, 164
Genesis 6:20, 66
Genesis 7–8, 164
Genesis 7:2, 265
Genesis 9:21, 164
Genesis 11:1–9, 164
Genesis 11, 20
Genesis 14:17, 254
Genesis 17:10, 264
Genesis 18:1, 128
Genesis 18, 126
Genesis 19:4–5, 111
Genesis 19:4–5, KJV, 127
Genesis 19:6–8, KJV, 127
Genesis 19:38, 128
Genesis 20:1, 254
Genesis 29:1–20, 255
Genesis 29:17, 255
Genesis 32, 255
Genesis 35:21, 107
Genesis 37–50, 255
Genesis 37:28, 206

Genesis 38:9, KJV, 43

Exodus 1:22, 235
Exodus 3:14, 236
Exodus 12:48, 264
Exodus 13, 21
Exodus 13:19, 256
Exodus 16:4–5, 265
Exodus 16:4ff., 20
Exodus 16:31ff., 283
Exodus 16:35, 21
Exodus 20:17, 103
Exodus 20ff., 164
Exodus 21:7, 19
Exodus 35:2, 19

Leviticus 11:7–8, 19
Leviticus 12:2, 95
Leviticus 12:3, 264
Leviticus 12:5, 95
Leviticus 15:19–24, 95
Leviticus 18:19, 96
Leviticus 18:22, 111, 121, 124
Leviticus 18, 124, 125, 126
Leviticus 19:19, NRSV, 124
Leviticus 19:27, 124
Leviticus 20:13, 111, 121, 124
Leviticus 20, 124, 125, 126
Leviticus 23:5–8, 265
Leviticus 23:15–21, 265
Leviticus 23:23–25, 265
Leviticus 23:26–32, 265
Leviticus 24:13–14, 19
Leviticus 25:44, 19

Numbers 10:11–13:26, 254
Numbers 20:1–122, 254

Numbers 27:14, 254
Numbers 33:36–27, 254

Deuteronomy 1:46, 254
Deuteronomy 21:18–21, 19
Deuteronomy 23:1, 296
Deuteronomy 34, 268

Joshua 10:12–15, 18
Joshua 13:14, 256
Joshua 17:7–18, 256

Judges 11:16–17, 254
Judges 13:5, 23
Judges 19, 130

1 Samuel 9:15–10:13, 221
1 Samuel 9, 257
1 Samuel 15:3, 18
1 Samuel 16:1–13, 221

2 Samuel 1ff., 257
2 Samuel 12:5, 269
2 Samuel 12:7, KJV, 269
2 Samuel 15:32–17:23, 206
2 Samuel 20:5ff, 206
2 Samuel 24:6, 254
2 Samuel, 268

1 Kings 1, 257
1 Kings 12:8–16, 21
1 Kings 12ff., 257
1 Kings 16:21ff., 257
1 Kings 17:8–16, 21
1 Kings 17:17–24, 21
1 Kings 17ff., 269
1 Kings 19:4–18, 25
1 Kings 21:12–13, 260

2 Kings 2:1–12, 235
2 Kings 4:8–37, 21
2 Kings 6:5, 21
2 Kings 19:14–28, 260
2 Kings 21:1ff., 260
2 Kings 21:14–15, 260
2 Kings 21:18, 261
2 Kings 21:23–24, 261

2 Kings 22:3–13, 261
2 Kings 23:15–27, 261
2 Kings 23:21–23, 262
2 Kings 24–25, 262

Psalms 2:7, 222
Psalms 8:5, KJV, 177
Psalms 18:2, 64
Psalms 19:4, 64
Psalms 22, 184
Psalms 29:8, 254
Psalms 31:2, 64
Psalms 41:9, 206
Psalms 42:9, 64
Psalms 62:2, 64
Psalms 71:3, 64
Psalms 77:19, 283
Psalms 80:17, 222
Psalms 124:10–30, 66
Psalms 124:29, 66
Psalms 130:2, BCP, 170
Psalms 137:3, 4, 263
Psalms 137:8–9, 18–19
Psalms 139:7–12, 295

Proverbs 8:22–31, 146
Proverbs 11:29, 3
Proverbs 12:20, 146
Proverbs 13:24, 143
Proverbs 22:15, 143
Proverbs 23:13–14, 143
Proverbs 25:21–22, 146

Ecclesiastes 1:2, 274
Ecclesiastes 3:19, 21, 66

Isaiah 4:6, 283
Isaiah 7:14, 23
Isaiah 11:1, 23
Isaiah 25:4, 283
Isaiah 29:10, 185
Isaiah 35:5–6, NRSV, 282
Isaiah 43:16, 283
Isaiah 53:5, 147
Isaiah 53:6, 147
Isaiah 53, 184
Isaiah 55:8–9, 294

Jeremiah 27:5, 65
Jeremiah 31:39, 4

Ezekiel 37:1–15, 64
Ezekiel 44:2, 84

Daniel 2:34, 275
Daniel 6, 275
Daniel 7:13, 275

Micah 4:8, 107
Micah 6:8, 270

Zechariah 9–14, 271
Zechariah 11:4–14, 271
Zechariah 11:7–17, 206
Zechariah 11:12–13, 206
Zechariah 14:21, 206

Malachi 1:11, 295

Apocrypha

4 Maccabeas 2:2, 137
4 Maccabeas 3:17, 137

The New Testament

Matthew 1:1–17, 294
Matthew 1:18–25, 21, 61, 280
Matthew 1:20, 280
Matthew 1:23, 23, 296
Matthew 2:1–12, 21, 291
Matthew 2:16–18, 235
Matthew 2:23, 23
Matthew 2, 20
Matthew 5:43, 294
Matthew 5:44, 290
Matthew 6:28, 3
Matthew 8:2–3, 291
Matthew 8:4, 20
Matthew 8:18–27, 61
Matthew 9:13, 20
Matthew 10:2–4, 199
Matthew 12:30, 211, 239, 240

Matthew 12:40, 225
Matthew 14:13ff., 283
Matthew 14:16ff., 61
Matthew 14:25, 61
Matthew 18:12, 293
Matthew 19:7, 20
Matthew 19:28, 201
Matthew 20:1–16, 293
Matthew 22:24, 20
Matthew 22:43–45, 20
Matthew 25:31–46, 163
Matthew 26:6–13, 104
Matthew 26:15, 202
Matthew 26:24, 206
Matthew 26:51–54, 202
Matthew 27:3–10, 202
Matthew 27:5, 206
Matthew 27:24–25, 181
Matthew 27:24, 208
Matthew 27:25, 185, 208
Matthew 27:62ff., 185
Matthew 27:63, 225
Matthew 28:16–20, 201, 295
Matthew 28:20, KJV, 296
Matthew 28, 291

Mark 1:1–11, 280
Mark 1:23–26, 20
Mark 1:44, 20
Mark 2:27, 292
Mark 3:14–19, 199
Mark 3:19, 200
Mark 4:39, 61
Mark 5:25–34, 291
Mark 6:3, 84
Mark 6:30ff., 283
Mark 6:37ff., 61
Mark 6:48, 61
Mark 8:31, 225
Mark 9:14–18, 20
Mark 9:31, 225
Mark 9:40, 239, 240
Mark 10:34, 225
Mark 12:36–37, 20
Mark 14:3–9, 104
Mark 14:10–11, KJV, 202
Mark 14:20, NRSV, 202

Mark 14:21, 206
Mark 14:44–45, 202
Mark 15:39, 290
Mark 16:8, 22
Mark 16, 291

Luke 1:1–4, 23, 278
Luke 1:5–25, 21
Luke 1:26–2:7, 61
Luke 1:26–38, 21
Luke 1:41–44, 21
Luke 1:51, 293
Luke 2:8–14, 21
Luke 2:41–52, 21
Luke 3:23–38, 294
Luke 5:14, 20
Luke 6:15, 207
Luke 6:16, 199
Luke 6:27–28, 290
Luke 7:36–50, 104
Luke 8:22–25, 61
Luke 9:12ff., 283
Luke 9:13ff., 61
Luke 9:38–42, 20
Luke 9:50, 239, 240
Luke 10:9, 296
Luke 10:29–37, 293, 294
Luke 10:38–42, 106
Luke 12:5, 163
Luke 14:12–24, 293
Luke 15:4, 293
Luke 15:11ff., 23
Luke 17:16, 294
Luke 17:21, 296
Luke 20:19–20, 202
Luke 20:28, 20
Luke 20:42–44, 20
Luke 22:3, 202
Luke 22:6, 202
Luke 22:22, 206
Luke 22:28–30, 201
Luke 22:53, 203
Luke 24:1–12, 22
Luke 24:13–27, 281
Luke 24:27, 20

Luke 24:50–53, 61, 223
Luke 24, 20, 291

John 1:1, 236
John 1:11, 191
John 1:17, NRSV, 197
John 1:45, 225
John 1, 236
John 2:19, 209
John 6:1–13, 283
John 6:9ff., 61
John 6:35, 234
John 6:42, 225
John 8:1–11, 108, 277, 291
John 8:12, 234
John 8:28, 234
John 8:39, 44, 181
John 8:44, 185
John 8:58, 234
John 9:22, 236
John 10:7, 234
John 10:10, 100, 297
John 10:11, 234
John 11:1–44, 105
John 11:25, 234
John 12:1–8, 105
John 12:6, 203
John 12:42, 236
John 13:18, 203
John 13:26, NRSV, 203
John 13:27, 203
John 13:27, NRSV, 203
John 13:30, 203
John 14:6, 211, 233, 234
John 14:22, 199
John 15:5, 234
John 15:6, 163
John 18:2–9, 203
John 18:10–11, 203
John 20:19–29, 281
John 20, 291

Acts 1:1–11, 61, 223, 225, 235
Acts 1:8, KJV, 296
Acts 1:15–18, 207

Acts 1:16–18, 203
Acts 1, 20
Acts 2:1–4, 296
Acts 2, 64, 210
Acts 7:58, 137
Acts 8:1, 137
Acts 8:26–40, 296
Acts 9:1ff., 137
Acts 9:2, 137
Acts 9:18, 102
Acts 10:9–16, 296
Acts 10:34ff., 237
Acts 11:26, 183
Acts 15, 235
Acts 16:14, 40, 102
Acts 18:2, 26, 102
Acts 22:3, 136

Romans 1:1–4, 280
Romans 1:21, 135
Romans 1:21, KJV, 135
Romans 1:22–27, 112
Romans 1:26–27, 135
Romans 1:26–27, KJV, 135
Romans 7:6, NRSV, 197
Romans 7:18–19, 139
Romans 7:23, 43, 139
Romans 7:23ff., 102
Romans 7:24, 43
Romans 7:24–25, 139
Romans 8:35–39, 292
Romans 8:39, 139
Romans 11:7–8, 181, 185
Romans 16:3, 103
Romans 16:6, 103
Romans 16:7, 103
Romans 16:13, 103
Romans 16:15, 103

1 Corinthians 1:11, 102
1 Corinthians 5:10, 140
1 Corinthians 6:9, 140
1 Corinthians 7:9, 102, 162
1 Corinthians 11:2–16, 22
1 Corinthians 11:5ff., 102

1 Corinthians 11:8–9, 69
1 Corinthians 11:23–24, 200
1 Corinthians 11, 205
1 Corinthians 13:12, 3
1 Corinthians 14:34, 102
1 Corinthians 15:1–6, 201

2 Corinthians 5:17, 210
2 Corinthians 5:18–19, 221
2 Corinthians 5:19, 279

Galatians 1:13–17, 137
Galatians 1:19, 84
Galatians 2:20, 279
Galatians 3:26–28, 101, 102
Galatians 3:28, 210
Galatians 4:4, 223
Galatians 5:12, 22

Ephesians 6:1–3, 22
Ephesians 6:5, 22

Philippians 3:5–6, 137

Colossians 3:20, 22
Colossians 3:22, 22, 155
Colossians 4:1, 155
Colossians 4:15, 103

1 Timothy 1:10, 141
1 Timothy 2:12, NRSV, 102

2 Peter 2:6, 141

1 John 4:16, 64

Jude 1:1, 199
Jude 1:3, 211
Jude 1:7, 141

Revelation 3:19, 169